BRITAIN BY BRITRAIL

Tour Britain economically and comfortably. *Britain By BritRail* shows you how to enjoy exciting do-it-yourself train touring by utilizing the economy of the BritRail Pass.

Everything you've always wanted to know about . . .
BritRail Pass ● Train Stations, Schedules, and
Reservations ● Tourist Information Offices
Money Exchanges ● City Transportation
Hotel Reservations ● Ferry Crossings

. . . day excursions to interesting points outside the major cities—each one completely detailed with *all* the facts and sightseeing tips to make it a complete adventure.

. . . the perfect travel companion—almost like someone who's been there before going along to hold your hand.

. . . a truly *useful* "take-it-with-you" train travel guidebook . . . takes the mystery out of do-it-yourself touring.

. . . a very entertaining and informative book that should be of great value to anybody contemplating exploration of Britain by rail.

BRITAIN *by* BRITRAIL
HOW TO TOUR BRITAIN BY TRAIN

Eleventh Edition

written by
George Wright Ferguson

edited by
LaVerne Ferguson

A Voyager Book

CHESTER, CONNECTICUT

Library of Congress Catalog Card Number: 87–658136
ISBN: 0–87106–539–8

Manufactured in the United States of America
Eleventh Edition/First Printing

FOREWORD

This 1991–92 Edition of *Britain By BritRail* extends a hearty welcome aboard to all who have joined the ranks of its readers since its first year of publication (1980) and to those who have made use of the author's first rail travel guidebook, *Europe By Eurail*. Adapting to British Rail's unique rail network throughout England, Scotland, and Wales, *Britain By BritRail* follows the format of its predecessor, *Europe By Eurail,* by adhering to the time-proven base city–day excursion format. Because of its adaptability, London has been selected as the base city for day excursions within England and Wales. The capital of Scotland, Edinburgh, with Glasgow as an alternative, serves as a base of operations for day excursions northward into the Highlands.

Readers are assured that everything written was learned through the personal research and experiences of the authors. Our pledge to check, revise, and improve each edition continues.

Ferry crossings from Britain to Ireland and to the continent of Europe form a very important part of travel within the British Rail system. Consequently, several chapters describing the various ferry crossings are a permanent part of *Britain By BritRail*'s format.

Britain By BritRail is dedicated to the rail systems of England, Scotland, and Wales. *Britain By BritRail* presents to its readers a compact yet comprehensive volume on British Rail travel. Armed with a BritRail Pass and a copy of the *Thomas Cook European Timetable,* its readers are ready to plan and then enjoy their British Rail itineraries.

THE FERGUSON TEAM

George Wright Ferguson was born in Philadelphia twenty minutes after his mother was taken from a Washington-New York express train. He grew up alongside the Baldwin Locomotive Works on the "Pennsy" main line, and trains have continued to play an important role in his life.

A graduate of Penn State, George served in Europe during World War II as a test pilot and engineering officer with the Eighth Air Force. His first European train ride was aboard a vintage 1918 "40-and-8" freight car between Munich and Antwerp, a trip that lasted four days and four nights!

After a stint as editor, and later publisher, of a farm-equipment magazine, George was recalled to active military duty, with assignments in Korea, Japan, and Vietnam and at the Pentagon in Washington, D.C. George retired from the Air Force in 1967 with more than 5,000 flying hours in his log book. As a senior Air Force logistician, he was commended by Defense Secretary Robert McNamara for his study of the Air Force's worldwide-movement capabilities.

George's international experiences continued with research assignments in Thailand, Iran, South America, and West Germany for the Battelle Memorial Institute, headquartered in Columbus, Ohio. There he met the other member of his "team," LaVerne.

LaVerne Ferguson, born LaVerne Woodrum in Marion, Ohio, first discovered her love for travel in a third-grade geography class. Determined to see "the world," she has collected brochures and information about various countries for many years. LaVerne majored in social studies and English at Ohio State University, then became an executive secretary and later a technical writer.

In addition to their annual collection of material for their travel publications and articles, the Fergusons act as consultants to various travel groups.

The Fergusons welcome correspondence from their readers. Please write to them at P.O. Box 194, Dublin, Ohio 43017.

CONTENTS

1 IN THE BEGINNING

As Edna St. Vincent Millay put it, "My heart is warm with the friends I make,/And better friends I'll not be knowing;/Yet there isn't a train I wouldn't take/No matter where it's going."

Britain By BritRail! You are about to embark on a unique and rewarding traveling experience. Like thousands of other discerning visitors, you are about to learn that the British Rail system offers a truly delightful way of vacationing throughout the length and breadth of Europe's only English-speaking nation—Britain.

In size, Britain is a rather compact nation. It's about two-thirds the size of California or approximately one-third larger than the New England area of Maine, Vermont, New Hampshire, Massachusetts, Rhode Island, and Connecticut—the North American area to which Britain has contributed much of her heritage since Colonial days.

London is a tourist magnet, but despite what other writers say, London is not Britain. Britain has some of the most beautiful countryside in the world. Its mountains are no match for the Alps; its seas are not azure blue like the Mediterranean. But what it might lack in spectacular scenery is offset by a magical quality of green so peaceful and picturesque that, in a mere glance, the visitor becomes aware that what he sees is history. A visit to Britain that does not include at least a few days in the countryside is unthinkable.

The difference in traveling along Britain's congested highways and on British Rail's InterCity trains must be experienced to be believed. By rail, it is a smooth, relaxing journey uninterrupted by traffic lights and traffic jams. Rent-a-car visitors are usually too involved with starboard steering and keeping a close watch on the car in front to appreciate much more about Britain than the fact that the road signs are in English.

In Britain, you'll find more than 15,000 trains traveling to more than 2,400 destinations daily. The service is so frequent that if you miss a train, chances are you won't have to wait more than one-half hour to an hour for another. The British frequently seize such an opportunity to nip into a nearby pub for a quick pint and a game of darts. So follow the adage, "When in Rome, do as the Romans do." It applies equally well in Britain, which inherited some of Rome's customs, too!

Aboard a British Rail train, the driver (that's what the British call their train engineers) takes care of all the driving while you sip on a beverage, enjoy an uninterrupted view of the countryside, and stretch out in a comfortable seat. You can even respond to "nature's call" at your own option rather than sweating out making it to the closest petrol (gas) station—many are closed on weekends and holidays!

There are few places in Britain that cannot be reached by train. By employing the base cities of London, Edinburgh, or Glasgow, the splendor of Windsor Castle, the academic aura of Oxford and Cambridge, the Old Course at St. Andrews, or the bonny banks of Loch Lomond are all but an easy, comfortable train ride away. It is true that a number of branch and feeder lines have been shut down in the past decade or so. The main lines, however, still connect all of the major cities and population centers throughout England, Scotland, and Wales—the three countries served by British Rail. Northern Ireland, by the way, is a part of Great Britain, but its railways are operated by a separate company that does not accept the BritRail Pass.

Millions of Americans have either forgotten or have never had the opportunity to learn what travel by train can be like. In the post–World War II days, when America was rebuilding its industries and highways, it failed to do the same for its railroads, which had provided the majority of the transportation needs throughout the conflict. The demise of the great passenger trains followed rapidly. Within a single decade, the Santa Fe's Super Chief, the Pennsy's 20th Century Limited, and the Southern's Crescent disappeared. Not so in the lands across the Atlantic. You may rest assured that in Britain, as well as in the rest of Europe, the passenger train is alive and well today.

Britain By BritRail is a train travel guidebook written for the purpose of bringing train and train-related information to its readers in a direct, pragmatic manner. *Britain By BritRail* does not rate or recommend hotels. A quaint coaching inn or a hotel's convenient location to rail services may gain comment. The book's primary purpose insofar as accommodations are concerned, however, is to point out the most convenient tourist information center or hotel booking (reservations) facility.

Restaurants are treated in the same manner. We appreciate good food, along with the service that complements it. But with few exceptions, the choice of what to eat and where to find it remains the option of the reader perusing the wealth of excellent publications catering to this most worthy pursuit.

Britain By BritRail, like its sister publication, *Europe By Eurail*, is devoted to the visitor who goes to Britain expecting that its train services will provide the necessary transportation for a holiday that is different. We have gone ahead of you, probed what can be done, and solved the problems of doing it long before you will arrive. Every city and day excursion has been personally experienced, and we are pledged to constantly recheck, revise, and expand subsequent editions. This is being accomplished by personal visits and correspondence with those tourist information offices in the areas described.

Britain By BritRail

Britain By BritRail presents a new concept for comfortable, unhurried travel by train in Britain. By utilizing the economy of the BritRail Pass, along with the innovative, *fully* described base city-day excursion method, you can really see Britain at its best—by train.

Britain By BritRail is the perfect traveling companion for visitors using the BritRail Pass. This book helps to introduce and establish the reader in the base cities of London, Edinburgh, or Glasgow. Once you are ensconced in affordable, comfortable accommodations and your sightseeing and shopping are attended to in the base cities, *Britain By BritRail* then introduces its recommended day excursions to interesting places based on train schedules that will assure your return each night to the same hotel room. With a BritRail Pass and a current copy of *Britain By BritRail*, you become your own tour guide and avoid the constant packing and unpacking that accompanies most bus tours attempting to cover the same territory. By BritRail, if it's Tuesday, it's London, unless you have made the decision to pack and move on to another base city. You are calling the shots, not the tour bus driver.

Britons and their Continental cousins have employed British Rail's services for "holiday-making" on the British Isles for decades. Train travel is too fast for any possible chance of boredom setting in, yet it is leisurely enough to enjoy fully the constantly changing scene of hills and hamlets, farms and forests, countrysides and cities—everything that forms Britain's fascinating landscape.

Should you pause to ponder why, for example, an English gentleman would leave his motorcar at home when he's "off on holidays," you will find the answer very quickly when your train parallels a major highway or flashes across a bridge through the center of a British city. The superhighways right down to the ancient, narrow streets are packed with vehicles—all proceeding at a much slower pace than you and your train.

In the chapters describing the base cities and day excursions, *Britain By BritRail* meets the traveler upon arrival at the base-city airport or train station and then methodically *leads* him—in a relative order of priorities—to those essential facilities such as currency exchange, hotel accommodations, and tourist information sources. *Britain By BritRail* does not dwell on all the sightseeing opportunities offered by the base city. It provides an overall picture and then gives *explicit* directions on how to get to the city's tourist information office to obtain the most current information available to visitors. Readers requiring advance information regarding the base cities of London, Edinburgh, or Glasgow should direct their inquiries to the closest British Tourist Authority office listed on page 290 of this edition.

Britain By BritRail does concentrate on the day-excursion opportunities made possible from the base cities' geographic locations and rail facilities. A resumé of the day excursions follows the book's introduction of each base city so that the visitor may begin sorting out those excursions personally preferred.

Whether you admit it or not, everyone has a problem budgeting vacation time. It's human nature to try to see as much as possible in as little time as possible. This "sightseers' syndrome" could be dangerous to your vacation. Avoid it by planning an itinerary that allows ample "free time." Also, vary the day excursions by going on a short one following a particularly long outing away from the base city. Press too hard by trying to see and do too much on your vacation and you will return home as a living example of the old adage, "A person who looks like he needs a vacation usually has just returned from one."

To avoid reader frustration when searching for a single item of information or a telephone number, *Britain By BritRail* groups much of this data in its appendix for ready reference. Along with addresses of information sources, useful telephone numbers are all compiled in the appendix. Station plans and maps of transportation lines can be located easily near the end of the book.

Train schedules between London and the base cities of Edinburgh and Glasgow in Scotland are listed on pages 79 and 81 of chapter 10, which describes London. This particular information should prove to be helpful when you are initially planning your BritRail trip. Train schedules for the day-excursion trips out of the base cities are provided in the text describing each day excursion. Trains departing from the base cities are normally on morning schedules; trains returning from the day excursions usually run in the late afternoon and early evening. Each day-excursion section begins with the distance and average train time for the trip, because we realize that there may be some days when you prefer a short trip rather than a great adventure. If the twenty-four-hour times shown in the train schedules boggle your mind, we suggest that you consult the "time converter" clock on page 313 of this edition.

Please remember that the timetables and schedules appearing in this edition are provided for planning purposes only. Every care has been taken to make the timetables and schedules correct. The information is checked with authoritative sources up to press time. *Britain By BritRail* and/or its publisher cannot, however, be held responsible for the consequences of either changes or inadvertent inaccuracies. Current rail schedules are posted in all British Rail stations, and timetables from the base cities to every day-excursion point are available for the asking in the base-city stations. Please consult them.

12

Travel Economy

"Know before you go," the slogan of the U.S. Customs Service pertaining to what you may return with, also applies to the financial aspects of vacation planning. The rise and fall of the dollar's purchasing power in Europe over the past few years has left a lot of us wondering whether or not we could afford a vacation on the other side of the Atlantic. Although the inflation rate in the United States has been reduced to what bankers term "acceptable," it is still difficult to determine what effect Europe's inflation will have on your dollars once you're there.

Advance planning and purchasing vacation needs in advance (particularly transportation) in American dollars are probably the most effective ways to combat inflation and price fluctuations. Basically, the program calls for buying as much of your vacation needs as you can before you go and planning to limit your out-of-pocket costs paid in foreign currency to a minimum. In this way, you are well protected against fluctuating currency values.

The idea of doing things that were previously thought impossible—like putting $40 worth of gas in a Volkswagen—emphasizes train travel in Europe as the best means of effectively stabilizing your travel dollars. Prepayment plans, such as the BritRail Pass, are ideal. Not only do you purchase the pass with American dollars prior to departure, but the BritRail Pass also provides the most inexpensive way to travel in Britain—the quickest, too!

American travel agents still have a penchant for wanting to sell a "fly-drive" program to any client who wants to vacation in Britain. But, in general, car rentals have one basic fault—"the price you see" is never "the price you pay," which is *always* higher. As a rule of thumb, add to the quoted price another 20 percent for personal accident insurance, collision insurance, and taxes. After that, consider fuel costs. Then, ask your agent to provide you with an economical BritRail Pass. If he doesn't sell them, you can order one by calling (800) 722–7151.

Accommodations almost always account for the greatest share of a traveler's budget. Low-cost air fares and transportation bargains like the BritRail Pass can get the traveler *to* and *around* the British Isles, but the real bite out of the buck comes when the visitor opens his wallet to pay for a night's lodging. Attractively priced accommodations packages are being offered by some American tour operators. But too few suit the needs of those preferring individual itineraries, as is the case for travelers on a BritRail vacation. With advance planning and advance payment, however, savings can be realized by those who are willing to put forth the extra time and effort.

Well ahead of your intended departure date—preferably two months in advance, but no less than six weeks—write to one of the British Tourist Authority (BTA) offices listed on page 290 of this edition and request information regarding lodging (including the "bed-and-breakfast" places) in the areas you intend to visit during your BritRail journey. You may make reservations, or "bookings," as the British call them, in various ways. Hotel accommodations may be arranged by mail with central booking offices in London and Edinburgh but generally not elsewhere. The best assurance that you will have a room waiting upon arrival is to make an advance deposit directly to the hotel, then take care of the balance with the hotel's cashier when checking out. By the way, always ask the hotel to confirm the room rate when you check in. This will avoid delays and possible financial embarrassment when leaving.

For the reader whose life-style absolutely precludes any preplanning, we suggest that you use the Best Western Worldwide Reservations System to assure reservations at least for your arrival date in Britain and for the night prior to your departure back home. Information is contained in the Appendix on page 303. With lodging assured for these two important nights, you can then arrange for the balance of your housing needs at a more leisurely pace.

As previously mentioned, *Britain By BritRail* does not rate or recommend hotels. We do, however, recommend the hotel-booking services of Best Western because it covers Britain and the rest of Europe with more available lodging accommodations than any other hotel reservation system presently accessible in North America by toll-free telephones. Its computerized central reservation service makes it possible to obtain instant reservations for any Best Western in Britain from North America, Europe, or from within Britain during your BritRail travels.

Contrary to the Best Western chain of motels in North America, the Best Western International organization represents a group of independent hotel affiliates, each having an individual character typical of its country and area. In many cities within England, Scotland, and Wales you can choose among several Best Western affiliates of various categories and price ranges.

The *Best Western International Atlas & Hotel Guide* will prove to be invaluable when planning a BritRail trip. It is available to *Britain By BritRail* readers free of charge. Just detach and mail the convenient postal card in this edition.

One final bit of advice on reducing the cost of accommodations in Britain—use your BritRail Pass. Too many of us overlook the fact that the BritRail Pass can actually provide exceptional savings in housing costs by permitting you to stay outside the base city's center, where hotel rooms, pensions, bed-and-breakfast housing, and the like are far less expensive than their downtown counterparts.

London particularly lends itself to such a suburban arrangement because there are many areas outside the city's center that are readily accessible by rail. Anytime downtown accommodations become difficult to find or too demanding on the budget, tell the housing people you have a BritRail Pass and can easily stay in the suburbs.

Staying in London's northern or western suburbs has other advantages, too. From many of the suburban stations, you can board a fast InterCity train for a day excursion without ever going into a London terminus. You can return to the suburbs in the evening, too, without becoming involved in London's rush hours.

Watford Junction, sixteen miles from London's Euston Station, is one of the stations in London's suburbs that offer excellent InterCity connections to such day-excursion points as Birmingham, Chester, and Coventry. Most InterCity departures from Euston Station on weekday mornings pick up at Watford Junction 16 minutes later. On weekday evenings, most InterCity trains set down at Watford twenty minutes ahead of their arrival times in Euston station.

Other rail points in London suburbs are Luton, for direct rail connections to Nottingham and Sheffield; Stevenage, along the main line to Edinburgh via York; and Slough or Reading, for connections to Bath as well as the Welsh cities of Cardiff and Swansea.

There are times when accommodations in the base cities are extremely limited. Edinburgh, during its annual festival every August to September, is an excellent example. Lodgings in the suburbs, à la BritRail Pass, can be more economical and just as convenient as those in the base cities.

If you have your heart set on lodgings in London when inquiring as to their availability, you will be asked the inevitable question, "Where do you want to be near to?" Naturally, when you're traveling by rail, your response will be, "Near the rail station." You are in for a surprise—at last count, London had fourteen rail stations. Because these terminals rim the vast, sprawling city, a better site-selection statement would be to ask for a hotel nearby one of the major lines of the Underground (subway). There are thirteen of these "tube" stations from which you can reach the British Rail stations. Of the ten Underground lines operating beneath London, the Circle Line serves the most rail stations. Confirmation of London's rail-station count may be made by turning to the map illustration appearing on page 296 of this edition. Opposite, on page 297, is a graphic presentation of the Inter-terminal British Rail Lines with the London Underground. The complete London Underground system is depicted on pages 298 and 299.

InterCity 125, the world's fastest diesel train, is British Rail's "Journey Shrinker." Along with speed, InterCity 125 trains offer air conditioning, soundproofing, automatic interior doors, and food services including buffet, bar, and restaurant with a wide choice of food and beverages.

2 PLANNING A BRITRAIL TRIP

Webster's Dictionary defines a plan as "a program of action." Plans vary in detail and complexity, according to the nature of the user. For example, one person may require a detailed, hour-by-hour, appointment-by-appointment schedule for a day's activities; another may merely plan to get up in the morning and see what happens after that. This example categorizes the two general types of rail travelers we have observed down through the years—one adventurous, the other conservative.

Time is the first consideration when planning any kind of journey. "Do I have enough time to go shopping today, or should I plan to go tomorrow?" That is a basic question we frequently ask ourselves. "Do I have enough time to visit Britain this year, or should I plan to go next year?" Basically, the latter question is the same as the former, the only variance being the time frame—one day or one year. Yet the second question has more impact than the first because the decision involves considerably more elapsed time than that for a routine shopping trip.

How long should your BritRail tour be? There are many factors bearing on such a determination, the most important being the individual. How much annual vacation time do you have? How do you use it—all at one time or in two or more segments? The folks issuing BritRail Passes are ready to accommodate just about anyone's personal needs, with passes ranging from eight, fifteen, and twenty-two days to one month. The passes permit travel on all scheduled British Rail trains, including the InterCity 125 train shown on the opposite page.

Travel magazines and the travel sections of the Sunday newspapers are usually loaded with one-week trips to almost anywhere—mainland Europe and the British Isles included. Based on our own experience, we believe that going to Europe for any period of less than two weeks is a waste of time and money.

In support of the foregoing statement, we invite you to take a look at the logistics involved in a European trip. It takes an entire day to reach Britain by air from North America and an entire day to return. Although the flying time aboard a jet airplane ranges from seven to eight hours, airport to airport, it will be day two before you arrive in Britain. (Most eastbound transatlantic flights depart at night during day one and arrive the following morning—day two.) During the flight, you will be exposed to a cocktail hour, a dinner hour, a break for an after-dinner drink, followed by a full-length, feature motion picture. In the morning, as the sun rises in the east over Britain, you'll be awakened an hour or so before landing to be served breakfast.

Add up the time consumed by all the scheduled events while en route, and you'll quickly conclude that your night spent in the sky over the Atlantic Ocean consisted of many things—except sleep. Even if you did manage to sleep during the entire trip instead of eating, drinking, and watching movies, your body and all its functions will be arriving in Britain a few hours after midnight by North American time. You will crave adjustment to a phenomenon known as "jet lag," which will be trying its best to interrupt your plans for a carefree vacation.

When you discount the two full days utilized for air travel, plus a minimum of one day to get your sleep-eat cycle functioning properly again, the number of days left in a one-week visit hardly seems worth making the trip. Most of the economical excursion fares for transatlantic air travel evolve around day fourteen, meaning that your minimum time spent in Britain after departing from North America must be fourteen days in order to qualify for the reduced fares. Consequently, in consideration of both time and money, we recommend your stay in Britain be a minimum of two full weeks.

Having determined the length of time you will have for your BritRail trip, the next step is to develop a clear idea of where you want to go in Britain, what you want to see, and what you want to do. This process of developing objectives should be completed well before your departure date. We disagree with those who feel that anticipation of travel is more rewarding than its realization. But we do agree that the planning phase can also form a fun part of your trip. Properly done, this "homework" will pay substantial dividends when travel actually begins.

To get things started, write to the British Tourist Authority and BritRail Travel International, Inc., for information. You'll find the appropriate addresses listed on page 290. *Be specific*. In your request, indicate *when* you will be going, *where* you wish to go within Britain, and *what* in particular you would like to see. If you have any special interests or hobbies, be sure to mention them in your request. Spelling out your information needs will produce better responses.

Don't overlook your local library as a valuable information source. For example, you will find an excellent condensation of British history in the Encyclopeadia Britannica. Back issues of *National Geographic* magazine are excellent sources for first-person explorations of the British Isles. Seek out friends and neighbors who have been to Britain. No doubt you'll find their experiences flavored with their own likes and dislikes. Nevertheless, any and all information you can gather prior to your trip will eventually find its place in your memory bank. Surprisingly enough, you'll find yourself recalling many of these fragments of information during your own journey.

You are now ready for the decisive phase of your trip planning—

constructing an itinerary. The moment of truth is at hand! Your only limitations during this portion of the planning phase are the lack of more than twenty-four hours in a day and the fact that the week does not contain more than seven days.

First, draw a blank calendar-style form covering a period from at least one week prior to your departure to a few days following your return. Make extra copies of the form—you'll need them. (Perfection is a long time coming in this project!) Now begin to block your itinerary into the calendar form, being mindful that the itinerary can be changed, but the number of days in a week remains fixed at all times. Possibly by the third time through the exercise, you'll begin to "see the light at the end of the tunnel." It's human to try to cram too many activities into a twenty-four-hour day, but it's better to discover your planning errors before starting your trip rather than during the middle of it.

With your itinerary in a calendar format, now you can determine your housing requirements, seat and sleeper reservations, and the other facets of your forthcoming trip. The days blocked out in advance of your departure can show your "countdown" items, such as stopping the newspaper, having mail held at the post office, and so on. Make several copies of your completed itinerary and leave some behind for the folks with whom you want to stay in touch. Above all, take copies of your itinerary with you—you'll refer to them frequently. If there have been any break-ins in your neighborhood, you should take steps to assure that it doesn't happen to you while you are gone. Alert the neighbors to keep a watchful eye for suspicious people and their activities. Many professional thieves have been known to park in a driveway in broad daylight with a moving van. The police should be advised regarding your absence. Also check with the insurance agency that writes your homeowner policy. "Am I covered?"— as they ask in television commercials—is what you ask. You may need additional coverage during your absence. One final caution. Don't have your forthcoming vacation plans announced in the newspapers. Thieves read, too. Save it for your return.

One item that you can't leave home without is a passport. If you do not have one or if yours has expired, write immediately to one of the U.S. passport offices listed on page 314 for information and applications. Allow a minimum of one month to obtain your passport. There are ways to expedite the process, but be safe by planning ahead and making this the first order of business when you've decided to make your trip abroad. U.S. citizens are admitted to Britain with only a passport. A visa is not required. Carry an extra certified copy of your birth certificate and two extra passport photos with you. If your passport is lost or stolen, go to the nearest U.S. Consulate.

Train travel is conducive to establishing new acquaintances or starting new friendships. When travelers (vacationers or business persons) are sitting next to you, they naturally will be inclined to strike up a conversation—if you are so inclined, too.

What to Take?

Obviously, the practical answer to this question is "as little as possible." A tourist tends to pack everything he conceivably might use during a vacation, lug it everywhere, use it very little, and return home with longer arms. In these days of wash-and-wear fabrics (and deodorants), this is no longer necessary. A good rule of thumb is to take one medium-size suitcase and a shoulder bag. Hold to this rule and you will have a more comfortable trip. Regardless of how comfortable the weather at your destination is expected to be, pack a sweater. Brief cold spells in Britain are not uncommon. Stow a small pocket flashlight in your shoulder bag together with a collapsible umbrella in the "unlikely event" that you may need them.

If you must take expensive jewelry with you, take as well a copy of its insurance appraisal as proof of purchase to customs officials upon your return. Same for watches produced by foreign manufacturers. You may have bought that solid-gold Rolex in a St. Louis pawnshop for a song, but the customs inspector may have you singing a different tune if you can't come up with the paperwork!

If you wear prescription eye glasses, take a copy of the prescription with you. The same applies for prescription medications. Even if you only use over-the-counter drug products, we suggest taking an adequate supply of the item. Many such products are not available in Europe or are sold under a different label or packaging.

Samsonite, one of the major manufacturers of quality luggage, has published an interesting booklet on the subject of suitcases and travel. With the catchy title *Lightening the Travel Load—Travel Tips and Tricks*, it is crammed with helpful tips, everything from analyzing your luggage needs and the basic points of safeguarding it through packing for a trip. Helpful hints on carry-on luggage, how to tip, how to clear customs, and how to stay healthy while on your trip are also included. For a free copy, write to Samsonite Traveler Advisory Service, P.O. Box 39603, Denver, CO 80239. Be certain to include a self-addressed business envelope with 45 cents postage affixed.

We also recommend the *Thomas Cook European Timetable* as part of your BritRail trip planning. An invaluable aid to anyone planning a rail trip anywhere in Europe, it contains complete timetables covering every major rail route in Britain honoring the BritRail Pass. We suggest you purchase a copy before departing on your BritRail trip and take it with you. It may be a bit bulky, but you'll find yourself constantly delving between its covers for information.

In the United States and Canada, copies of the *Thomas Cook European Timetable* can be purchased from the Forsyth Travel Library, whose full services are described on pages 305 and 306.

How to Get There

Transatlantic air traffic is so frequent and varied today that no description of it—short of an entire book—could do it justice. Excursion fares are still available in a multitudinous variety. Charter flights are available, too, and they are still mostly money savers. But some excursion rates are less expensive than charters. It is not uncommon on a regularly scheduled airliner winging its way to Europe to find that every passenger in your row of seats paid a different fare for the same flight on the same schedule with the same service!

We refer readers to their travel agents for airline information. But there has been an erosion of such information in travel agencies, brought about in general by the proliferation of air fares. The agencies face the almost impossible task of keeping tabs on the rapidly changing airline industry. Let's put it this way. If you've dealt with a reputable travel agency over the years, contact them the moment you've decided to BritRail through Britain, and ask them to come up with some air-excursion-fare options. At your leisure, call the various airlines' "800" telephone numbers and ask them for suggestions and fare information. Don't be disturbed if you receive a variety of responses. Sift them out until you find what you're looking for. Even if your travel agent didn't suggest the air fare you prefer and found through your own research, employ the agent's services in getting the tickets. You will pay the same price whether you obtain the tickets directly from the airline or from your travel agent. So give him the opportunity of collecting the commission and at the same time realizing that you are a pretty savvy client, and he will probably give you more personal service on your next trip.

Long-distance calls can be made in the United States without charge when calling businesses that have "800" service numbers. Obtaining the proper "800" number to call is easy: Dial (800) 555–1212 and tell the special operator the name of the airline information office with which you wish to speak. Icelandair is well known for its money-saving fares. Icelandair's toll-free number is (800) 223–5500. Some other airlines you may want to call are Air Canada, British Airways, British Caledonian Airways, Continental, Pan Am, and TWA.

Regarding charter flights, inquire about them but investigate them thoroughly before making any final decisions. Here again, get your travel agent involved, even if it's only to obtain the tickets. Even some of the most reputable air- charter carriers still operate on a "Go—No Go" basis. This means that if enough passengers sign up for the flight, it will go as scheduled; if there are not enough passengers booked, the flight will be scrubbed.

The BritRail Pass

The BritRail Pass is a ticket for any train operated by the British Railways in England, Scotland, and Wales. You don't have to purchase a BritRail Pass to travel by train in Britain. Having one, however, is very convenient. For example, with a BritRail Pass, you do not have to purchase a ticket every time you want to make a trip somewhere by train in Britain. Just board any British Rail train that is going your way and travel whenever, wherever, and as often as you like throughout the period in which your BritRail Pass is valid.

BritRail Passes may be purchased for first class or for economy class, with special reduced rates for youths and senior citizens. First-class seats are wider; consequently, the first-class coaches are more spacious because they accommodate fewer passengers. British Rail's economy class, however, is also comfortable. With the exception of a few local lines on which some "vintage" equipment is still in operation, the economy-class seats are fully upholstered, and space is plentiful. One thing is common to both classes—the view. Either in first or economy class, you can lounge in comfort while watching the countryside glide by.

A Senior Citizen BritRail Pass may be issued to anyone age sixty or older. The holder travels in either first-class or economy class at a reduced rate. Youth Economy BritRail Passes are available for those ages sixteen through twenty-five; youth passes, however, are not available for first-class travel. BritRail also issues child passes for those ages five through fifteen for travel in first class or economy class at 50 percent of the adult fare. See page 309 for BritRail Pass prices and ordering information.

If you obtain your BritRail Pass through a travel agent, you may be given an airline ticket–style coupon together with instructions for where in Britain you can exchange the coupon for a BritRail Pass. These offices are located at the Gatwick and Heathrow airports outside of London as well as forty-seven other locations listed in the instructions.

When traveling in Britain on certain peak days, holidays, or summer Saturdays, seat reservations are recommended. You may make them at any British Rail station for $5 per person per trip. Reservations are usually obtainable up to the day of travel.

Any visitors going to Britain should consider purchasing a BritRail Pass if they plan to travel primarily by train. To help you decide whether or not to purchase a BritRail Pass, we have included a selection of British Rail one-way fares on page 311. The fares are listed in British pounds. To obtain the rate for converting pounds into dollars, consult the financial section of your newspaper or the international department of your bank. Compare the individual fare costs with the BritRail Pass costs shown on page 309 for your itinerary.

British TV favorites, The Muppets, shown here by floral designs in Bath's city park, attest to the strong ties existing between Britain and North America in culture, art, and entertainment.

Keep in mind, when comparing the straight rail fares to the cost of the pass, that convenience in travel has a value, too. Standing in line ("queuing") to purchase train tickets is an inconvenience that can be avoided. With a BritRail Pass, you need do this only once—when you validate your pass. The rest of the time, you need only to board the train and you are on your merry way.

Even short-time visitors to the British Isles may find it advantageous to purchase a BritRail Pass in lieu of point-to-point tickets if they plan to make more than one or two medium-length rail journeys. For example, the cost of point-to-point tickets for a circuitous journey—like a quick dash out of London for a look around Edinburgh, Aberdeen, and Glasgow—exceeds the cost of an eight-day economy adult BritRail Pass; the economy of the pass becomes immediately apparent. Consider, too, that the London-Edinburgh-Aberdeen-Glasgow-London round trip could be made comfortably in as little as three days, leaving five more days of unlimited rail travel available to the pass holder. Even though you might not be able to change your plans to extend your stay, you would still save money, in this case, by purchasing the BritRail Pass.

Some travelers may prefer the flexibility of a BritRail Flexipass. It is available for first-class or economy travel, offering the same privileges as the conventional BritRail Pass. With a BritRail Flexipass, you can travel any four days within an eight-consecutive-day time frame or choose any eight days of travel within a fifteen-day period or any fifteen days within one month. Senior citizens can purchase a Flexipass at reduced rates, and special rates are available for youths (ages sixteen to twenty-five). Children (ages five to fifteen) pay one-half the adult fare.

Casual, short-term, or business visitors to Britain may all benefit from a BritRail Pass tucked in their pocket before leaving home. BritRail has come up with a combination package it calls the "Capital Travel Pak," which has been designed with this type of visitor in mind. The Capital Travel Pak consists of a special "network Southeast" Rail Pass (Economy Class) for four or seven days combined with a four- or seven-day London Visitor Travel Card—the pass that permits you to travel unlimited on London's red double-decker buses and the Underground (subway). It also includes Gatwick or Heathrow airport transfers. With this combination in your pocket, you have up to four or seven days to roam about London as well as the entire southeast British Rail network.

The London Visitor Travel Card is also available separately for increments of three, four, or seven days. BritRail Pass *must* be purchased in North America prior to departure. Expand your horizons—don't leave home without one!

Trip-Planning Tips

Don't carry more cash than you can afford to lose; carry traveler's checks. Whenever possible, cash your traveler's checks at the branch-bank facilities located in or near railway stations and airports. The currency-exchange services operated by Thomas Cook are also acceptable. The banks and the official currency-exchange services are government supervised and are required to pay the official exchange rates. Hotel and store cashiers, in contrast, seldom give you the full exchange value and often add a service charge.

Take a credit card with you. It usually proves to be an important adjunct to your en route finances. American Express is a popular card to carry. The privilege of cashing personal checks at the American Express offices is invaluable. Card members may cash checks for up to $1,000 ($200 in local currency and $800 in traveler's checks). MasterCard and Visa have gained popularity in Europe and can be used in a number of places, mostly stores and restaurants. Diner's Club and Carte Blanche are also accepted by most establishments.

Concerning credit cards, be aware that there's a "plastic war" being waged against American Express by MasterCard and Visa. *International Travel News* reports some readers have had to pay a supplemental charge to cash American Express traveler's checks at some British banks. Until the dust settles, it might be discretionary to inquire before presenting any card company's traveler's checks for cashing or credit cards for payment of services or purchases.

Picking pockets is an art that is practiced throughout Europe. Gentlemen's breast pockets are the main targets. Foil the thief by sewing a medium-size button both above and below the pocket opening. Loop a piece of shoestring or other strong string around the buttons when carrying valuables. Avoid carrying anything more valuable than a handkerchief in hip pockets. Ladies' pocketbooks should be of the shoulder type and carried that way at all times. Don't let the thought of someone picking your pocket alarm you. Just be aware of it and protect yourself against it. Actually, it is mild compared to what could happen to you on Main Street in your own home town in broad daylight.

Don't leave your cash, cameras, and other valuables in the hotel room or locked up in a suitcase. Take them with you or leave them in the hotel safe.

If you normally bathe with a washcloth, take your own; most European hotels don't have them.

3   EN ROUTE—THE FUN OF GOING

With all the luxuries of flight that modern aircraft offer, there is still something about flying that makes it a bit more demanding on your system than a similar amount of time spent at home or in the office. A transatlantic trip with a minimum of incidents and inconveniences is what we're after. Here are some suggestions that we have found helpful on our flights; perhaps they may help on yours.

Cash, Cards, and Credentials

You'll need some cash on your flight to pay for tips, snacks, refreshments, and taxi fares at your arrival point. U.S. currency will do very well, but don't carry it all in one big roll—distribute it around in pockets, a briefcase, or a money clip. A money belt is an ideal way to carry the larger notes. Taxis plying the airport-hotel routes have no problem converting dollars to local currency. Check with the driver, however, before entering his cab.

List the number of each credit card you plan to take. Leave a copy at home and pack one in your suitcase or carry-on bag. List passport numbers, too. When anything is lost or stolen, the police are interested primarily in its serial number. A certified copy of your birth certificate and a few extra passport photos will save you days of delay if you lose your passport.

Luggage

One suitcase, one shoulder bag. Check the suitcase and carry the shoulder bag. Be sure the carry-on bag has a small supply of toilet articles, stockings, and underwear—just in case the suitcase disappears.

In-Flight Comfort

If you plan to catch some shut-eye en route, ask for a seat alongside a bulkhead. Bulkheads don't mind being leaned on, but passengers do. Passengers in the forward section of the airplane generally experience less vibration. Wear loose clothing. Unfasten your shoes, but don't take them off. Your feet will swell following several hours of immobility. The best remedy is to walk the length of the aisle in the airplane every hour or so. Try deep knee bends.

Flying dehydrates your body. Drink lots of water and watch what you mix with it—alcohol dehydrates, too. Special meals for special diets are no problem with the airlines, but requests should be made at the same time as reservations.

Cameras, Film

If you plan to take a foreign-made camera with you that you purchased in the United States, save yourself a lot of headaches by taking the sales slip with you. Otherwise, go to a U.S. Customs Office before leaving the country and have your equipment registered. Carry a copy of the sales slip or the registration form with your passport and a spare copy tucked away in the camera case or shoulder bag.

Despite what airport officials tell you, their electronic luggage-checking devices can fog your film. The best way to avoid it is to report for check-in early and ask that your cameras and film be inspected by hand. Special lead-lined bags are available at most camera stores. Color film in Britain includes processing and is usually more expensive than that which you can buy at home. Solution? Take all the film you'll need with you.

Tax-Free Purchases

Every international airport has a "tax-free" shopping service. The routine is generally the same. You select your purchases, pay for them and add them to your carry-on luggage, find safe storage for it during the flight, and then haul it off the airplane. Yet there are variations. For example, at JFK in New York, you select the items from a sample or catalog. The items are then delivered "for your convenience" to your departure gate for pick-up. The hazards of this system are many. If the delivery person gets things mixed-up and fails to make the right gate at the right time, you'll be off into the wild blue yonder sans purchases. Or if you are late passing the pick-up point, sometimes an unknown "benefactor" tries to help by taking your purchases on board the plane ahead of you. Finding this so-called "benefactor" can prove to be difficult. Solution? Buy your "booty" aboard the airplane while en route. Most international airlines carry aboard a good stock of "tax free" items, which you may purchase from the cabin crew. It's always best to check at the airline counter, however, to be certain that this "in flight" service will be available on your particular flight. "Tax-free," by the way, is a misused term. Most items, with exception of alcohol and tobacco, normally can be purchased cheaper in the arrival city.

Keep in mind that everything you purchase, "tax free" or otherwise, is subject to customs duty when returning home. Consequently, know your quotas and attempt to stay within them to avoid paying duty and the ensuing delays involved. Good luck with customs. Honesty is always the best policy!

Prior to Landing

Fill out all the customs forms your flight attendant gives to you and keep them with your passport and airline ticket. Keep this packet handy, but secure, until the credentials are required by the customs officials at the arriving airport.

Jet Lag and What to Do About It

Earlier, we mentioned jet lag. It can seriously affect your transatlantic trip unless you know how to deal with it. The following explanation of what jet lag is and some means to combat it should prove helpful to any traveler undergoing four or more hours of time change.

The human body has numerous rhythms; sleep is one of them. Even without sunlight, as in a cave, the body will still maintain a twenty-four-hour awake/asleep cycle. The heart rate falls to a very low ebb in the early hours of the morning, when you are usually asleep. Body temperature, which affects the mental processes, also drops during this time. Consequently, if an air traveler is transported rapidly to a time zone five or six hours ahead of that of the departure point, even though it may be eight or nine o'clock in the morning at the arrival point in local time, the traveler's body functions are at a low ebb. As a result, the traveler feels subpar, and this feeling can persist for as long as two or three days unless something is done to correct it.

To cope effectively with jet lag, start varying your normal sleep-eat-work pattern a week or so before your departure. If you are normally up by 7:00 A.M. and in bed around 11:00 P.M. or so, get up earlier and go to bed later for a few days. Then reverse the procedure by sleeping in a bit in the morning and going to bed ahead of your normal time. Vary your meal times, possibly putting off breakfast until lunch time. What all this erratic life-style will do is condition your body to begin accepting changes in routines. In turn, when the big transatlantic change comes, it won't be as much of a shock on your system.

To lessen the effects of jet lag en route, avoid excessive drinking and eating. After your arrival, exercise the first day by taking a vigorous walk, followed by a long nap. You should have set your watch to local time at your destination as you departed on your flight. By doing this, you subconsciously accelerate your adjustment to the new time zone. For example, how many times have you looked at your watch and then realized you were hungry? Get plenty of rest on the day of your arrival, and begin doing everything you normally do back home according to the new local time. Respect jet lag by taking these precautions and you'll enjoy your vacation.

Prestwick Airport is Scotland's international air terminal. Positioned twenty-nine miles southwest of Glasgow, the airport serves scheduled transatlantic air carriers as well as charter flights. Rail connections to Glasgow and Edinburgh are available from the train station in the nearby town of Prestwick.

4   ARRIVING IN BRITAIN

That big moment is about to happen. Years of dreaming, months of planning, and weeks of anticipation are about to become a reality. The "No Smoking" and "Fasten Seat Belts" signs have been illuminated, and the cabin attendants advise that the aircraft will be landing in a few minutes. If this is your initial visit to Britain, you'll be straining to get your first glimpse of the land from your window; if you have been to Britain many times before, you'll be straining to get a glimpse of the land right along with the other passengers. There is always an unexplainable thrill about arriving in a foreign country. Enjoy this emotion; it's part of the reason for your journey—to experience the adventure of travel, to probe beyond the normal confines of your environment, to meet other people, to enjoy a bit more of the world than you did before the "Fasten Seat Belts" sign came on.

The Airports

Within Britain, there are seven airports managed by the British Airports Authority—Heathrow, Gatwick, and Stansted in the London area; Glasgow, Edinburgh, Prestwick, and Aberdeen in Scotland. Your destination depends on the routing you selected and the air carrier taking you there. If your destination is London, you could arrive at either Heathrow or Gatwick. Check with the air carrier to be certain.

Should you need specific information regarding your arrival or departure airport in Britain, such as travel to and from the airport, airport services, or information services, ask your travel agent to check in the European edition of the Official Airlines Guides "Travel Planner." Another way would be to ask your agent to send a FAX to Gatwick Airport, (0293) 50413; Heathrow Airport, (01) 745 4290; Scottish Airports, (041) 887 1699; or Stansted Airport, (0279) 81655. A FAX message will ensure that the latest and most specific information will be obtained.

Transportation between London and the Heathrow and Gatwick airports is described on page 69. Similar information for Prestwick Airport in Scotland may be found on page 222.

Clearing Customs

The customs-information cards given to you by the cabin attendants before landing will expedite your clearance through arrival formalities. Actually, you will go through two processes—customs and immigration— although they appear to be integrated. Immigration officials will want to examine your passport.

This is usually conducted at a barrier gate en route to the baggage-claim area in the airport. After collecting the checked baggage, you should proceed to the customs-inspection area, where you will find two color-coded lanes—green for "Nothing to Declare" and red for "To Declare." Everyone has some apprehension about passing through customs. For the most part, the apprehension is based on the question, "Am I doing it properly?" Doing it properly in Britain consists of going straight through the "Nothing to Declare" channel (unless you are asked to stop by an officer) and moving through into the airport's general-assembly area.

If the customs officials want to examine your luggage, they will indicate so as you approach them. Don't go through the "To Declare" lane unless you have brought amounts of tobacco or liquor with you that exceed the duty-free limits or have purchased a gift that you will be leaving with someone in Britain with a value exceeding £28.

The type and amount of duty-free goods that you may bring into Britain vary with your point of departure—a European Common Market country or otherwise. For transatlantic passengers, the limit is 400 cigarettes and a liter bottle of liquor or two bottles of sparking wine and two bottles of still wine. You will have plenty of advance advice on duty-free imports posted in your departing airport and you can check with the cabin attendants on the airplane as well. Know before you go, and the clearing procedures in Britain will present no problem.

The phrase "know before you go" also applies to your return to North America. The U.S. Treasury Department publishes an informative booklet containing customs hints for returning residents. Write to the Department of the Treasury, Washington, DC 20229 for the *Know Before You Go* booklet. For U.S. Customs information while in London, telephone 499–1212 at the American Embassy.

When clearing through foreign customs, keep in mind that the average customs inspector is more interested in the luggage of a returning national than in yours. Always carry your customs declaration along with your passport and in full view as you unlock your luggage in case it has to be inspected.

British Currency

British currency is based on the pound sterling. The pound is divided into one-hundred pence, just as the U.S. dollar is divided into one hundred cents. When exchanging money in Britain, you will receive paper notes in denominations of £5, £10, or £20. Coins of 50p (seven sided), 20p, 10p, 5p, 2p, and 1p will be exchanged for amounts less than one pound. The £1 coin replaced the £1 note.

British paper notes, like the majority of world currencies, vary in size according to their value, and a variety of them can wreak havoc to the orderliness of a North American's wallet. Certain notes, the £10 and £20 in particular, will require folding before they will fit into a wallet designed to hold dollars. Use discretion when engaged in this folding process, especially in public.

British Telephones

Old-timers who first toured the British Isles under the auspices of General Dwight D. Eisenhower and their local draft boards will find that the British telephones with the dreaded "A" and "B" buttons are long gone. Many people thought that when the British removed all their road signs to confuse possible invaders during World War II, they added "A" and "B" buttons to the telephones to confuse—possibly even eliminate—telephone communications by invaders and visitors alike. We've even heard it whispered by off-duty State Department personnel that Britain was denied participation in the Marshall Plan because of the huge amounts of money the Americans had "hung up" in the British pay phones somewhere between the "A" and "B" buttons.

All that is legend. The modern, public, coin-box telephones now in operation throughout Britain are simple—with a bit of explanation, that is. Basic differences still exist between British phones and ours, particularly in the signals they make. A ringing signal is two short rings, followed by a pause. The busy signal sounds the same—only busier. An all-circuits-busy signal is a rapid series of high-low tones, but when you have reached a telephone number not in use, a high-pitched continuous tone reminiscent of a World War II air-raid siren is heard.

To master the modern British pay phone, arm yourself with an ample supply of decimal coins. Lift the receiver, listen for the dial tone (a purring sound), and drop a coin into the appropriate slot. Then dial the number you want. The ringing signal will be heard until you are connected with your party. If a series of rapid pips occurs during your conversation, you need more coins. Don't despair if you can't master the system. Merely lift the receiver and dial 100 for the operator. Do not insert money until the operator tells you to. To summons emergency services (fire, police, or ambulance), dial 999. Do not insert money.

British Traditions

Some visitors entering Britain for the first time may find some of the British traditions, customs, and way of life a little difficult to understand. Perhaps what follows may assist in the transition.

If a Scot from Edinburgh, a Welshman from Cardiff, and an Englishman from London were traveling together in North America, they would describe themselves as being "British." But among themselves, they would be Scot, Welsh, and English. These three nationalities, joined by the

Ulstermen of Northern Ireland, make up what we refer to as the United Kingdom. Since the BritRail Pass is not accepted for rail travel in Northern Ireland (as previously mentioned), references in this book are to *Britain* rather than the *United Kingdom*, and the term *British* refers to the peoples of England, Scotland, and Wales.

The British character will wear well on you after a few days. If you are taken by the strangeness of their manners, remember that the British are a well-disciplined people. If anything is at fault, more than likely it is the visitor, not the host. You might spill your tea the first time a waitress calls you "Dearie," but you'll learn very quickly that these figures of speech are actually a kind of politeness. You'll also learn very quickly that the British queue is the quintessence of "first-come, first-served."

On the surface, Britons may appear to lack a sense of humor. Once their facade is penetrated, however, you will find them capable of the highest mark of humor—they can laugh at themselves. This becomes most evident in their observations regarding their weather. "The way to ensure summer in England," snapped Horace Walpole, "is to have it framed and glazed in a comfortable room." Byron's observation was perhaps more terse: "The English winter—ending in July to recommence in August." Britain does have a tendency to be damp at times. You won't regret taking a small folding umbrella.

The Language Barrier

By now, you'll notice that there is one! It has often been said that the two great countries of America and Britain are divided only by a common language. Terminology, more so than pronunciation, appears to be the problem whenever an American and a Briton cannot communicate effectively. Several of our readers report that *British Self-taught, with Comments in American* by Norman W. Schur (New York, the Macmillan Company, 1973) can be most helpful during an initial visit to Britain.

Reading the daily newspapers and listening to the British Broadcasting Corporation (BBC) or watching the telly (television) are quick remedial methods for learning the language. These media communicate through a (more or less) middle-of-the-road lexicon. Regional and local dialects can be extremely difficult to comprehend on occasion. It has been said that if an Oxford graduate and a Cambridge graduate were locked together in the same room, neither would be able to converse with the other—even after being properly introduced.

One of the first things a visitor from "the Colonies" will notice is the manner in which directions are given. Americans geographically locate a point within a city by referring to the number of blocks distant from the point of inquiry, for example, "two blocks down the street." Britain's early road builders, however, never thought too much about a grid system and permitted their streets to wander along the easiest gradient. Consequently, directions given by a constable or a man on the street will usually be in terms of linear directions, that is, "straight-away for one-hundred yards," "a quarter-mile," "a mile or two," and so on. Visual objects are employed as well: "straight-away to the pub," "keep walking till you come to the third traffic light," and the like. Cabbies (taxi drivers) are particularly good sources for directional information and advice. Every cabby carries a street map in his taxi and will be glad to assist you.

Nuances in the American/British vocabulary can sometimes lead to trouble. In a public place, such as a train station, those in search of toilet facilities will do well to employ the term *lavatory* in their quest. The *WC* (water closet) seems to be losing its effectiveness in Britain, although it still brings direct results when used in Continental Europe. But if you want to be up on slang expressions, you might ask for the *loo*—that's where the "in crowd" goes to "spend a penny." Requesting directions for the *bathroom*, particularly in a train station, might lead you to the public showers. So take our advice and stay with lavatory.

Terminology in a train station should not present much of a problem. The baggage room is *left luggage*, and *lost property* translates easily into lost and found. Elevators are labeled *lifts,* but *subway* means a pedestrian, underground street crossing. The Underground, or *tube,* is the British version of our subway.

A *carriage* is a (rail) coach, and a *coach* is a long-distance bus. Should you hear the term *goods wagon* or *goods train,* that translates to a freight car or a freight train in American terminology. Aboard a train, the conductor usually is referred to as the *guard;* the engineer becomes the train *driver*.

The British measure their body weight in stones—a stone being a unit of fourteen pounds. A person weighing fourteen stone six pounds would gross out at 202 pounds avoirdupois. A popular measurement of elapsed time is *a fortnight,* meaning fourteen days or two weeks. Britain's conversion to a decimal currency system has not changed the slang for the pound sterling— it's still a "quid." You may hear a price quoted in *guineas,* a holdover from the old days meaning one pound and one shilling.

British Pubs

The pub is uniquely British and can be found only on the British Isles, because the ingredient that makes a true "public house" is not its construction, architecture, furniture, or the spirits it dispenses—it's its clientele. The "local," as most British pubs are lovingly referred to, is an organic part of the community. It ranks in importance along with the local

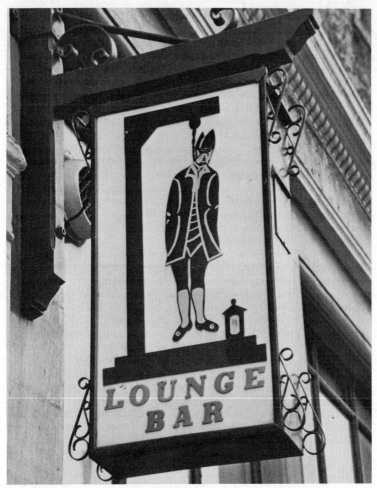

LOUNGE
BAR

Local Hangout, The Gallows Pub in Edinburgh takes its name from the fact that it is located on the site of Gallows Hill, where executions by hanging were held in days not too dim in the city's past. British public houses frequently have taken their names from the activities previously conducted in the area, like Smugglers—or from folklore— George & Dragon. The Wicked Lady near St. Albans, however, has us puzzled.

postal office and the town hall—perhaps even higher. It is supported by "locals," who generally prefer to stand when they imbibe, for pub etiquette must be observed at all times. Pub etiquette also dictates that you pay for the "round" when served and if you accept a drink, you are expected to buy a round in return.

The term *public house,* means just that. Everyone is welcome—even Americans and Australians. To accommodate the differences in drinking etiquettes of these visitors, most pubs have a second bar area, which is identified as a lounge or a saloon. There are more seats and usually the drinks cost a bit more.

When are the pubs open? Licensing hours now generally permit English pubs to remain open from 1100 to 2300 Monday through Saturday and Sundays from 1200 to 1500 and again from 1900 to 2230. You must be over eighteen to buy or consume alcoholic beverages in a pub. Children fourteen years and older may be admitted legally to a pub and may consume nonalcoholic drinks. Children of all ages are usually admitted to licensed restaurants; they are also admitted to "beer gardens" and family rooms, which many pubs have.

Closing time in a pub is quite an event and frequently can create confusion among the uninformed and the uninitiated. At the appointed hour, the owner or head barkeep announces, "Time, gentlemen!" in a loud, authoritative voice. At that instant, a bar towel is draped over the beer pumps, and everyone quickly attends to drinking up and hastily departing the premises. Without prior knowledge of this procedure, visitors have frequently mistaken closing time for a fire drill and have begun evacuating the building via the closest window!

A pub is usually rated by the congeniality of its owner, and unless "on holidays," he or she is usually found on the premises during operating hours. An entrepreneurial lot, many owners offer "pub grub" in their establishments. Visitors find it a good alternative to Wendy's or McDonald's for a snack or a lunch because a Frosty can never really compete with a good pint of ale or porter.

A pub's personality greets you at the door. You can tell in an instant whether or not it's your kind of place. If its ambience reaches out to you, enter. No doubt a local or two will note your entrance with a friendly nod as the barmaid beams at you and asks, "What'll you have, governor?" When advised, she'll then indicate with a slight directional nod of her head that it will be served in the lounge area. Pay when served. Tip the barmaid, but never tip the owner in the event he brings the drinks to the table to bid you welcome. He's the host; you are the guest. Later, you might join the locals at the bar; but remember, remain standing and pay for a round when it's your turn to buy. Who knows, the locals might suggest that you drop around again.

Food on the move includes a variety of service and menus. InterCity trains (above) feature three types of menus: Gold Star, Main Line, and Grill. Buffet service (below) offers a wide range of snacks and drinks. Food-service cars (carriages) are identified by an exterior red band above the windows.

5 BRITISH RAIL SERVICES

Over the last decade, the services on the British Rail passenger network have come a long way—with yet a long way to go. There is still a discernible difference between the operating speeds and the passenger comforts of the railroads of Continental Europe and those of the British, the latter being inferior; yet the gap is narrowing.

The front runner of British Rail's stable is its High Speed Train (HST), the InterCity 125. Nicknamed the "Journey Shrinker," the world's fastest diesel train is shrinking journeys on many of the main routes out of London. From King's Cross Station, for example, the Flying Scotsman, an InterCity 125, covers the 393 miles between London and Edinburgh in four hours and thirty-five minutes—an average of eighty-seven miles per hour, and that includes a station stop at York and Newcastle in England before crossing the Scottish border. Hourly service by 125s links the two capitals. InterCity 125 service also extends from London to Plymouth and Penzance. Leading the 125 fleet to England's west is the Golden Hind, appropriately named after Sir Francis Drake's famous sailing vessel.

InterCity 125 trains offer comfort as well as speed. They have a whole range of luxury features, including air conditioning, soundproofing, automatic interior doors, and a wide choice of meals, snacks, and drinks. The trains are powered by two 2,250-horsepower diesel-electric engines—one at each end of the train. The 125 coaches are identified by letter (A, B, C, etc.), and the stations they serve have their platform positions marked accordingly.

The mainline between London and Edinburgh, which is particularly popular with overseas visitors, is being electrified. The use of electric locomotives, due for completion in 1991, will cut the time for the 393-mile journey to only four hours and fifteen minutes. The light at the end of BritRail's tunnel grows brighter and brighter. By InterCity 125 service from London, you can now reach Cardiff, in Wales, in two hours and twenty minutes; York, in one hour, fifty-one minutes. Running times are being slashed on all major British Rail lines. A train trip from London to Glasgow used to take six hours; now you're there in only four hours and fifty-three minutes!

Aside from the InterCity 125s and the equally fast and comfortable all-electric passenger trains operated by British Rail on its major routes (the London-Glasgow line is completely electrified), there is a paucity of modern commuter-type trains on many of its intermediate lines. For example, although train service south of London is completely electrified, for the most part it is served by four-car units, some of which have already passed their thirty-eighth "birthdays." These trains have seen yeoman duty through the years and show more than a fair amount of wear and tear.

Along with Beatlemania, graffiti arrived in Britain accompanied by modern packaging, which produces litter in abundance. The older trains, however, were designed in the days when cleaning labor was plentiful and cheap. Washing as many as eighty windows on a single coach wasn't a problem then, but it is now. Moreover, air conditioning is nonexistent in the older trains, although that's no great problem because summers in the British Isles are generally milder than those in North America. But heating can be a problem. Not many years ago, train passengers set out on their journeys wrapped in heavy overcoats and shod with thick-soled shoes. Full heat in the coach brought complaints of stuffiness. Today's grumbles from thinly clad travelers are very much the opposite.

The ''old units'' are gradually being replaced by new suburban-type trains, and some of the vintage units are being refurbished with more comfortable seats, better lighting, heating, and soundproofing. Nevertheless, it will be a while before the ''generation gap'' in British Rail's rolling stock is overcome.

Possibly on a day excursion off the main lines, you may ride in a locomotive-hauled coach with an exit door for each compartment. We've counted as many as nine doors to a side on some coaches. These cars are relics from the days when station porters opened and closed the doors for passengers. Consequently, you won't find any door handles inside the compartment. To get out, lower the window and open the door from the outside.

Sleeping, restaurant, buffet and Pullman cars are operated by British Rail, along with the standard passenger carriages (coaches). British Pullman cars differ from the Pullmans of North America in that they do not convert at night to provide sleeping accommodations. Instead, British Rail Pullmans are the elite of the line, the best in daytime comfort, and exclusively first-class. Even travelers holding first-class BritRail passes are required to pay a supplemental fare for occupancy, and seat reservations are obligatory. This luxury service operates on the London-to-Manchester/Liverpool route. Basically, it is designed to offer the businessman morning and afternoon services between England's capital and its leading commercial center. It is worth the experience, but we suggest that you dress appropriately for the occasion if you want to engage in tycoon-to-tycoon conversations with other passengers. In London, the Pullman trains depart from Euston Station. When accommodations are available, last-minute reservations and supplementary payment can be arranged with the conductor.

First-class sleeping cars have single-berth compartments; economy-class sleepers have two-berth compartments. Sleeping-car charges in Britain are economical—$40 per person for first class and $35 per person for economy class. Sleeping-car passengers are served with morning tea or coffee and biscuits free of charge, and they generally can remain in the sleeping cars at destination until 7:30 A.M. The charge is standard for all destinations regardless of the distance.

With such attractive prices, an overnight trip aboard a sleeper may outweigh the alternative of seeking a night's lodging in a city and an early morning departure in order to make your destination on time. Consider the sleeping cars for excursions to Plymouth, Penzance, and Inverness.

Sleeper services operate between London and the main centers in Scotland, the north of England, south Wales, and the west of England. "Nightcap" service is available, too, in case you're interested.

Most InterCity trains haul restaurant cars. If not, there usually is a buffet car from which you can obtain snacks and beverages. Aboard the InterCity fleet, restaurant cars offer a wide range of freshly prepared traditional dishes. Gold Star restaurant service is available on many 125s and on selected "business" trains—the Manchester/Liverpool Pullman, for example. Passengers holding first-class tickets who wish to take meals can reserve seats in the restaurant car or in adjacent coaches. Breakfast aboard British Rail trains has always been a great attraction. It's hearty and generally very good.

Some buffet cars offer "grill" meals, which you may enjoy either there, or back at your seat. Seating in the buffet cars is not assignable, thereby providing a reasonable opportunity to be seated while you select from the bill of fare. One innovation found aboard many British Rail food-service cars is beer and lager on draft. This, according to many railroad buffs, is an outstanding stride forward in the annals of railroad engineering!

Admittedly, dining aboard a speeding train is an unusual gastronomic experience, but it can be on the expensive side. Although British Rail's food catering aboard is far more economical than similar services on the trains of the Continent, those seeking less expensive food may want to utilize the food facilities found at most rail stations in Britain. They range in service from complete restaurants servicing a variety of hot and cold dishes to a snack bar–type operation. Some have off-license provisions allowing you to purchase alcoholic beverages for consumption elsewhere, but all bars operating in the stations, unlike those on the trains, must observe the local licensing hours for drinks.

The most economical food you may enjoy on a train in Britain is, of course, that which you bring aboard yourself. Many of the station restaurants will prepare box lunches for you to take on your trip. Ask for the "buffet-pack" service. Your hotel or bed-and-breakfast probably can provide the same service. We suggest that you make your initial inquiry a day ahead of your first planned day excursion.

First Class, Economy Class?

On most British Rail trains you have a choice of first- or economy-class travel. BritRail Passes are sold for both classes. First-class seats are wider and more spacious. If that is the sort of accommodations you want, then it is worth paying the extra price. Economy class (also referred to as standard class) is, however, an excellent standard. All the facilities aboard the trains, such as restaurant and buffet services, are available for both first- and economy-class travelers.

The average British citizen usually travels by economy-class carriage (coach). In fact, it is so much the custom that if you want to purchase a first-class ticket, you must specifically state "first-class"; otherwise, you will automatically receive an economy-class ticket. This does not mean that you will find the economy-class carriages crowded, while the first-class sections remain vacant. First class offers extra comfort and is less crowded. First-class accommodations for weekend and holiday travel are particularly desirable. Seats may be reserved in both classes, which is a wise move if your journey is a "must" and the distance is great. "Riding the cases" (sitting on your suitcase for lack of a seat) is not a comfortable way to travel.

Seat reservations may be made in any major train terminal throughout Britain. If you purchase a BritRail Pass, you may obtain advance reservations prior to arriving in Britain through BritRail Travel International, Inc., which represents the British Rail system. For the office nearest you, consult page 290. The charge for seat reservations is $5.00 (U.S.) per person per trip.

Travelers holding first-class BritRail Passes may travel in either first- or economy-class carriages—which is a nice option for bachelors when the good looking "bird" you've been yearning to chat with boards the economy-class section. It's a disaster, however, if she moves to the first-class section while you're holding an economy-class ticket!

You will find some single-class trains operating on branch lines. This means that the first-class accommodations are not available aboard that particular train. It is a nice, polite British way of avoiding the somewhat unrefined term *second class only*.

Similar to those on the Continent, first-class British Rail cars are marked distinctively by a yellow band running the length of each car above its doors and windows. On other-than-mainline service, where both first- and economy-class accommodations may be provided in the same car, a yellow band will be shown for only the first-class portion of the car. Restaurant cars, buffets, and cars containing other forms of food-catering facilities are identified by a red band above their doors and windows.

Except for those of the InterCity 125s (page 39), it is difficult to determine exactly where the first-class coaches will halt during an en route station stop. The non-English-speaking nations of Europe generally provide a diagram of each train's composition and where it will stop in the station.

Not so in Britain. According to the equipment in use, the first-class section of a British train can be at the head, the rear, or the middle of the train. Station porters (there are a few left) generally speculate on where the yellow-striped cars will stop. But few are accurate, even if they are handling your luggage. Through experience, we have devised a system that is relatively effective.

Position yourself midway on the platform and scan for the yellow band as the train enters the station. Should it pass you, take off to the head of the train; if it doesn't, head in the other direction. Should the yellow-striped car stop directly in front you, fate has been kind to you this day, but you can bet it won't happen again soon.

There is an increase in the nonsmoking accommodations aboard British trains. The overall percentage of nonsmoking seats currently is about 75 percent, reflecting the noticeable change in the public attitude toward smoking. There is a stiff fine for violating the rule. So if you are a smoker, keep your eyes alert for the red nonsmoking signs and smoke only in the areas so designated.

Train Schedules

British timetables are generally divided into sections according to the pattern of services provided. A typical two-part division is "Mondays to Saturdays" and "Sundays." You may run across a mix, however, including "Mondays to Fridays," "Mondays to Saturdays," or "Saturdays and Sundays." All days stated are inclusive. In other words, "Mondays to Saturdays" includes all six days. (The schedules appearing in *Britain By BritRail* are stated as "Mondays *through* Saturdays.")

Always be certain that you look at the correct part of the schedule for the particular day of the week on which you wish to travel. Another caution: Services may be modified on days preceding and immediately following bank holidays. Best bet for a "must" trip, a late night return, or an early morning departure is to check your plans with the British Rail personnel in the station travel centers. Extensive engineering work is often conducted on the British Rail system on weekends, which frequently affects passengers' schedules. Telephones may also be employed for inquiries. Useful telephone numbers are given on the *Britain By BritRail* schedules for this purpose.

You should experience little difficulty in verifying the departure time of your selected train or locating the platform from which it departs once you've made it to the station—providing that in London you've gone to the proper station. Airport-style digital displays are the usual source for such information in most British stations. You will find them in the main station halls and also on the train platforms in many stations. Even the old-fashioned train bulletin boards (page 288), however, can still provide the needed information. Augmenting displayed train-departure information are the usual vocal announcements in the station halls and on the platforms. For the most part, they differ from those made by Amtrak because you can understand them. Perhaps it's the accent that makes it possible.

Ask The Guard

Every British Rail train travels with a conductor aboard. As previously explained, his official title is guard. This gentleman carries with him—in either his handbook or his head—a potpourri of valuable information. For example, if you are required to change trains in order to arrive at your final destination, ask the guard. The London day excursion to Lincoln is one in which you should change trains at Newark Northgate, approximately one and one-half hours after departing London. Will the train departing there for Lincoln Central be standing across the platform from the train you arrive on from London, or will a platform change be necessary? The guard has this information, and it's yours for the asking.

Perhaps en route you learn that the train you are traveling on will be passing a famous British landmark, say a castle. On which side of the train will it pass? If you are a castle buff, maybe you would like to come back on another day to visit the castle. Is there a local train station near the castle? Is there a local bus to take you there if the castle is beyond walking distance? Is there a pub or inn in the vicinity? Surprisingly, you'll probably get responses to all of the above plus a condensed history lesson on the castle and its surroundings—all from the guard.

The guard becomes invaluable when you decide to change your itinerary or vary the time to return to your hotel. With a quick reference to his handbook, he will be able to tell you the time of the next train or the last one you may take that evening. He's also an excellent source of the correct time, for his watch is always set to the second and checked with British Rail's master clock daily. In many ways, the guard becomes your unofficial tour guide—or guardian angel, as the case may be.

BritRail/Drive

Britain is compact, which makes it convenient to take the train and see the sights. There are but a few nooks and crannies within Britain that cannot be reached by train. Some vacationers to Britain, however, find an occasional need to go sightseeing by car. As a consequence, BritRail has devised a system with Hertz to fill this need.

BritRail/Drive combines a BritRail Flexipass with the rental of a Hertz car with unlimited mileage for four or eight twenty-four-hour periods depending upon the validity period of the BritRail Flexipass. There are six different types of car models to choose from—three types with automatic transmissions, an absolute must for any driver experiencing the transition to "starboard" steering for the first time.

If you decide upon the BritRail/Drive package, along with your pass you will receive car-rental vouchers (one for each day's rental). Hertz has more than 200 convenient locations throughout Britain. One hundred are located in the major British Rail stations; eleven at airport locations; and 105 at downtown locations throughout England, Scotland, and Wales. When you are ready to reserve a car, you contact the nearest Hertz office. It is suggested that you make these reservations as early as possible, particularly if you want a car with an automatic transmission.

Since your car-rental vouchers may be used only during the validity period of your BritRail Flexipass, the most economical way of using them is to arrange for a car to meet your train at a day-excursion point, do your exploring, and return the car to the same station before returning to your base city by train. By the way, prebooked requests for a car to meet your train will be honored seven days a week.

Each car-rental voucher includes a twenty-four-consecutive-hour rental with unlimited mileage, government tax (VAT) of 15 percent, insurance, and emergency car-replacement coverage. The renter is responsible for collision damage, personal accident insurance, and gas. Payment of these charges may be made by credit card or a deposit at the start of each rental period. Aside from the gasoline, the other charges average about $9 U.S. per day.

If you are traveling alone, a single supplement will be charged in addition to the per-person price. The amount of the supplement varies according to the duration of the BritRail Flexipass and the car category. BritRail/Drive rates are based on two adults per car. The minimum age for rental is twenty-one.

Complete rate information and a *Go BritRail* catalog may be obtained from your travel agent or by calling (800) 722–7151.

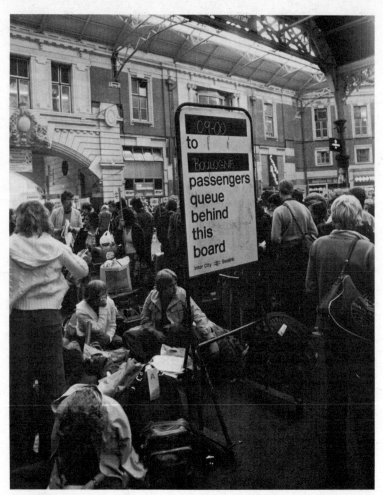

09.00
to
BOULOGNE
passengers
queue
behind
this
board

Inter City Sealine

Weekend/holiday travel need not be avoided on British Rail services as long as you accept the fact that trains will be crowded. Seat reservations in advance will help. Aids to passenger control, such as this queue marker, do much to expedite boarding for holiday destinations.

6 TRAIN-TRAVEL TIPS

"What affects men sharply about a foreign nation," wrote G. K. Chesterton, "is not so much finding or not finding familiar things, it is rather not finding them in the familiar place."

For many of us coming to Britain for the first time, we find a confusion of terminology and learn too late that what we sought was really available throughout our visit. Our problem was merely not knowing the proper place to look or the proper name to ask for. Perhaps some things might be set in better order for the pleasure of your BritRail adventures with the following train-travel tips.

Handicapped Travel

One important tip to mention first is that British Rail is leading the world in providing facilities in its stations and aboard its trains for the disabled and the handicapped. Through such efforts, rail travel is becoming more and more a chosen method of transportation and recreation for disabled persons. Many aids for the handicapped have been incorporated into British Rail's code for station design. Trains are being designed with wider doors for wheelchair access; some even have a removable seat to make room for a wheelchair. Ramp access to toilets, buffets, and other facilities is being provided. Folding wheelchairs are also available at main stations so that occupants may be transferred to a regular seat once aboard the train. British Rail is most eager to provide as comfortable a journey as possible for the disabled passenger. To do this, prior advice of the intended travel plans would be most helpful to both the traveler and the authorities.

For those readers who want to learn more about this innovative approach to travel for the disabled and the handicapped, we suggest writing to the Royal Association for Disability and Rehabilitation, 25 Mortimer Street, London, W1N 8AB, England, for details. The association has published *A Guide to British Rail for the Physically Handicapped*.

If you plan to travel in Britain with a handicapped person, write or call BritRail Travel International, 1500 Broadway, New York, NY 10036–4015 (telephone 212–575–2667) as soon as you establish your itinerary and begin making arrangements. The same applies to the airline you'll be using for your transatlantic flight. Provide them with all the details of your itinerary, the nature of the disability, and any other information that will help them to help you.

Specifically, special diets, medications, and toilet and medical-attention requirements should be made known. With these details attended to, you can look forward to a pleasant journey.

Baggage Carts

Many otherwise able train visitors to Britain impose a severe disadvantage upon themselves by arriving with more luggage than three men and a small boy could possibly carry. Train porters are an endangered species, and their demise is being expedited by the luggage trolley—Britain's version of our baggage cart—an elusive device that, whatever your position on the train platform, haunts the extreme opposite end. Our number-one tip (repeated from chapter 2) to all train travelers is to "go lightly." At most, take one medium-sized suitcase augmented by a modest shoulder bag. There still will be times when you will wish you could completely unburden yourself by discarding your suitcase. If you have purchased a model with built-in wheels, however, it usually will follow at your heels like a well-trained dog as you apply minimum pulling power. Unlike a dog, the wheeled suitcase cannot climb stairs, so be prepared to lift it on and off the train.

Rather than relying upon the trolleys in the train stations, you might consider investing in your own baggage cart to take with you. You will see more and more train travelers proceeding through rail stations in Europe with such equipment. There are many types of carts on today's market. Airports and travel specialty shops are the best places to look for them. Like most items, the better ones cost a little more, but they're usually worth it. For our money, there is only one baggage cart worth buying—the Cart-A-Bag. It's collapsible and holds up to 150 pounds of luggage. It folds small and packs into its own vinyl case. When not on the road, we even use it around the office to cart books and things to the post office. TWA's Flight Shop sells them, and most of the better luggage shops do, too. Cheaper carts are available, but not for long. Within days of their purchase, you'll find parts of their wheels scattered about in some airport or train station and the rest of the device in a dustbin (that's British for trash can).

Another tip regarding the loading of your luggage onto a baggage cart, or one of British Rail's station trolleys, is to keep the load as narrow as possible. You must pass through ticket barriers going to and coming from the trains. The barriers are rather narrow. A Samsonite suitcase loaded sideways on your baggage cart or one of the station's trolleys will just clear, but a full-figured lady with a wardrobe case is in trouble every time. The trolleys provided by the station should not be taken aboard the train, although we've seen it tried. Again, if you are taking your own cart with you, fold it before boarding. If you don't, you may spend an embarrassing ten minutes or so on the station platform extracting a hapless fellow traveler from it as your train eases out of the station without you.

Using the Lifts

The greatest problem in using the train station's luggage trolleys (or your own baggage cart) is traversing the station hall to the platform area, because practically every station has stairs. You can overcome this problem by using the station's lift (elevator). This polite announcement is found posted in most British Rail stations: "Lifts are available for passengers who have difficulty in using the stairs. Please contact station staff if assistance is required." In searching for a lift, don't keep looking for a modern, automatic-door elevator brightly lit with soft music playing. What you will find instead is the old-fashioned, double-door, manually operated freight elevator, large enough to hold a Mack truck and usually illuminated with a single, bare light bulb—but it works. As the sign says, station staff will assist you. If you use the lifts frequently, however, you will develop the knack of handling them all by yourself. One word of caution: The lift will not operate until *both* barriers (usually a door and a gate) have been closed securely. Furthermore, the lift will be left inoperative if you fail to close the doors after you have used it. Be considerate of other passengers and the station staff by making certain that the lift is left operable for the next user.

As a matter of interest, if your rail journey takes you to Continental Europe, the use of rail-station lifts by passengers is strictly forbidden.

Porter Services

Porter service is on the wane but still available in many train stations throughout Britain, particularly in the larger ones. The best way to locate a porter is to inquire at the "Left Luggage" (baggage storage) area or at the station's incoming taxi stand. If your luggage has been checked in at the station, there will be a handling charge, but the tip remains a personal item between you and the porter. We suggest 25 pence per parcel (with a 50-pence minimum) as a reasonable gratuity. Most porters will take your bags to the train and place them aboard in the luggage racks over your seats. Porters are rather scarce on arrival platforms. If you must have assistance, approach the stationmaster's office or the train conductor prior to departure with the request that a porter be asked to meet your train upon arrival at your destination.

If you are transferring between base cities or changing hotels from one city to another, you can request the hall porter at the hotel you are leaving to arrange for the arriving hotel's hall porter to meet your train upon arrival. A small tip should arrange everything.

The BritRail Difference

Readers who have traveled on the trains of Continental Europe will note a few basic differences between Eurail and British Rail operations. Car (carriage, if you please) markings include the standard pictographs for smoking or nonsmoking. First-class conveyances are appropriately identified with the yellow band, but unlike their Continental cousins, British Rail cars do not display the destination panel on their sides. (Eurail cars are marked with the name of the city from which they originated, the final destination, and the major in-between stops.) Nevertheless, British Rail trains do "split." Dual-destination trains in Britain will be identified in the departing station by dividing boards—first at the ticket barrier, where a bulletin board will state the train's composition. (For example: "First 4 cars—Dover. Remaining Cars—Ramsgate.") At the head of the first four cars, you will find a platform sign advising "Ramsgate Ahead. Turn Back for Dover." The best solution we have found in a situation like this is to *ask the train conductor before boarding and again on board the train when you present your BritRail Pass or ticket.*

Another thing missing on the BritRail scene are the vendors, trackside as well as aboard the train. The construction of the "four-car unit" makes access impossible to the other units making up the train. So the vendor and his "goodies cart" moving through the train while en route is automatically ruled out.

Most of all, we missed the trackside vendors who can provide all the essentials of life—food and beverage alike—through an open train window during a two-minute station stop. BritRail's counter to the trackside vendor are the snack-bar kiosks located on the train platforms. But leaving the train to make a purchase at one of the kiosks is a bit risky—particularly if spouse, kids, and *your* suitcase depart without you!

A Few More Trip Tips

A few more train, travel tips to make your trip more enjoyable: "Mind the doors!" British Rail cars of the vintage class appear to provide a door for each passenger. There is a great din of door slamming prior to departure and an equal amount of confusion each time the train makes a station stop. If you are waiting at an en route station for a train, stand well back from the platform edge. Passengers impatient to alight from the train are prone to open the doors before the train comes to a complete stop. In so doing, they're actually extending a bludgeon that could kill you, maim you for life, bruise you, or just scare the daylights out of you—the last being preferred over any of the others. British Rail has posters, positioned in all of its stations where these multi-door cars are in service, asking folks to "please don't open the carriage door until the train has stopped" and "please don't stand close to the platform edge." Most of the posters are illustrated by a picture showing a person being struck by a door. Be certain that you are neither the hapless victim nor the careless culprit by observing the rules.

50

The final caption on the poster sums it up succinctly: "A moment's impatience, a lifetime of remorse."

Train Etiquette

Show your BritRail Pass, or ticket, upon request, and in the case of the pass, have your passport handy should the conductor like to see it. Don't place your feet on the seats of the train unless you have removed your shoes or have provided a protective covering for the seat. Place your luggage in the overhead racks provided for that purpose—not on the seats so that other passengers won't be able to crowd you. Observe the smoking/nonsmoking areas and rules. There are rather stiff fines that can be imposed for those smokers who violate the nonsmoking areas.

Observe seat reservations. Seating that has been reserved is marked. Even though it is apparent that a seat is unoccupied, if there are other passengers seated opposite, ask if the seat is open. It will avoid embarrassment later if the person holding the reservation happens to return.

Regarding dining-car reservations, on long-distance trains it is best to arrange for them soon after boarding. Inquire from the guard (conductor, remember?). If he cannot make them for you, a member of the dining-car crew will do so. Generally, they pass through the train prior to the first serving for that purpose. Usually, there are two servings, so be prepared to select the one to your liking. You can also inquire regarding the menu at the same time. The second serving is scheduled so that the dining-car crew has time to tidy up before the train reaches its destination. Therefore, the first serving is preferred by many because it does not seem to be rushed.

If you plan an overnight journey on a sleeper, ask the attendant to explain the manner in which the equipment in your compartment operates. For example, the newer sleeping cars have electric shades. A push of the button and they open; another push of the same button and they close. If you did not know the button's function, you just might try pushing the button while the train is standing in a station and you are not dressed for the occasion! It's proper to tip the attendant for his services; the proper time to do so is when he serves breakfast.

Hovercraft skim across the English Channel between England and France in thirty-five minutes or less at speeds exceeding sixty miles per hour. Rail transportation, combined with hovercraft service, has reduced running time between London and Paris to five and one-half hours. Victoria Station serves as the London terminal. In Paris, connecting trains arrive and depart at the Gare du Nord (North Station) or nearby Gare St. Lazare. With the opening of the rail tunnel under the English Channel in June 1993, running time between the two capitals will be reduced to three hours. Photo from British Rail.

7 SPECIAL ITINERARIES

In addition to the day excursions offered by this edition of *Britain By BritRail,* there are some special itineraries that are made possible through the unique features of British Rail services and its associated transportation facilities. Two of them, the Continental Quickie and the BritRail By Night excursions, are our own concoctions. Britainshrinkers have been offered by British Rail since 1973.

Continental Quickie

If you have never been to Continental Europe before, here's an opportunity to set foot on French soil, explore the seaport city of Boulogne, and yet return to London in time for a 9:00 P.M. dinner appointment. Hoverspeed's services makes this day excursion possible by skimming across the English Channel in one of the company's Super 4 hovercraft between Dover and Boulogne in less than thirty-five minutes port to port! Train connections are made out of London's Victoria Station (page 59) to Dover's Priory Station, where a transfer to the hoverport on Dover's Western Docks is accomplished by a special bus. Consult Table 50 of the *Thomas Cook European Timetable* for schedule information and read more about the amazing hovercraft on page 57 of this edition.

Boulogne is the largest fishing port in France. It was from Boulogne that Caesar set out to conquer England. Boulogne is really two towns—the Basse Ville that lies along the waterfront is very modern, while the Haute Ville poised on the hillside is much older and has a fine medieval wall surrounding it. You may want to include a side trip to Calais on this excursion. Rail and bus services between the two cities are frequent and convenient. If interested, make inquiry with the Boulogne tourist information center at the hoverport when you arrive.

If you are planning a day trip to France during the valid period of your BritRail Pass, you will need to purchase a Port-to-Port round-trip ticket. Your BritRail Pass will get you to the port and return you to London once you are back on British soil. If you plan to spend several days on the Continent, however, you should consider the BritFrance Railpass, which allows you to travel on both the British and the French rail networks. You can choose from any five days of travel to be completed within a fifteen-day period ($249 adult economy class, $335 adult first class) or any ten days travel within one month ($375 adult economy class, $495 adult first). The BritFrance Pass also includes round-trip Hovercraft travel between Dover and Boulogne or Dover and Calais, which must be completed during the time the pass is valid.

Britainshrinkers

This sounds like it could be the title of a James Bond thriller—and well it may be. BritRail's *Go BritRail* brochure describing this program states: "You'll travel on a special network of BritRail trains and comfortable motor coaches. Because our trains are fast, we can show you much more on each tour . . . all in a relaxed, leisurely way. At your destination, a motor coach awaits to whisk you off to the 'must see' sights in the area."

Britainshrinkers is a program of fully escorted tours leaving London after breakfast and returning in time for dinner. Lunch in a genuine pub is included, as are the entrance fees to places of interest that you will visit. The tours are easy to take—just arrive at the London rail station indicated on your ticket. A guide in a red uniform will take your ticket at the Britainshrinkers check-in point, which is easily identifiable by its sign.

The Britainshrinkers also offer two-day tours called overnighters. These enable you to visit places more distant from London. They include first-class hotel accommodations for one night, along with dinner and breakfast. Two-day tours venture into scenic Scotland and to north Wales and Chester. Or you can opt for the three-day tour, which combines York with Scotland.

The Britainshrinkers and overnighter programs differ from *Britain By BritRail's* day excursions and out-and-back excursions only in that the Britainshrinkers are fully escorted. The BritRail Pass is accepted as supplemental payment for the rail portion of the Britainshrinker tours—you could save up to 40 percent of the cost of each Britainshrinker tour you take if you have a BritRail Pass. As British Rail officials point out, the Britainshrinkers program was devised to serve the needs of visitors to London who were unable to take more than a day or two to visit the British countryside.

Another Britainshrinker program, The Great Britain Express, features an escorted six-day (five nights) tour of Britain from as far south as Plymouth up to Edinburgh, Scotland. Probably the most famous of the Britainshrinker programs is the luxury day trip from London on the most celebrated and romantic train in the world—the Orient Express. These tours are operated by the Venice Simplon-Orient-Express, a private company, so remember that the BritRail Pass is *not* valid on the Orient Express.

For a complete BritRail catalog and details on purchasing Britainshrinkers programs, BritFrance Railpasses, and/or BritRail Passes, write to George Ferguson & Co., Box 194, Dublin, Ohio 43017. You may also telephone toll-free (800) 722–7151 or FAX your request to (614) 764–0711.

BritRail By Night

Here's something that you can do with your eyes closed. As a rule, we do not advocate using sleeper cars when traveling by train in Europe. In the case of the excellent sleeper services offered by British Rail—and their moderate cost—however, we are making an exception.

British Rail operates its sleeper services between London and the main centers in Scotland, the north of England, south Wales, and the west of England. First-class sleepers accommodate one person; connecting bedrooms are available. Economy-class sleepers offer double accommodations—the two berths are stacked one over the other like bunk beds. Both services provide wall-to-wall carpeting, hot and cold running water, soap and towel, a comfortable mattress, and that all-important call button that will bring you a nightcap or your wake-up coffee.

The cost of sleeper accommodations based on single occupancy is $40 for first class; $35 for economy class. Usually, you can take occupancy thirty minutes before departure time and stay aboard until 7:30 A.M., even if the train arrives at your destination several hours earlier.

The major sleeping-car routes to points described in this edition are: Paddington Station to Penzance and Plymouth and to Cardiff in Wales; Euston Station to Glasgow, Inverness, Edinburgh, and Aberdeen. Sleeper service also is available from either Edinburgh or Glasgow to Inverness.

Overnight sleeper service opens a new door to the adventurous rail traveler. The sleeper charge compares favorably to economical hotel rates, so you can make the sleeper your "hotel on the move." By reserving sleeper accommodations for successive nights, an itinerary could be planned for a night on the train; a day at the destination; a night on the train returning to London; sightseeing, shopping, or a short day excursion out of London; and a night to another destination.

Expanding on the above, an adventurous traveler could depart London's Paddington Station about midnight, arriving early morning in Penzance to begin an all-day sightseeing trek extending to Land's End. Back in Penzance, the adventurer could board the sleeper that evening for London, spending an entire day there before boarding another sleeper in King's Cross Station for Edinburgh. After spending the day in Edinburgh, our traveler would board the Inverness-bound sleeper and search for the monster "Nessie" on Loch Ness the next day before boarding a sleeper bound for Glasgow. After devoting the following day to sightseeing in Scotland's largest metropolis, a fitting finale to this whirlwind tour would be to board a sleeper and arrive back in London, where it all began *only* a week ago.

Sealink ferries provide vehicle and passenger transport between Great Britain and the Continental seaports as well as to Ireland and the Channel Islands. Sealink services out of Dover include the French ports of Calais (one hour, thirty minutes) and Boulogne (one hour, fifty minutes).

8 CROSSING THE ENGLISH CHANNEL

The most convenient way of crossing the English Channel between Britain and the Continent is by the services of the British government subsidiaries of Sealink and Hoverspeed. Sealink is the conventional ferry service; Hoverspeed utilizes the hovercraft. For either service, you will be required to leave the train to board the water-borne conveyance. Unlike the European rail-ferry services from Denmark to Germany and Sweden, the rail coaches are not transferred aboard the ferries or hovercraft.

Private shipping lines such as the Sally Line also provide channel service. All of the cross-channel and North Sea schedules and destinations will be summarized later in this chapter.

Sealink

Sealink services on the English Channel are one class only; both first- and second-class accommodations, however, are available on the boat trains between London and Dover or Folkestone. The BritRail Pass is accepted for the rail portion of the journey from London to the ports. Separate tickets, however, must be purchased for the sea portion. These tickets are available at the ticket offices of London rail stations or at the Sealink Travel Centre at the head of platform 2 in the Victoria Station. Seat reservations are advisable throughout the year for the boat trains departing from this station. The term *boat train* applies to those trains departing from Victoria Station for direct connection at either Dover's Western Docks or Folkestone's Harbor terminal with Sealink ferries crossing to the French ports of either Calais or Boulogne. (See Table 50 of the *Thomas Cook European Timetable* for details.)

These boat trains go directly to the pier. Boat trains going to the port of Folkestone do not stop at Folkestone's Central Station. Regular train service is available to Dover, terminating at Dover Priory (Dover's main station), and to Folkestone, where trains call at Folkestone Central but not at Folkestone Harbor. For an expanded overview of these various land-terminal-only services, consult Tables 500 and 501 of the *Thomas Cook European Timetable*. Sealink also operates a service between Newhaven and Dieppe. For details, refer to Table 1003 of the timetable.

Due to the myriad of sailings to the Continent, we suggest that you check with the Sealink Travel Centre at the head of platform 2 in the Victoria Station for additional information, reservations, and current schedules.

Hoverspeed

Without doubt, the hovercraft is the most spectacular form of public transportation ever devised by man. Watching it in operation, you'll find it hard to determine if the hovercraft's origins are from *Star Wars* or *Close Encounters of the Third Kind*. Nevertheless, it is an ideal means of crossing the English Channel, which it can do between Dover and Calais in thirty-five minutes from pier to pier.

Hoverspeed is the trademark of Hovercraft, Ltd. Rail passengers have the option of either Sealink or Hoverspeed passage to and from the Continent. The fares are the same for both transportation modes, and both offer "one class only" accommodations.

Hoverspeed hovercraft depart on their "flight" from the hoverport on Dover's Western Docks. Travelers intending to use Hoverspeed rather than Sealink should be aware that *the boat train for hovercraft service does not terminate at the hoverport*. Hoverspeed hovercraft passengers should leave the train at Dover Western Docks, where a bus is available for transfer to the hoverport. The train for direct connections with the Hoverspeed hovercraft service departs from London's Victoria Station. When in London, check in with a British Rail Travel Centre for full details, reservations, and current schedules for a hovercraft crossing. For planning purposes, consult Table 50 in the *Thomas Cook European Timetable*. Another source of information for hovercraft services is the previously mentioned Sealink Travel Centre, located adjacent to platform 2 in London's Victoria Station.

"Ladies and Gentlemen, Hoverspeed's flight 715 is about to depart for Boulogne." That's the announcement you'll hear soon after boarding a hovercraft, for it literally flies just above the surface of the water, supported on a cushion of air generated by a series of aircraft jet engines. A foursome of directional propellers provide the lateral thrust to move the hovercraft at speeds up to sixty-five miles per hour.

Cabin attendants will check to see that you have fastened your seat belt, and you will be expected to remain in your seat for the duration of the "flight." Each hovercraft carries a duty-free locker, and it will open moments following departure from the hoverport. Your selections will be brought to your seat by one of the cabin attendants.

If weather conditions interrupt the hovercraft service, passengers will be transferred to the next car ferry. Connecting trains will be retimed to maintain the connections, with correspondingly later arrivals at destinations. The Super 4 series of hovercraft carry 424 passengers along with fifty-five passenger cars. Since you have the option of either Sealink or Hoverspeed for a channel crossing, we suggest you opt for the latter. There's no attraction at Disney World that can match it!

Choosing a Channel Crossing

Since there are various ways of crossing the English Channel and the North Sea en route to Europe, which one should you select? The fastest means of crossing the English Channel for direct rail connections between London and Paris is by hovercraft. If time permits, however, you may want to select a Sealink crossing by regular displacement vessel. The ultra-modern fleet of Sealink ferries plies the waters between England and the French port of Calais in an elapsed time of one hour and thirty minutes, compared to the thirty-five-minute crossing aboard a hovercraft. The slower crossing provides more time for shopping in the ship's duty-free store, however, and time to enjoy a leisurely meal as well.

Duty-free items are also available on the hovercraft crossing, but shopping is hectic in such a limited time. If the channel is rough, the hovercraft's stores are stowed and you might have to forgo restocking your larder until later—and not at popular duty-free prices, either.

As previously described, London to Paris by Sealink ferry takes you from London's Victoria Station to Dover or Folkestone by special boat train right to the dock. After the crossing, a French National Railroads' train will be waiting in Calais for you to continue your journey on to Paris. You will arrive in the Gare du Nord (North Station) of Paris approximately three hours after you reach the French port. The entire trip can be completed in no more than seven hours and twenty minutes via Sealink; via Hoverspeed, the journey will average about six and one-half hours. If you are returning to London following your visit to Paris, we suggest that you go by one means and return by the other.

Other Crossings

Dover–Oostende. The Belgian marine services of Regie des Transports Maritime (R.T.M.), in conjunction with P&O European Ferries, cross between Dover and the Belgian port of Oostende with train service connecting with Brussels and Koln (Cologne). A Jetfoil service is also available on this route. A supplementary fare of approximately $10 U.S. is payable for travel by Jetfoil. The ferries and the Jetfoil are one class only; connecting rail services are both first and second class. Refer to Table 52 of the *Thomas Cook Continental Timetable* for complete rail, ferry, and Jetfoil schedules.

Train departures for the boat ferries and Jetfoil leave from Victoria Station. Jetfoil passengers must report to the Jetfoil Lounge at track 14 for a boarding card at least twenty minutes before train departure. This route is the most direct connection with Brussels. By rail and Jetfoil, the average time between London's Victoria Station and Brussels Midi (South) Station is five hours and fifty-eight minutes; travel by the rail and ship combination requires seven hours plus forty-three minutes.

Newhaven–Dieppe. If you are looking for an alternate route between Britain and France, Sealink services are available from the English port of Newhaven, east of Brighton, to the maritime terminal of Dieppe in France. The sea route is seventy-one miles and the crossing takes four hours. Night crossings, made throughout the year, take five hours.

If the English Channel is not in a huffy mood, this can be a very pleasant crossing. Victoria Station is the point of departure from London. The boat train calls at Gatwick Airport en route to the Newhaven harbor. The French National Railroads' express-train service between Dieppe and Paris takes slightly more than two hours. St. Lazare is the rail terminal in Paris. The entire trip takes eight hours and fifty-three minutes by day; at night, it's completed in an even nine hours. Table 50 of the *Thomas Cook European Timetable* carries all the details of this route, including the connecting British and French train schedules.

Harwich–Hook of Holland. This is an excellent routing for travelers ranging between Britain and the Netherlands. It is the most direct sea link between London and Amsterdam. Convenient connections may also be made from the Hook of Holland (Hoek Van Holland) to Brussels, Belgium.

Both day and night crossings are available on this route. Sleeping accommodations aboard begin at modest prices. Reservations for the night crossings are obligatory and should be made well in advance of your journey. Departure out of London is from the Liverpool Street Station.

In the *Thomas Cook European Timetable,* Table 66 carries schedule information on the service between London and Amsterdam and features EuroCity name trains, the Admiral De Ruyter and the Benjamin Britten. Many famous express trains utilize this North Sea crossing, such as the Warszawa (Warsaw) Express, the Scandinavian Express, and the Loreley Express to Switzerland, as well as regular through-train service to Brussels, Munich, and Moscow. If you are looking for international intrigue, you'll be most likely to find it on the Harwich–Hook of Holland crossing. Running between the Liverpool Street Station and the Harwich harbor takes one hour and ten minutes. Once aboard, the daytime crossing is completed in six hours and thirty minutes; passage at night requires up to eight hours and thirty minutes.

BritRail Passes are not accepted by Sealink, Hoverspeed, or any of the privately owned shipping companies operating on either the English Channel or the North Sea. In addition, BritRail Passes cannot be utilized for rail travel in Continental Europe. Point-to-point tickets must be purchased for all sea voyages and continuing rail travel once you have departed Britain. If you hold a Eurailpass, you may have it validated at the rail station of the European port upon arrival and then continue your rail trip without the inconvenience of having to purchase point-to-point tickets.

Portsmouth–Cherbourg/Le Havre. Details of this crossing are listed on Table 1007 of the *Thomas Cook European Timetable*. Tables 507 and 511 provide rail-schedule information between London and Portsmouth; Table 122 describes rail schedules between Cherbourg and Paris. Table 120 should be consulted for train times between Le Havre and Paris. Arriving in Portsmouth, passengers are advised to use the bus service from the Portsmouth Continental Ferry Port to the Portsmouth Harbor rail station. The crossing from Portsmouth to Cherbourg takes four hours and forty-five minutes; the sailing to Le Havre requires five hours and thirty minutes. Although the sea leg of the Portsmouth-Le Havre route takes more time to complete, the elapsed time between London and Paris via this routing is nine hours and five minutes, compared to nine hours and thirty minutes for the Cherbourg route with its shorter sea leg. Both routes to the French capital pass through Normandy, where the Allies stormed ashore on 6 June 1943 in the invasion of Hitler's "Fortress Europe."

Ramsgate–Dunkerque. After departing from Ramsgate Harbor at the most easterly point of Kent County in England, the ferries operated by the Sally Line provide two and one-half hours at sea (where the English Channel meets the North Sea) before docking at Dunkerque, the French port where German military forces held off the Allies throughout World War II until VE Day on 9 May 1945. After going ashore, roam the restored streets of Dunkerque before proceeding on to Lille, France, and connections for Brussels, Paris, or Strasbourg. Dunkerque has witnessed more than its fair share of human conflict, including the heroic retreat of the British forces in 1940. More than 350,000 men were evacuated by a mixed fleet of naval and civilian ships and boats while being battered relentlessly by the combined forces of the German army and air forces.

The Channel Tunnel. If all goes as planned, "the Chunnel," as it is sometimes called, is scheduled to begin operating between Britain and France in June 1993, giving Europe the finest rail transport network in the world. Passengers will be able to board a passenger train in London's Waterloo Station and reach the Gare du Nord (North Station) in Paris nonstop in only three hours total time—or the Brussels Gare Midi (South Station) in two hours and forty-five minutes—less than half the present time by the fastest rail and water transportation combinations now available between the three European capitals.

Termed the most extraordinary engineering feat of this century, the tunnel is the largest privately financed project in the world to date. With a total length of 32.2 miles between its terminals at Folkestone in England and Calais in France, 23.6 miles of the tunnel is under water. By the year 2003, the tunnel planners expect the system will be handling up to 44.6 million rail passengers a year.

Sealink's combined fleet of British, French, and Netherlands registries is one of the world's largest passenger-carrying fleets. They link London to Amsterdam, Brussels, Dublin, and Paris. Augmented by Hoverspeed, these shipping services carry the bulk of the passenger and vehicle traffic passing in and out of Britain.

9 CROSSING THE IRISH SEA

Many of the ferry crossings on the Continent of Europe involve loading the passenger-rail cars aboard the ferry. When this occurs, the passengers need not disembark. But at all ferry ports in Britain, passengers are required to leave the train and board the ferry. Then they board another train after landing. You will find that this change of transportation mode is no great hardship. In fact, it can be a very enjoyable experience by including drinks and dinner aboard the ferry, followed by a chat with fellow passengers. The salon of a ferry is a good place for meeting people. Everyone has a common interest in travel, and everyone is going to the same destination.

Crossing the Irish Sea is very much like crossing the English Channel, except you cannot forward your luggage on to the Republic of Ireland. What you take is what you carry. So again, adhere to our admonition to "go lightly" when it comes to luggage. Porter service is available at all of the marine terminals. The number of porters available, however, has diminished drastically in the past decade. It is best not to expect porter service. Furthermore, the trolleys (baggage carts) found in the majority of British Rail stations are missing at the piers because their use is impractical on the sloping ramps and gangways used for access to the vessels.

When you visit Ireland, keep in mind that the Republic of Ireland and Northern Ireland are two separate political states. Northern Ireland is a part of Britain, while the republic is independent. There are no customs to contend with when arriving in Northern Ireland from England, Scotland, or Wales. On the other hand, customs formalities entering the Republic of Ireland should present no problem for the bona fide traveler. The efficient "declare" or "nothing-to-declare" system is used by Irish Customs.

Duty-free shops are operated on all of the shipping lines crossing the Irish Sea between Britain and the Republic of Ireland. Crossing times are adequate enough to permit shopping at leisure. Except for tobacco and alcoholic beverages, however, there are few bargains. Check with the salespersons to be certain that you are not exceeding the import limits. Duty payments on excesses can be stiff. Tax-free shops are not available on routes to Northern Ireland.

Sealink provides services to Northern Ireland through Stranraer in Scotland to Larne, with train connections from there to Belfast. From Holyhead in England, Sealink ferries cross to Dun Laoghaire, a suburban port of Dublin; from Fishguard in England, Sealink connects with Rosslare, one-hundred miles south of Dublin, for direct train connections to southern points. Fares are listed on page 65.

Sea Links to Ireland

Stranraer–Larne. A short crossing of two hours, fifteen minutes port to port, this is the most direct route to Northern Ireland. Access to England, Scotland, and Wales by rail is through Glasgow. Larne to Belfast takes another forty-five minutes on the train. The BritRail Pass is *not* accepted on trains in Northern Ireland because rail services are operated by Northern Ireland Railways, not British Rail. Food and beverage services are available aboard. No customs formalities for entering Northern Ireland from Scotland. No tax-free shops aboard. Train connections from London through Euston Station with overnight-sleeper service are available between London and Stranraer. First- and second-class accommodations are available aboard ship. Direct train service from the Glasgow Central Station to Stranraer Harbor takes two and one-half hours. Details are found on Tables 591 and 610 of the *Thomas Cook European Timetable*.

Holyhead–Dun Laoghaire. This crossing is from Holyhead in Wales to Dun Laoghaire (a suburb of Dublin). The elapsed time from port to port averages three hours and thirty minutes. Connections from the port into Dublin can be made by train, city bus, or taxi. All three transportation modes are available at the pier. The BritRail Pass cannot be used for transportation in the Republic of Ireland. The Eurailpass is accepted on the railroads. It would not be economical to validate your Eurailpass for the short ride into Dublin, however, if you plan to spend a few days sightseeing there before traveling to other parts of the country by train. Food and beverage services are available aboard the ferries, and tax-free shops are open during the crossing. Customs formalities are observed upon disembarkation. Train connections from London's Euston Station to Holyhead provide through-coach and sleeper accommodations. The ferries offer first- and second-class accommodations. Consult Tables 555 and 605 of the *Thomas Cook European Timetable*.

Fishguard–Rosslare. This Sealink ferry crossing is recommended for train travelers bound for Cork, Killarney, and the Shannon Airport. Crossing takes three hours and forty-five minutes. Food, beverages, and tax-free shops are available during the voyage. One-class service only aboard ship. Customs formalities are observed at disembarkation. Daytime train service only from Paddington Station in London. Train time between London and Fishguard is six hours. From Rosslare Harbor, connecting time to Dublin is three hours by train; to Limerick for connections to the Shannon Airport, three hours and fifty minutes. Transportation time to the airport from the Limerick rail station is forty-five minutes. Tables 531 and 607 of the *Thomas Cook European Timetable* have details.

SAILING TO THE CONTINENT
One-Way Fares (1990) in U.S. Dollars

	First Class	Economy Class
London to Brussels, Paris, Amsterdam:		
*Brussels (see Note A)	$ 82.00	$ 67.00
*Paris	102.00	79.00
†Amsterdam (Via Hook of Holland)	**93.00	66.00
*Amsterdam (see Note A)	119.00	92.00
†The Hague	**85.00	60.00
†Rotterdam	**80.00	57.00
London to European Continental Ports:		
*Boulogne/Calais	59.00	49.00
*Dieppe	58.00	49.00
*Oostende (see Note A)	65.00	55.00
†Hook of Holland	74.00	53.00
Port to Port:		
*Dover/Folkestone to:		
Boulogne/Calais	—	29.00
Oostende (see Note A)	—	35.00
*Newhaven to Dieppe	—	32.00
†Harwich to Hook of Holland	46.00	35.00

SAILING TO IRELAND

	First Class	Economy Class
London to:		
*Dublin	92.00	76.00
*Rosslare	92.00	76.00
*Belfast (via Stranraer)	101.00	80.00
*Larne	99.00	78.00
Glasgow to:		
*Belfast (via Stranraer)	50.00	41.00
*Larne	48.00	39.00
Port-to-Port:		
*Holyhead to Dun Laoghaire	—	38.00
*Fishguard to Rosslare	—	38.00
*Stranraer to Larne	—	22.00

Round trip: Double one-way fares. All prices subject to change. Reservations required on all services during peak travel periods; $3.00 per reservation each journey.

*   One-class ship or hovercraft
**   First-class train and ship
†   Sleeping accommodations available in both classes from $16.00.
Note A: Via Oostende, both ship and Jetfoil service available; $14.00 supplement for Jetfoil service, by reservation.

Big Ben, London's most famous landmark, stands in the clock tower of the Houses of Parliament (officially known as the Palace of Westminster). Actually, it's the bell, not the clock, which is called Big Ben. The thirteen and one-half-ton bell's name honors Sir Ben Hall, Commissioner of Works in 1858.

10 LONDON

"Why, Sir, you find no man, at all intellectual, who is willing to leave London. No, Sir, when a man is tired of London," wrote Samuel Johnson, "he is tired of life; for there is in London all that life can afford." London is a wonderful mixture of ancient elegance and modern technology, of outdated traditions and contemporary inconveniences. While plumed guardsmen mount jet black horses in Whitehall, bankers examine computer printouts on Lombard Street.

London sits astride the Thames River about forty miles inland from its estuary on the North Sea. One of the largest cities in the world, London, like a typically modern megalopolis, has failed to come to terms with the present century yet has managed to preserve many of the virtues of those past. Presumably a consort to kings, London appears to many as being ruled by the Cockneys of the city's east end, and the shouting down of the prime minister in Parliament is observed by visitors in total disbelief that a government could operate in this manner.

It's difficult to get the first-time visitor to Britain interested in anything other than London until he has seen the great city. Although London is Europe's largest city, most of its historical sights are clustered around a compact area. A reasonable stroll will take you past the Houses of Parliament and its clock tower housing Big Ben, Westminster Abbey, Whitehall, Downing Street, Buckingham Palace, and Trafalgar Square. If strolling is not your thing, then take the advice that Prime Minister Gladstone once gave a group of American tourists: "See London from the top of a bus." London Transport makes it very convenient by running buses around a twenty-mile circular tour in about one and a half hours, and they pass most of London's major landmarks.

If you would like a personally guided tour of London, hail a taxi—any taxi. London's taxicab drivers are a special breed. They are not issued a taxi operator's license just because they can drive a car. An extensive knowledge of the city and its history is an important part of their taxi-licensing examination. Cabbies usually have fixed rates for such sightseeing excursions. Hail one and make inquiry. We're sure that you'll be pleased with the outcome.

After you have seen London, see more of this wonderful country where, among many of its advantages, everyone speaks your language—well, almost everyone. You cannot get to know the country without experiencing the charms of its other cities and seeing first-hand the loveliness of the rural areas that separate them. There is no better way to do that than aboard a train, viewing the passing scene and conversing with the British themselves.

Day Excursions

Like the road builders of Rome, Britain's rail builders laid their tracks leading to London—or, more properly, out of London. Picture, if you will, London as the center of a somewhat lopsided spider web with its radials running east and south to the sea on the short side of the web and the longer extensions running west to Wales and north into Scotland. Thirty-two day excursions from London await your pleasure. They have been selected for a variety of reasons. Varied reader interest was the main consideration, but any "mix" should certainly provide the desired cross section of this green and pleasant land.

Like a knight of old, perhaps you would prefer to sally forth on a short sortie or two before departing on a crusade. In that case, you will find the Greenwich, Windsor, and St. Albans day excursions to your liking. Ranging southeast out of London, Kent beckons with its towns of Canterbury, Dover, Folkestone, and Ramsgate. Southward, rail trails lead along the English Channel to the port/resort towns of Hastings, Brighton, Portsmouth, and Southampton and to the Isle of Wight.

Having whetted your appetite with the excursions above, you should be ready now to venture farther afield. Everything you plan to see has been there for quite some time—usually at least a century or two—so relax and enjoy your further travels throughout Britain.

West from London, excursions to Salisbury and Stonehenge, Bath, Gloucester, and Cardiff (Wales) await the train travelers. Ready to crusade? Go farther west to the pilgrims' Plymouth or the pirates' Penzance. You may want to make these "out-and-back" visits. If so, make arrangements with your hotel. If you plan to return, pack light and have the hall porter store your bulky luggage. In the heart of England you will find awaiting you excursions to Birmingham, Stratford-upon-Avon, Coventry, Nottingham, Sheffield, Lincoln, and York. From farther west beckons Chester.

Northeast of London is East Anglia, where historic King's Lynn, Bury St. Edmunds, and Ipswich wait to greet you. East Anglia was the area from where the U.S. Eighth Air Force staged its massive attacks on the Third Reich in World War II. It abounds in museums and memories relating to the conflict. For the academic flavor of the country, you may want to visit Cambridge or Oxford (or both) for the cap-and-gown atmosphere. School-tie types will appreciate Eton, a stone's throw away from Windsor.

Select your day excursions carefully. Don't rush—take time to enjoy the flowers. Time flies when you're having fun, so keep in mind that the land of Scotland to the north is also looking forward to the honor of your visit. Budget your time accordingly.

Arriving and Departing

By Air. London has two major international airports, Gatwick and Heathrow. A third air terminal, Stansted, is being developed. Be certain to ask your airline which airport you'll be using for your flight.

Heathrow, fifteen miles west of the city, is connected to London's Underground (subway) system. If you are not overloaded with luggage, the Underground provides fast and frequent service between Heathrow and Central London. The journey time is about fifty minutes; trains depart every five to ten minutes. The Underground station at Heathrow Terminals 1, 2, and 3 is situated in the center of the airport complex and directly linked to the terminal buildings. The Underground station at Terminal 4 is located within the terminal itself. The one-way adult fare is £2.10; children (ages five to fifteen), 80 pence. If you are burdened with luggage, consider the airbus system. This fast and frequent door-to-door service by deluxe double-deck coaches between all four Heathrow terminals and Central London offers convenient en route stops in London's major hotel areas. All coaches are equipped for handicapped travelers. There are two lines: Airbus A1 terminates at Victoria Station (Grosvenor Gardens); Airbus A2 connects Heathrow and Russell Square via Euston Station. Service is every twenty minutes in the morning and every thirty minutes throughout the afternoon and evening. Airbus tickets can be purchased from the driver or in the London Transport Tourist Information Centres at Heathrow, Euston, and Victoria stations. One-way fares: adults £5.00; children £3.00. Taxi journey time to Central London is about one hour; fares range from £20.00 to £25.00. Additional information is available from the London Tourist Board offices throughout the airport, 0900–1800 daily.

Gatwick, 27 miles south of London, has its own rail station in the airport's South Terminal. The Gatwick Express departs every fifteen minutes from early morning until late evening for Victoria Station. Journey time is thirty minutes. For late arrivals, an hourly night service runs until 0600. One-way fares: adults £6.30; children £3.15. Bus transport between Gatwick and Victoria Station is provided by Flightline 777 service from both the North and South terminals at Gatwick. Service is every thirty minutes from 0600 until 1800, then every hour through 2000. The en route time is approximately seventy to eighty minutes. One-way fares: adults £6.00; children (ages five to fifteen) £3.00. Bus services to most points in England depart from the coach station on the ground floor of the South Terminal. There is a bus and coach information desk on the arrivals concourse in both terminals, open from 0730 to 2030 daily. Taxi and limousine service from Gatwick to Central London is available—but *expensive*. Rates range from £35.00 to £55.00. More information? Check with the South-East England Tourist Board office on the South Terminal arrivals concourse. It's open 0600–1800 daily.

By Train. London has a plethora of rail stations; however, you need only be concerned with five of the city's major stations when arriving from, or departing to, the Continent, the Irish Republic, or Scotland.

Crossing the English Channel by the most direct routes from either France (Calais/Boulogne) or Belgium (Oostende), your ferry, hovercraft, or Jetfoil will dock at Dover or Folkstone. From there, the "boat trains," as they are termed, proceed to London's Victoria Station. As previously mentioned, the majority of air travelers arriving in the Gatwick Airport proceed either by train or bus to Victoria Station. As a matter of future interest, Victoria Station will also be the English terminus of the tunnel running under the English Channel, which is scheduled to begin operation in June 1993.

The voyage time for crossing by ferry between Dover and Calais is under two hours; the time is the same for ferry crossings between Folkestone and Boulogne. On the other hand, the same crossings by hovercraft are made in forty minutes or less. Hovercraft seat reservations are required since space is limited. Ferry crossings between Dover and Oostende take about four hours; a Jetfoil crossing takes one hour plus thirty-five minutes. Reservations are required.

There are several land-sea routes that may be taken between London and Dublin, capital of the Irish Republic. The rail route linking the two capitals through the English port of Holyhead and the Irish port of Dun Laoghaire, however, is the most traveled. The ship crossing takes three hours and thirty minutes. The English terminus is London's Euston Station, which also shares honors with London's Kings Cross Station for rail traffic to Glasgow and Edinburgh in Scotland.

London's Liverpool Street Station is the gateway for rail and ship traffic between the Netherlands, northern Germany, and Scandinavia. Trains departing Liverpool Street bound for that part of Europe proceed to Harwich, where passengers then embark from the Parkeston Quay by ship to Hoek of Holland, a small peninsula jutting out into the North Sea. There, trains are waiting to take them to further destinations such as Amsterdam, Hannover, Berlin, or the Scandinavian capital cities of Copenhagen, Oslo, and Stockholm. The ship crossing is made in eight hours and thirty minutes.

For those who can recall Robert Taylor and Vivien Leigh bidding good-bye in the Waterloo Bridge Station, the same nostalgia can and probably will sweep your imagination whenever you enter a London rail station. The clouds of wet steam are gone, as is the huffing of the coal-burning steam engines at the head of the platform as they stand waiting

London taxi stands briefly in front of Eros Fountain in the center of London's most celebrated traffic circle, Piccadilly Circus. The steps of the fountain were at one time the "marketplace" of London's flower sellers. Officially, the fountain is a memorial to the philanthropist Lord Shaftesbury.

to take passengers on to their destinies. *But the electricity of the moment still survives*. Sense it. Enjoy it. After all, that's what rail travel is all about!

London's Railway Stations

If the major cities of the world were to enter a train-station contest, London would win. Perhaps a glance at the London Station Plan on page 296 would be helpful at this point as we try to put things into order verbally. You will note a total of fifteen stations listed in the plan, which looks very much like a quarterback's option play for the Pittsburgh Steelers. For the sake of brevity, we will reduce the number of station descriptions to the manageable number of eight—those stations of major arrivals, departures, and *Britain By BritRail* day excursions from London. Take heart—at least all of the major train terminals are linked by the London Underground, principally by the Circle Line. For a quick reference, check the Inter-Terminal Plan on page 297 of this edition.

Victoria Station's train services cover the south and the southeast of England in addition to the sea-rail services to Belgium and France. A special Sealink Travel Centre is located in the station, at the head of platform 2, to cater to the more than two million passengers who transit Victoria every year en route to and from the Continent. As the gateway rail station for the Gatwick Airport, Victoria operates a "Next Train to Gatwick Airport" indicator between platforms 9 and 15 to assist air-rail travelers. Train departures for connections to the Continent are also displayed in this area.

Most important to *Britain by BritRail* readers is the London Tourist Board Centre located in the station forecourt. From the second week of April through the first week of November, it's in operation daily 0800–2000. To reach it, follow the corridor running out from train platform 15. This is the *only* tourist information center located directly *in* a London rail station. It is also one of the few London stations providing currency-exchange facilities.

Euston Station is closely grouped with St. Pancras and King's Cross stations for rail services to England's Midlands, northern England, and Scotland. One of the most modern facilities in the British Rail system, it is the Sealink terminal for services to Belfast via Stranraer and to Dublin via Holyhead. It is also the London departure point for the all-electric-hauled InterCity trains to Glasgow. Train departures and arrivals are displayed in digital format on an easy-to-read display board over the train entrance doors. As you face the train departure/arrival announcement board in the Euston Station, the travel center will be on your left. In general (although some functions operate at different hours), the travel center is open year-round, Monday through Saturday 0700–2330 and Sunday 0800–2330. Waiting rooms, restaurants, and other conveniences are located on the far side of the station hall from the travel center. A Barclays Bank is located on a pedestrian esplanade beyond the restaurants. It is open Monday–Friday 0930–1530.

The train information windows are 12 and 13; hotel bookings (for Dun and Bradstreet-rated hotels only) may be obtained at windows 16 and 17. Other windows, according to their signs, provide sleeper and seat reservations, air tickets, special-events reservations—there is even a special information window for travel to Ireland.

St. Pancras Station is the London terminal of the Midland Mainline of the British Rail system serving *Britain By BritRail*'s day excursions to St. Albans, Nottingham, and Sheffield with both diesel and electric service. Directional signs for the Euston and King's Cross stations, as well as the London Underground, are found throughout the station.

Charing Cross Station is London's rail terminal for direct train service to Folkestone, Dover, and the ports for Sealink and Hoverspeed hovercraft services to Boulogne and Calais on the Continent.

King's Cross Station is the London terminal for InterCity 125 train service to Aberdeen and Edinburgh. The station's travel center provides its major services from 0700–2300 daily, with its hotel-bookings section closing at 1900. Full information, reservations, and advance ticketing services are available. Outside the station, to the left, a Bureau de Change is open daily 0800–2000.

Paddington Station serves the west with its InterCity 125 service through Plymouth to Penzance. It is also the London terminal for Sealink services to Ireland via the ports of Fishguard and Rosslare. All facilities operated within the station are exceptionally well marked with overhead signs and directional signals. Paddington's travel center stands in front of platforms 1 and 2 and operates 0800–2130 Monday through Saturday and 0900–2000 Sunday. Three banks (Barclays, Midland, and Westminster) are close to the station.

Liverpool Street Station, one of the oldest rail terminals in London, is under extensive renovation. In the meantime, a profusion of signs is scattered throughout the station to assist arriving and departing passengers. Perhaps the most important sign is the one reading, ''Look around you. The next century starts here.''

Waterloo Station is primarily for trains to the south of England, including the Isle of Wight. Its travel center is located at the end of tracks 15 and 16, opposite the Underground entrance. The center is open 0800–2200 seven days a week. A Westminster Bank facility is between tracks 18 and 19. A map is positioned at track 13. The latest revisions in the channel tunnel program now designate Waterloo as the primary station of the network. Understandably, there will be much construction work and many inconveniences in preparing the terminal for this service.

London's Tower Bridge has remained in constant service since its construction between 1886 and 1894. The huge bascule sections of the drawbridge remain in operation, and the footbridge at the top is now a major tourist attraction.

London's Visitor Information Services

"Everything should be made as simple as possible," wrote Albert Einstein, "but not simpler." Apparently, this is the organizational pattern of London's tourist information services. Regardless of the office and the service, you will find that its personnel are trained to respond professionally to the basic questions most visitors ask: "Where can we stay tonight?" "How do we get there?" "What's going on in London?" "Where are the sights?"

The following are the primary points of contact with the London Tourist Board offices and their hours of operation:

Victoria Station: Streetside in the forecourt, outside platform 15. Operating hours are 0800–2000 daily from the second week in April through the first week in November. Services available include visitor information, hotel accommodations, free and saleable publications, and tourist tickets for buses and the Underground. To get there, use the Underground Circle Line to the Victoria Station stop; proceed to street level and the front of the main entrance.

Heathrow Airport: The office is at the bottom of the passenger ramp in the concourse leading to the Underground station in Terminal 2. For directions, inquire at any one of the airport information desks in Terminals 1, 2, 3, or 4. Operating hours are 0800–1830 daily. Services available are the same as those at Victoria Station, except the airport office does not handle tourist ticket sales.

Selfridges: This office is located in Selfridges basement services arcade of the Oxford Street store. Open during regular store hours. Services available: visitor information, free and saleable publications, tourist tickets for the bus and the Underground. To get there, exit at the Oxford Circus station of the District or Central lines of the Underground.

Harrods: The office is located in the basement banking hall of Harrods Knightsbridge store. Open during regular store hours. Services available are the same as at Selfridges. Use the Knightsbridge Station of the Underground's Piccadilly line to get there.

Tower of London, West Gate: This information center is in operation from the second week in April through the first week in November. Operating hours are 0930–1800 Monday through Saturday and 1000–1800 on Sunday. Services available are the same as those at Victoria Station.

London Telephone Information: The London Tourist Board also operates a telephone accommodations and tours reservation service (credit card holders only). Ring up (071) 824–8844. It operates 0900–1800 Monday through Friday. You also may call (071) 730–3488 for general information from Monday through Friday 0900–1800.

In addition to its tourist information services in London, the London Tourist Board maintains a mail order service for advance hotel reservations provided that you write ahead at least six weeks prior to your arrival date. Direct requests and inquiries to: Correspondence Assistant, Distribution Department, London Tourist Board & Convention Bureau, 26 Grosvenor Gardens, London SW1W ODU, England. A £5.00 booking fee plus a £12.00 deposit must be paid to confirm the reservation. The deposit is deductible from the hotel bill; the booking fee is nonrefundable.

Accommodations may be booked on the day of arrival at the London Tourist Board's information centers at Victoria Station or Heathrow Airport. The same booking fees and deposit are required.

British Tourist Authority Services

Additional tourist information services are provided in London by the British Tourist Authority (BTA). The BTA offices in North America are listed on page 290 of this edition.

British Travel Centre (BTA): Located at 12 Regent Street, SW1, just a few minutes walk south of Piccadilly Circus. The center houses the offices of the British Tourist Authority, British Rail, and American Express. Facilities, such as Roomcentre (for hotel accommodations), and a tax-free shopping center also are on the premises.

The center books rail, air, and car travel, reserves sightseeing tours and theater tickets, and provides information on all of Britain. A currency exchange also is available. The center is open daily 0900–1830 Monday through Friday, 1000–1600 Saturday, and Sunday (summer only) 1000–1600.

The BTA also operates a telephone information service on (071) 730–3400 Monday through Friday 0900–1830, Saturday from 1000–1600, and Sunday (summer only) 1000–1600.

Roomcentre will assist you in finding accommodations in London for any date you require. Booking fees and room deposit are the same as the London Tourist Board's. Roomcentre also operates a Book-A-Bed-Ahead service, which enables visitors to reserve their hotel accommodations for any area in Britain.

British Rail Travel Centres

In addition to the office located in the British Travel Centre described above, British Rail has many offices throughout Greater London where you can buy tickets, make seat and sleeper reservations, and obtain information. Locations in Euston, King's Cross, Liverpool Street, Paddington, St. Pancras, and Waterloo stations open daily at 0800. Go to a station in person or call the British Travel Centre on (071) 730–3400 for directions.

Getting Around in London

London has been described as "a whole world wrapped up in a unique city." For sightseeing in London during your visit, London Transport has many convenient, time-saving ways for you to see the city. The fastest get-acquainted mode of seeing London's highlights is London Transport's "Round London Sightseeing Tour" by red double-decker bus. This one-and-a-half hour guided tour passes most of London's major landmarks. After your "orientation" tour, you can then go back to those places of particular interest for a closer look.

You may start your London sightseeing tour from any one of four points: Piccadilly Circus, the Speakers' Corner at Marble Arch, Baker Street outside the Forecourt Underground station, or Victoria Street outside the Victoria Underground station. The tour covers a twenty-mile circular course. The adult fare is £8.00; children under sixteen years, £4.00. A family ticket for two adults with two children is £20.00. Buses run daily except Christmas Day, spring through autumn every hour from 1000 to 1700; winter (mid-October–April) from 1000 to 1600. The tour is not included with the London Visitor Travelcard. Tickets may be purchased at any of the London Tourist Board Information Centres, London Transport Travel Information Centres, or American Express at the British Tourist Authority Office, 12 Regent Street.

A London Visitor Travelcard will make your London visit smoother, faster, and more enjoyable. It gives you three, four, or seven days of unlimited travel on all London red double-decker buses and the Underground. The Travelcard is also good for unlimited round-trips from London to Heathrow Airport on the Underground during the time of its validity.

The Travelcard, like the BritRail Pass, isn't sold in London. You must purchase it, in conjunction with your BritRail Pass, before leaving home. (See page 309 for ordering information.) You will be issued an airline ticket–style coupon upon purchase, plus a ticket jacket listing the London Transport Travel Information Centres throughout the city where you may exchange the coupon for the Travelcard. At that time, you will also be given a set of discount vouchers to many of London's top attractions and a free Underground map.

"Whilst" in London, you should not deny yourself the opportunity of traveling in one of the city's taxis. The London taxi is an institution in itself. It is designed so that it can virtually turn on its own wheelbase and has an amazing amount of space for passengers and their luggage. Taxis may be hailed if the yellow "For Hire" sign is illuminated. Fares and supplemental charges are displayed inside the cab. Fares within London are on the meter. Each driver is thoroughly examined before being licensed. Many American cities should take note of this!

Royal Guardsmen, hallmark of Britain's allegiance to her sovereign, stand duty at royal buildings and residences. The regimental identification of the guards, who traditionally wear the bearskin hat, scarlet tunic, and dark blue trousers, is distinguished by badges, buttons, and various insignia.

LONDON-EDINBURGH TRAIN SERVICE
(First- and second-class accommodations for all services listed)

DEPART FROM KING'S CROSS STATION*	ARRIVE IN EDINBURGH			NOTES
	MON–FRI	SAT	SUN	
0600	1115	1115	—	(1)
0730	1220	1225	—	(1)
0800	1250	—	—	(1)
0830	—	1316	1457	(1)
0900	1341	1356	—	(1)
0930	—	1440	1528	(1)
1000	1432	1447	1609	(1)
1030	1455	1519	—	(1)
1100	1534	1600	1703	(1)
1130	1616	1636	—	(1)
1200	1628	1640	1729	(1)
1230	—	1736	1756	(1)
1300	—	1755	1830	(1)
1330	1819	1834	1904	(1)
1400	1831	1846	1922	(1)
1500	1941	1956	2025	(1)
1600	2036	2050	2117	(1)
1700	2138	2207	2233	(1)
1800	2249	2301	2325	(1)
1830	2332	—	—	(1)
2200 (2)	—	0700 + 1	—	
2215 (2)	0525 + 1	—	—	
2315 (2)	—	—	0600 + 1	
2345 (2)	0600 + 1	—	—	

Distance: 393 miles/632 km
References: Thomas Cook Tables 550 and 570

*   See Appendix, page 296, for London station plan.
(1) High-speed train, food service available
(2) Departs from Euston Station; sleeping cars only

USEFUL PHONE NUMBERS

Tourist Information Centre	*Train Information*
All Scotland: 031–332–2433	London: 071–278–2477
Edinburgh: 031–557–1700	Edinburgh: 031–556–2451

Churchill's War Rooms

Few Americans are aware that a memorial to their World War II president, Franklin Roosevelt, exists in London's Grosvenor Square. Fewer perhaps are aware that the place where Prime Minister Winston Churchill of Britain held telephone conversations with him is now open to the public.

In 1936 when the storms of the war were gathering, the British government began constructing a communications center, or war room, beneath the government offices in Whitehall. Building a ten-foot layer of concrete above a labyrinth of wine cellars and connecting tunnels, workmen toiled at night so as not to arouse suspicions of what was being constructed. Virtually bombproof, facilities for electrical power, water, and air from one primary plus two alternate sources were installed. Anticipating that the prime minister and his staff might be required to spend extended periods of time underground without the benefit of sunlight, a room was equipped with ultraviolet machines.

The Nazis captured Warsaw in September 1939. With the stage set for the ensuing conflict, Churchill's staff moved in. Essentially, the Allies' direction of the war was conducted from this communications center until the war ended. The center was sealed in 1945 and not reopened until it was removed from the British official secrets list in 1975. Today, it is the Cabinet War Rooms Museum. A visit there will place you in the exact location where some of the most dramatic decisions in the history of mankind were made.

In a small, soundproof room, you can see the telephone on the British end of the "hotline" connected with the White House in Washington. It was here that Churchill spoke with Roosevelt over a secure line that was made possible by a scrambler invented in 1943 by the Bell Telephone Laboratories. The clock on the wall was equipped with two sets of hands: one set in black for London time, the other set in red for the time in Washington.

Nearby, Churchill's bedroom is maintained in much the same manner as it was when occupied by the prime minister. Seated at the desk in the bedroom, Churchill delivered many of his famous radio broadcasts that helped so much in maintaining morale throughout the free world. Of equal interest is the Map Room, where information from all over the world regarding the war was collected and displayed. The scene visitors view today depicts the situation during the last few months of the war; it was left in place when the center was closed down and sealed.

The entrance to the Cabinet War Rooms Museum is located at the Clive Steps on King Charles Street, across from St. James Park. Open daily, 1000–1800; admission is charged. For information, call (071) 930–6961.

LONDON–GLASGOW TRAIN SERVICE
(First- and second-class accommodations for all services listed)

DEPART FROM EUSTON STATION*	ARRIVE IN GLASGOW CENTRAL			
	MON–FRI	SAT	SUN	NOTES
0725	1252	—	—	(1)
0835	1422	—	—	(1)
0845	—	1422	—	(1)
1000	—	—	1735	(1)
1015	—	1508	—	(1)
1025	1508	—	—	(1)
1115	—	1654	—	(1)
1125	1654	—	—	(1)
1300	—	—	1929	(1)
1315	—	1854	—	(1)
1325	1854	—	—	(1)
1415	—	1030	—	(1)
1425	1939	—	—	(1)
1515	—	2040	—	(1)
1525	2040	—	2159	(1)
1615	—	2124	—	(1)
1625	2124	—	—	(1)
1725	—	—	2310	(1)
2205	—	0720 + 1	—	(2)
2320	—	—	0615 + 1	(2)
2350	0615 + 1	—	—	(2)

Distance: 402 miles/647 km
References: Thomas Cook Table 550

*   See Appendix, page 296, for London station plan.
(1)   High-speed train, food service available
(2)   Sleeping cars available

USEFUL PHONE NUMBERS

Tourist Information Centre
All Scotland: 031–332–2433
Glasgow: 041–227–4880

Train Information
London: 071–387–7070
Glasgow: 041–204–2844

The great Roman bath attracted visitors from all parts of the Roman Empire between the first and fifth centuries. It was constructed around a natural hot spring with waters rising from the ground at 116°F. The abbey church tower of Bath looms in the background.

A DAY EXCURSION TO BATH
DISTANCE BY TRAIN: 107 miles (172 km)
AVERAGE TRAIN TIME: 1 hour, 20 minutes

Bath has been in the limelight of social attention during two eras of recorded history—once during the Roman occupation of Britain and again in the eighteenth century when Bath became the "in place" for royalty and other well-to-do's. Development of the only hot spring in Britain is attributed to the Romans soon after the Emperor Claudius invaded the land in A.D. 43.

To the Romans, the city's name was *Aquae Sulis*—literally translated, "the waters of Sul." By the end of the first century, the Romans had established a great bathing facility. The magnificent hot baths were said to have curative powers. Although modern scientists are doubtful of the waters' purported healing properties, there is no doubt that the only hot mineral springs in Britain played a major role in establishing Bath as the "hot spot" for socializing.

The baths made Aquae Sulis famous throughout the empire. Its fame lasted 400 years until the rising sea level and the fall of the Roman Empire brought the city's prosperity to an end. By the end of the seventh century, the city was described as "a ghostly ruin with crumbled masonry fallen into dark pools, overgrown and bird haunted, but still a wondrous sight."

The second revitalization of the city, a cultural one, began in 1705 with the arrival of thirty-one-year-old Richard Nash. Like the Romans, he, too, conquered, but not by force. Nash was Bath's first public relations expert. It was during his "reign" that Queen Anne visited Bath and it again became an elegant and stylish resort for the wealthy. When Nash died at the age of eighty-eight, he had created a kingdom of taste and etiquette over which he reigned as Beau Nash, King of Bath.

Although the hot springs were used again during the Middle Ages, the Roman ruins remained buried even during the times of Beau Nash, when the gilded bronze head of Minerva was uncovered by workmen while digging a sewer in 1727. Although the statues and columns of the present-day Roman bath were added by Victorian restorers, the original bath area still has the lead floor and limestone paving installed by the Romans.

The restoration of Bath's Roman past and the combining of the city's two eras of fame finally began in 1878 when the city engineer, while investigating a water leak, came upon the Roman reservoir and the huge complex of baths that it fed. In other words, someone finally called a plumber.

BATH—*ROMAN ENGLAND*

A Day Excursion from London

DEPART FROM PADDINGTON STATION*	ARRIVE IN BATH SPA STATION	NOTES
0815	0934	(2)
0830	1005	(4)
0845	1006	(2)
0915	1034	(2)
0930	1105	(4)
1005	1115	(1)
1015	1134	(2)
1030	1205	(4)

(Plus other frequent service)

DEPART FROM BATH SPA STATION	ARRIVE IN PADDINGTON STATION	
1327	1448	(2)
1412	1547	(4)
1427	1553	(2)
1512	1645	(4)
1527	1657	(2)
1557	1710	(1)
1612	1748	(4)
1627	1748	(2)
1657	1820	(2)(4)
1727	1848	(2)

(Plus other frequent service)

Distance: 107 miles/172 km
References: Thomas Cook Table 530
* See Appendix, page 296, for London station plan.

(1) MON–FRI	(3) SAT
(2) MON–SAT	(4) SUN

Train Information: 0225–463075
InterCity Services: 071–262–6767
Bath Tourist Information Centre: 0225–461111

The Roman baths are one of Britain's major tourist attractions and draw visitors from all points of the globe to their waters. The baths rank a close second to England's number-one attraction, the Tower of London, and are well worth the short train ride to see them and the "glory that was Rome"—transposed to England.

The City of Bath abounds in sightseeing opportunities. We suggest that upon arrival in Bath you proceed immediately to the Bath Tourist Information Centre located at The Colonnades on Bath Street and let it assist you in your visit. To reach the center on foot, proceed up Manvers Street directly in front of the Bath rail station until you cross North Parade Road. At this point, you will see the Bath Abbey tower to your left. Pass the Abbey on its right side and proceed through the Abbey church yard. At the columns, turn left and then take the first right into Bath Street. The center is at the end of Bath Street. Should you want to telephone ahead from the rail station, "ring up" on (0225) 462831. This will connect you with the Inquiries Office of the center.

The center has a wealth of information about the City of Bath and its surroundings. You should consider purchasing at least two of their publications. The first we can recommend is the beautifully illustrated *Official Guidebook*. You'll want to show it to the folks back home. The second publication we recommend is the pamphlet *Bath Mini-Guide*. This informative piece contains a city map and lists the places of interest to visitors.

The *Official Guidebook* devotes a part of its pages to "Wandering Through Bath," which will prove most helpful to you when you explore this beautiful city. Bath has won many awards for its floral displays, and its natural beauty makes a walking tour through the city a real pleasure.

On the subject of tours, you should check to see if you may avail yourself of the Mayor's Corps of Honorary Guides. They conduct guided tours at various times throughout the summer season at no charge. These tours, which depart from the Abbey church yard, take approximately one and one-half hours. For advance information, ring up (0225) 461111 and ask to be put through to extension 2785. By the way, we'd appreciate having you mention *Britain By BritRail* when the Guides' office asks who recommended their services. We've been mutual admirers for years.

If you are on a tight schedule, the best sights in the city are cloistered about the Roman baths. The baths and the abbey practically adjoin each other. Upstairs from the baths, you may visit the Pump Room and sample its water. During your visit, take time to touch the worn paving and dip your hand in the water. In that moment, you can recall the glory that was Rome.

A stately statue of Britain's Queen Victoria overlooks the plaza fronting Birmingham's Council House. One of the World's great industrial cities, Birmingham has made spectacular strides in developing itself as a beautiful residential city and is no longer England's "ugly duckling."

A DAY EXCURSION TO BIRMINGHAM
DISTANCE BY TRAIN: 119 miles (191 km)
AVERAGE TRAIN TIME: 1 hour, 30 minutes

Birmingham has more canals than Venice. This is rather unusual because Birmingham claims to be Britain's "city at the center." Although it is in the approximate geographic center of the British Isles, it was once the center of England's waterways, which carried most of the nation's industrial traffic. With the development of other forms of transportation, particularly rail, canal transportation dissipated. Many canals have been developed into recreation areas with walks, pubs, and restored buildings along their right-of-ways.

For decades, Birmingham has been recognized internationally as one of the world's great industrial cities. Along with the recognition came the image of a smoke-filled, grimy Victorian sprawl of a city. Since World War II, Birmingham has made spectacular progress in developing a beautiful residential city. The center of the city has been completely rebuilt. One of the newer landmarks marking the city center is the Rotunda, a 250-foot tower. Beneath the tower is the "bull ring," the world's first under-one-roof-shopping complex. The multilevel, temp-erature-controlled bull-ring shopping center is completely traffic-free and linked by subways with major shopping streets of the city. It connects directly with the New Street railway station, where you will arrive from London on your day excursion. If you experience difficulty in gaining your bearings in the vast New Street Station, consult the travel center (train information) in the station's main hall on the extreme far right as you exit from the train platforms.

Something unusual in the development of a modern city is Birmingham's National Exhibition Center. For years the exhibition centers in Continental Europe lured the larger trade fairs. Now Britain has its own showcase at Bickenhill, only one hour and twenty minutes from London by InterCity trains. This modern exhibition-and-conference center is on a 310-acre site readily accessible by rail. Rail connections to the exhibition center may be made through the New Street Station on any trains departing in the direction of London. The stop, Birmingham International, is a short, seventeen-to-twenty-minute ride. Obtain full details from the tourist information center. With 1.2 million square feet of air-conditioned exhibition space in nine halls, it is by far the largest complex in Britain, and it's still growing. With the opening in 1991 of the International Convention Centre Birmingham, Britain's first international meetings complex can compete with any in Continental Europe.

BIRMINGHAM — *HEART OF ENGLAND*

A Day Excursion from London

DEPART FROM EUSTON STATION*	ARRIVE IN BIRMINGHAM NEW STREET STATION	NOTES
0740(5)	0918	(2)
0800	1010	(4)
0840(5)	1015	(2)
0940(5)	1118	(2)
0940	1146	(4)
1040(5)	1214	(2)
1040	1246	(4)
1140(5)	1319	(2)
1200	1406	(4)

(Plus other frequent service)

DEPART FROM BIRMINGHAM NEW STREET STATION	ARRIVE IN EUSTON STATION	
1440	1644	(4)
1448	1628	(2)
1540	1733	(4)
1548	1729	(2)
1618	1803	(2)(4)
1648	1829	(2)(4)
1718	1858	(2)(4)
1748	1929	(2)(4)
1818	1959	(2)(4)

(Plus other frequent service)

Distance: 119 miles/191 km
References: Thomas Cook Table 540

* See Appendix, page 296, for London station plan.

(1) MON–FRI   (3) SAT
(2) MON–SAT   (4) SUN
                               (5) Departs 10 minutes earlier on Saturday

Train Information: 021–643–2711
InterCity Services: 071–387–7070
Birmingham Tourist Information Centre 021–623–2514

To reach the Birmingham tourist information center at 2 City Arcade, make your way to Corporation Street from the station, and behind the Superstore C&A, you will find the tourist information and ticket shop. The office is open 0930–1730 Monday through Saturday and is closed on Sunday.

Check with the city tourist information center concerning a sightseeing tour. Despite a massive redevelopment program after World War II, the best of the old has been carefully preserved. The city has an interesting skyline. Historic buildings appear unexpectedly among new ones in a way that emphasizes the quality of both.

Also located in the Victoria Square vicinity and worthy of a visit for its classic elegance and Victorian style is the Town Hall. Opened in 1834, it was designed by Joseph Hansom, the inventor of the Hansom cab. It houses the concert hall in which Mendelssohn conducted the first performance of *Elijah* in 1846. Many distinguished musicians have appeared there since.

Other historic buildings close to the city center are the Sarehole Mill at Hall Green, an eighteenth-century water mill restored to working order, and Blakesley Hall, a seventeenth-century timber-framed yeoman's house furnished in period style and with an interesting garden. For rail buffs, a visit to the science museum is a must. It houses the first English locomotive, which was built in 1784, and displays of early machinery, engines, and motorcars.

Birmingham's Civic Centre is a modern contribution to the city's skyline. It includes a repertory theatre and one of the largest and best stocked libraries in Europe, featuring a comprehensive Shakespeare collection. The city's Central Museum and Art Gallery houses paintings and sculpture by Van Gogh, Botticelli, and Gainsborough.

After all the sightseeing, you may develop a thirst. You came to the right city. Birmingham has long been one of Britain's major brewing centers, and its beer is recommended highly by both locals and visitors. One pub, The Old Crown on Digbeth, has been in business since 1310!

Birmingham is justly proud of its restaurants, which cater to every palate and purse. The city has stylish theater-restaurants with entertainment by international cabaret stars, as well as a wide selection of eateries providing French, Italian, Spanish, Greek, Indian, Chinese, and traditional English cuisine. There's no reason to leave Birmingham with an empty stomach.

Birmingham has undergone many structural changes in recent years, and, undoubtedly, it is becoming one of Europe's outstanding cities. Birmingham is proof positive that an "ugly duckling" can be transformed into a swan.

Brighton's Royal Pavilion, onion-domed creation and seaside home of England's King George IV, still contains most of its original furnishings. The Banqueting Room is set out with period glass and gold plates in the festive style of an era past.

A DAY EXCURSION TO BRIGHTON
DISTANCE BY TRAIN: 51 miles (82 km)
AVERAGE TRAIN TIME: 55 minutes

Brighton is, and always has been, much more than a traditional seaside resort. Since the earliest days of travel, visitors have been attracted by the resort's unique sense of style and architectural splendor. These special qualities are as strong as ever. But they are only part of a continuing success story that secures Brighton's position as Britain's leading resort area.

Perhaps Brighton would have remained a tiny, humble fishing village originally known as Brighthelmstone if it were not for the efforts of Dr. Richard Russell and the Prince Regent (who later became King George IV). In 1750 Dr. Russell, a Brighton resident, published a book extolling the magical effects of sea air and saltwater. This started a fashionable trend that brought royalty and commoner alike to Brighton. The good doctor prescribed bathing in the sea and drinking a pint and a half of seawater daily as a cure for glandular diseases. Such a prescription, incredible as it seems, must have initiated a whole new series of maladies. Chronicles of that period, however, have failed to note them.

The gifted and wayward Prince Regent first visited Brighton in 1783. Enamored by it all (and well heeled with royal funds), he ordered his Royal Pavilion constructed there. Completed in 1822 from an architectural style taken somewhere east of Suez, it has been termed the most bizarre and exotic palace in all Europe. The Royal Pavilion's ostentatious onion-domed exterior, looking very much like a series of hot-air balloons about to ascend, is only surpassed by its even more amazing interior. It is fully furnished in its original style and open to the public daily. Queen Victoria, not at all amused by the pavilion's architecture, calculatedly was permitting it to fall to ruin when Brighton's citizenry saved it from demolition in 1850. The Royal Pavilion recently underwent a £10 million refurbishment to restore the seaside palace to its original condition.

The city maintains "The Lanes," where you take a step backwards into the old fishing-village days. The buildings in these narrow, twisting passages were fishermen's cottages in the seventeenth century. Today, they are quaint and fascinating antique and jewelry shops, pubs, and cafés.

Part of the changing scene in Brighton has been the introduction during the last decade of English-language schools, which attract international students from a score of foreign lands. This youthful input has made it one of the most vibrant resorts in Britain.

Brighton's train terminal was refurbished in 1986. A landmark, the wooden, manually operated dispatch board now rests in York's National

BRIGHTON — *COLORFUL SEASIDE RESORT*

A Day Excursion from London

DEPART FROM VICTORIA STATION*	ARRIVE IN BRIGHTON STATION	NOTES
0750	0855	(1)
0756	0911	(4)
0832	0945	(2)
0856	1011	(4)
0902	0957	(2)
0942	1040	(4)
1005	1057	(2)
1042	1140	(4)
1105	1157	(2)
1142	1240	(4)

(Plus other frequent service)

DEPART FROM BRIGHTON STATION	ARRIVE IN VICTORIA STATION	
1546	1639	(2)
1608	1723	(4)
1646	1739	(2)
1708	1823	(4)
1746	1839	(2)
1846	1939	(2)
1908	2023	(4)
2000	2116	(2)
2008	2123	(4)
2335	0056	(2)

(Plus other frequent service)

Distance: 51 miles/82 km
References: Thomas Cook Table 505

* See Appendix, page 296, for London station plan.

(1) MON–FRI	(3) SAT
(2) MON–SAT	(4) SUN

Train Information: 0273–206755
InterCity Services: 071–928–5100

Brighton Tourist Information: 0273–23755, 0273–27560 (Accommodations)

Railway Museum. Its digital replacement is at the head of the train platforms. The station's rail information center is located at the head of platform 6. As you exit the station, you'll find the taxi queue ahead and on the left. A bus departs for the tourist information center every thirty minutes, or you can begin walking down Queens Road to the sea and stroll along the boardwalk.

The tourist information center is located at 54 Old Steine Road. Old Steine begins at the gate to the Palace Pier. The Palace Pier is one of two such structures extending into the English Channel like silent sentinels. The tourist information center is open every day (except Christmas Day) from 0900 to 1700, with extended evening hours in the summer. It's housed in another of Brighton's historic buildings—Marlborough House.

If you would like to participate in a guided walking tour of Brighton's "Old Town," obtain details from the information center. From June through mid-September, the tours start at Marlborough House. Or you can pick up the Brighton "Mini Guide" at the information center. The "Mini Guide" features a town plan showing where to go and what to see.

Brighton's shopping center, including the Churchill Square Pedestrian Precinct, is one of the largest in southern England. The kids will love the aquarium, dolphin pool, and Peter Pan's playground. Because of the city's number and variety of shopping areas, Brighton is sometimes referred to as "London by the sea." Swank shops can be found in Brighton's east side and the adjoining Regent Arcade. For the more bizarre, shop the Upper Gardner Street junk market on Saturday mornings.

Young and old alike should take a ride along the sea front on the Volks Railway, Britain's first public electric railway. Open daily between Easter and Labor Day, the railway travels along the beach on Madeira Drive to Black Rock. Lacking the speed of British Rail's InterCity 125s, the Volks Railway makes up for it with its nostalgia.

Brighton's marina is the largest in Europe. Whether you are a boating enthusiast or not, a visit there is well in order. A complete new village is now the centerpiece of the marina with elegant shops, quayside restaurants, and, of course, traditional British pubs on the waterfront. The marina also stages many colorful events, such as boat shows and sailing regattas throughout July and August.

If you're caught up in Brighton's buoyancy, check with the tourist information center for hotel accommodations and catch a morning train back to London.

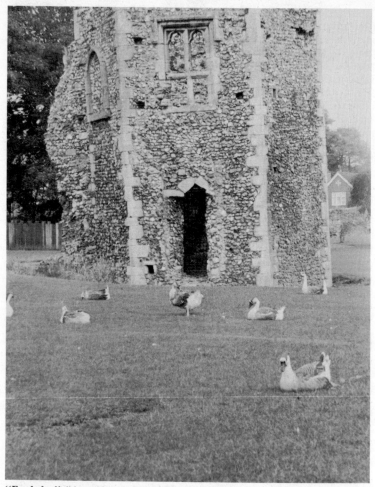

"Fowl play" did not this tower tumble! In 1327 the Abbey of St. Edmunds was destroyed by townspeople protesting against monastic control. Earlier, in 1214, English barons swore before the abbey's high altar to force King John to ratify the Magna Charta—which he did the following year at Runnymede.

From London . . .

A DAY EXCURSION TO BURY ST. EDMUNDS
DISTANCE BY TRAIN: 74 miles (119 km)
AVERAGE TRAIN TIME: 2 hours

For centuries, the East Anglian town of Bury St. Edmunds has been the scene of a fight for freedom of conscience, speech, worship, and the rights of the individual man.

In his *Pickwick Papers*, Charles Dickens described Bury St. Edmunds as " . . . a handsome little town of thriving and cleanly appearance." So it remains today. A monastery was built on the present site of Bury St. Edmunds in A.D. 633. The town gained its name in 903, when thirty-three years after King Edmund of East Anglia was killed by the Danes at Hoxne, his body was brought to the town by Bishop Theodred. The first abbey church was built soon afterwards to honor the memory of the king. For many, Bury St. Edmunds is regarded as one of the most famous towns in all England. In 1214, barons gathered at the high altar of the abbey to take a solemn oath to force King John to grant a charter of liberties, one of the events leading to the granting of the Magna Charta in 1215.

The town center is most notable for its pleasant Georgian atmosphere, recalling the days when the town was a leading social center within East Anglia. The great abbey was one of the largest in Europe at one time. It was sacked in 1327 by townspeople protesting against monastic control and again in 1381 during the Peasants' Revolt. In 1465, a severe fire damaged the church, which had to be extensively repaired. It was subsequently robbed of much of its stone for use in building materials in the town. A placard on the abbey gate indicates that the gate was destroyed along with the abbey by the townspeople in 1327 but was rebuilt in 1347. It is apparently the only structure that was rebuilt out of the entire enclosure compound.

Across from the abbey gate is the Angel Hotel, more than 500 years old, known for its association with Charles Dickens. His room, No. 15, is preserved exactly as it was more than a century ago. The hotel was originally one of three East Anglian inns on the site. A unique attraction of the Angel Hotel is its tavern room, dating back to 1433—59 years before Columbus discovered America.

During World War II, Bury St. Edmunds was ringed with American air bases. Today, the Third Air Force of the U.S. Air Force European Command operates RAF Mildenhall, west of Bury St. Edmunds. Visitors are welcome at the base but are advised to contact the base information office or its community relations advisor before proceeding there. The tourist information center can provide complete details.

BURY ST. EDMUNDS — *MAGNA CHARTA*

A Day Excursion from London

DEPART LIVERPOOL STREET STATION*	ARRIVE IN CAMBRIDGE	NOTES	DEPART CAMBRIDGE	ARRIVE BURY ST. EDMUNDS STATION**	NOTES
0718	0849	(2)	0910	0948	(2)
0902	1012	(2)	1100	1138	(2)
1102	1219	(2)	1255	1338	(2)

DEPART BURY ST. EDMUNDS STATION	ARRIVE IN CAMBRIDGE	NOTES	DEPART CAMBRIDGE	ARRIVE LIVERPOOL STREET STATION	NOTES
1325	1410	(2)	1439	1537(3)	(2)
1519	1600	(2)	1613	1722	(1)
1700	1745	(2)	1803	1916	(2)

Distance: 74 miles/119 km
References: Thomas Cook Tables 581, 585

* See Appendix, page 296, for London station plan.
** Via Cambridge, service through Ipswich also available
(1) MON–FRI   (3) Arrives King's Cross Station
(2) MON–SAT

Bury St. Edmunds Tourist Information Centre
0284–763233
Evenings and Weekends: 0284–764667

The tourist information office is located at 6 Angel Hill, immediately opposite the abbey-gate entrance to the ruins of St. Edmunds Abbey, a short distance from the train station. Station personnel will gladly provide directions. The information office is open during the summer months from 0900 to 1730 Monday through Thursday, 0900–1800 Friday, 1000–1630 Saturday, and 1000–1200 Sunday (July–August only). Winter hours are 0900–1700 Monday–Friday and 1000–1200 Saturday.

Sightseeing in Bury St. Edmunds is, of course, highlighted by the abbey ruins and gardens. St. Mary's Church, which borders the southern boundary of the abbey grounds, is also a popular visiting spot. The Burrow Museum is an interesting building, constructed in the latter part of the twelfth century as Moyses Hall. It is a fine example of Norman domestic architecture. Before becoming a museum, the hall was used for many purposes, including a house of correction and a police station.

There are two distinct parts to the town. As was customary in most medieval towns with a monastic foundation, there was a physical division between the monastery and the townspeople—possibly the first example of separation of church and state. This division resulted in the business section and public buildings standing on a hill to the west of the abbey ruins today.

The Theatre Royal, one of the three surviving Georgian playhouses in Britain, was built in Bury St. Edmunds during 1819 by England's famous architect, William Wilkins. He also designed Downing College on the campus at Cambridge. The Theatre Royal's architecture displays in elegant fashion the style and form for which the Georgian architects were famous. This historical theater's repertoire features a broad scope of entertainment, plays, dance, opera, and every form of music ranging from classical to jazz and rock. In 1892, the Theatre Royal made international headlines by presenting the world premiere of *Charlie's Aunt*, a comedy that is still performed in every major language throughout the world.

Bypassed by time, Bury St. Edmunds is essentially a country town that was spared the industrial expansion of the Victorian Age. But the town stands tall in history. The principles of the Magna Charta, which had their foundation in Bury St. Edmunds and developed over the centuries by English Common Law, have become the heritage not only of the British Isles but of countless millions throughout the world. As history records, the grant of the Magna Charta by King John is the basic source of the constitutional liberties of English-speaking peoples, forming a common bond of peace between them.

One of Bury St. Edmunds's local products is ale. Although the city boasts numerous pubs, we suggest that you sample a pint in the Nut Shell, the smallest pub in England. Its single bar room measures twelve feet by seven feet.

King's College Chapel in Cambridge, universally known as one of the world's finest architectural structures, took seventy years to build.

The "backs," that portion of the River Cam passing the college buildings and gardens, is ideal for a placid boat tour of Cambridge.

A DAY EXCURSION TO CAMBRIDGE
DISTANCE BY TRAIN: 56 miles (90 km)
AVERAGE TRAIN TIME: 1 hour

Oxford graduates often refer to Cambridge as "the other place." Both universities hold one thing in common—organized along the classic federal structure, they house a number of largely autonomous colleges. Comparisons stop here. Cambridge is Britain's "university city." It is said that if you visit only one other English city besides London, it should be Cambridge.

Cambridge is situated on the River Cam around the original bridge over which all trade and communications passed between central England, East Anglia, and Continental Europe 1,000 years ago. It was a natural spot for travelers to pause to exchange news and opinions, thereby preparing the ground for a center of learning.

King's College was founded by Henry VI in 1441. Several other Cambridge colleges, like King's College, are more than 500 years old. It was not until the nineteenth century, however, that Henry VI, considered the founder of Cambridge University, was honored with a statue in the courtyard of King's College.

There are daily walking tours of the colleges with qualified guides who can tell you about the university and its colleges. Schedules and tickets for the tours may be obtained from the tourist information center. A note of academic etiquette: College members are happy to welcome you to the grounds and their historic buildings, but they ask you to respect their need for quiet and privacy.

Arriving by rail from London, take the bus located immediately in front of the railway station to Market Square, which lies between the two main streets of Cambridge, one of which is devoted to commerce and shopping, the other being the academic "main drag." Cambridge is a complex blend of market town, regional center, university, and tourist attraction and defies neat analysis. Consequently, after dismounting the bus in Market Square, ask for directions to the tourist information center on Wheeler Street (behind the Guildhall) a few short blocks from the market.

The tourist information center is open Monday through Friday 0900–1800 (1900 July and August); Saturday, 0900–1700; and Sunday 1030-1530 (Easter–September). Winter hours vary. Ask for the pamphlet *Cambridge, City for All Seasons*. It provides basic information about the colleges and museums and includes a street plan of the city. The *Official Guide* is available (for £1.95) for those wanting to know more about the history of Cambridge and places of interest outside the city.

CAMBRIDGE — *UNIVERSITY CITY*

A Day Excursion from London

DEPART FROM LIVERPOOL STREET STATION*	ARRIVE IN CAMBRIDGE STATION	NOTES
0828	0930	(1)
0845	1020	(4)
0932	1100	(2)
0945	1120	(4)
1002	1119	(2)
1032	1200	(2)
1045	1220	(4)
1102	1219	(2)
1132	1300	(2)
1145	1320	(4)

(Plus other frequent service)

DEPART FROM CAMBRIDGE STATION	ARRIVE IN LIVERPOOL STREET STATION	
1613	1722	(1)
1655	1819	(4)
1702	1810	(2)
1730	1852	(1)
1755	1919	(4)
1803	1916	(2)
1845	2006	(1)
1902	2015	(2)
1955	2119	(4)

(Plus other frequent service)

Distance: 56 miles/90 km
References: Thomas Cook Table 585

* See Appendix, page 296, for London station plan.

(1) MON–FRI	(3) SAT
(2) MON–SAT	(4) SUN

Train Information: 0223–311999
InterCity Services: 071–928–5100
Cambridge Tourist Information Centre: 0223–322640

If you plan to see Cambridge on your own, planning an itinerary may be difficult because there is so much to see. King's College Chapel is regarded universally as one of Cambridge's finest architectural structures. It was constructed in stages over a period of nearly seventy years and was completed in 1515. The chapel, which is open to the public, displays the carved coats of arms of Henry VIII. His initials, along with those of Anne Boleyn, can be seen on the screen. The chapel's stained-glass windows depict the story of the New Testament. Rubens's *Adoration of the Magi* is the altarpiece.

Trinity College's great court is one of the largest collegiate quadrangles in England. It's so large that much of its detail goes unnoticed. It is said that taking advantage of this situation, Byron bathed nude in the fountain and shared his room with a pet bear, which he claimed he kept for the purpose of taking examinations. Sir Isaac Newton first measured the speed of sound in the great court by stamping his foot in the cloister along the north side.

The admission qualifications to the University of Cambridge are exceptionally demanding. Each year, approximately 8,000 students apply for admission. In the end, however, only about 20 percent are admitted.

The Cam River, the source of Cambridge's being and delightful throughout every season, deserves a portion of your visit. A tour of the city by boat along the "backs," as the placid stretch of the river is called, is an experience not to be missed. You can hire a punt, rowboat, or canoe to boat along the backs. If your selection is the punt—which is propelled with long wooden poles—be aware that these poles frequently stick in the mud and have been known to vault a punter into the river. A "chauffeur punt" service is also available.

Visitors have a wide choice of museums covering a wide range of interests. Allow yourself time to wander in at least one of them. The Fitzwilliam Museum on Trumpington Street features medieval and Renaissance objects of art, arms, and armor. The Folk Museum on Castle Street contains a vast array of domestic articles. Another point of interest is Kettles Yard Art Gallery at Castle Street on Northampton with its fine collection of modern paintings and sculpture.

Steeped in history, Cambridge has a reminder of a more recent historical event—Duxford Airfield, which is located eight miles south of the city. Now the site of the Imperial War Museum, Duxford was one of the many airfields from which Allied aircraft flew raids into Continental Europe during World War II. A visit to the museum is recommended. The American Military Cemetery, four miles from Cambridge, contains the graves of 3,811 American airmen who operated from bases in Britain. The cemetery and the museum may be reached by bus.

The Old Weaver's House in Canterbury owes its name to Flemish and Huguenot weavers who came to the city in the sixteenth century and set up looms in private houses along the River Stour. Now a small but attractive stream, the river played an important role in Canterbury's earlier times.

A DAY EXCURSION TO CANTERBURY
DISTANCE BY TRAIN: 62 miles (99 km)
AVERAGE TRAIN TIME: 1 hour, 25 minutes

Canterbury was originally a huddle of huts that the Romans captured as they penetrated inland from the Kentish coast. They fortified the area and built their roads to London and beyond, and along these roads came the Roman legions of occupation. Although the Romans' domination of England ended in the fifth century, the road between London and Canterbury remains heavily traveled even today.

In early times, the River Stour meandered through the valleys, creating a large boggy area. At Canterbury there was a ford for crossing the watery barrier. The selection of the Canterbury site for settlement probably was dependent on its natural advantage as a ford and on the consequent communications that spread out from it.

Canterbury has had a hectic history. In the year 1011, it was sacked by the Danes. It was again invaded by the Normans, who founded the city of Canterbury as we know it today. The victory of William the Conqueror began an era during which the city developed in an orderly manner until the Reformation. In England, the Reformation lasted several decades, during which time there were martyrs in Canterbury on both sides of the dispute.

Thomas á Becket was made Archbishop of Canterbury in 1162. A close confidant to King Henry II and an advisor in matters of state, Becket chose, upon his ordination, to disregard the wishes of the king and transferred all of his efforts to trying to establish the claims of the Church. Invoking the ire of the monarchy, Becket spent some years in exile, but returned in 1170 to a tumultuous welcome from the populace. On 29 December 1170, he was murdered in his own cathedral after King Henry II mused aloud in the presence of four knights, "Who will free me from this turbulent priest?" Horrified by the murder, Christendom immediately declared Becket a saint.

Becket's murder induced vast pilgrimages to Canterbury, enriching both the cathedral and the city's development during the Middle Ages. These pilgrimages, conducted in a boisterous spirit from all parts of England, have been portrayed by Chaucer in his *Canterbury Tales*.

During World War II, Canterbury was the victim of air raids and bombings, which destroyed about one-quarter of the city. The most severe raid occurred in 1942 in reprisal for British raids on Cologne. The West Gate, however, the only one of seven medieval gates not destroyed more than one-hundred years ago, survived the raids.

Canterbury has two railway stations—West Station and East Station.

CANTERBURY — *AND THE CATHEDRAL*

A Day Excursion from London

DEPART FROM VICTORIA STATION*	ARRIVE IN CANTERBURY EAST STATION	NOTES
0723	0913	(2)(4)
0823	1013	(2)(4)
0920	1040	(2)(4)
1020	1140	(2)(4)
1123	1313	(2)(4)
1223	1413	(2)(4)

(Plus other frequent service)

DEPART FROM CANTERBURY EAST STATION	ARRIVE IN VICTORIA STATION	
1606	1733	(2)
1706	1833	(2)
1706	1855	(4)
1806	1932	(2)
1806	1955	(4)
1906	2055	(2)(4)
2006	2155	(2)(4)
2106	2255	(2)(4)

(Plus other frequent service)

Distance: 62 miles/99 km
References: Thomas Cook Table 501

* See Appendix, page 296, for London station plan.

(1) MON–FRI	(3) SAT
(2) MON–SAT	(4) SUN

Train Information: 0227–454411
InterCity Services: 071–928–5100
Canterbury Tourist Information Centre
0227–766567

Trains departing London's Charing Cross and Waterloo stations arrive at Canterbury West. Those departing London's Victoria Station arrive at Canterbury East. For simplicity, day-excursion schedules are given for Victoria and Canterbury East stations only.

Arriving in Canterbury East Station, use the pedestrian bridge to reach the city walls. There's a taxi queue just outside the station entrance, or you can walk to the city center and the cathedral in about fifteen minutes. From the station entrance, you'll see a sign across the street that says, "City Centre-Marlowe Theatre-Cathedral." A blue sign showing a person walking indicates where to cross the highway. Proceed along the city's old Roman walls, which enclose Dane John Park. Climb the mound in the park for a view of the town and the cathedral. Farther along, you'll come to the city bus station. Descend from the wall at this point onto St. George's Street. Turn left and walk until the cathedral is in view on your right through the Christ Church Gate. Passing through the gate will bring you onto the cathedral grounds.

Not far from the Christ Church Gate is the Longmarket, a paved pedestrian area beginning at the intersection of Rose Lane and St. George's Street. Walking directly away from the Christ Church Gate on St. Margaret's Street will bring you to the Canterbury Visitor Information Centre at No. 34 (telephone 766567). The center is open Monday through Saturday year-round and on Sunday in the summer. City tours depart from this point.

From High Street, where it intersects St. Margaret's Street, walk down until you pass over a narrow bridge on the River Stour. On the far right of the bridge you will see the Old Weaver's House, built in 1500. Canterbury was the background for Dickens's novel *David Copperfield*, so your imagination can take over here for a few fleeting moments and transport you back into English history and literature. The structure houses a beautiful collection of English Church brass rubbings from the medieval and Tudor periods. Unfortunately, as of press time it is closed to the public temporarily due to a change of ownership.

Following World War II, Canterbury became an educational center of great importance. In 1962 Christ Church College was opened adjacent to St. Augustine's College. More recently, the University of Kent was established on a hill overlooking the cathedral and city from the west. Its buildings are designed in a modern idiom; in keeping with the theme of Canterbury, however, it was organized on the basis of colleges with emphasis on artistic and cultural development.

Canterbury, proud of its historical past, is nonetheless eager to respond to the demands of present "pilgrims"—visitors who come to see the cathedral and the other historical landmarks. The city of Canterbury has done an excellent job by exhibiting its history as a living part of a modern, living community.

Castle Clock Tower, an outstanding feature of Cardiff, was designed by Victorian architect William Burges. Commissioned by the Marquis of Bute in 1865 to restore Cardiff Castle, Burges replaced a turret of the castle with this magnificent clock tower as part of the restoration.

From London . . .

A DAY EXCURSION TO CARDIFF
DISTANCE BY TRAIN: 145 miles (233 km)
AVERAGE TRAIN TIME: 1 hour, 46 minutes

A triple treat lies in store for those who take this delightful day excursion to the Welsh capital of Cardiff. The first is the opportunity to travel on one of British Rail's "journey shrinkers"—the fabulous InterCity 125 trains. As an example, the 0900 InterCity out of London's Paddington Station will set you down in Cardiff Central Station exactly 107 minutes later, averaging an amazing speed of eighty miles per hour along the 145 miles separating the two capital cities. As an added bonus, you can savor a delicious English breakfast while watching the western English countryside glide by.

Arriving in Cardiff, your second treat is sampling the scenery of a historic city of the empire that has cast off its grim mantle of industrialism to reveal a sparkling center of shopping arcades, a glistening white array of impressive civic buildings, a most memorable museum (well worth the trip), and smack in the middle of town, a genuine 1,900-year-old castle with walls dating back to the Roman occupation of Britain.

If you recover in time, you'll be off on a fifteen-minute train ride from the city's Queen Street Station for the third treat to nearby Caerphilly Castle, second in size only to Windsor Castle. Covering thirty acres and remarkably well preserved, it's crammed with interesting things, including a tower that even Oliver Cromwell's gunpowder couldn't topple—at least not completely.

Cardiff was first developed by the Romans, then by the Normans. Both left their marks in the form of formidable fortifications. The Romans fought their way into south Wales, reaching the area that is now Cardiff about A.D. 76. At first they erected a wooden fort; but as Cardiff grew in importance as a Roman naval base, a stone fortress was erected, parts of which still exist today as a portion of Cardiff Castle. Following the conquest of England in 1066, the Normans arrived in Cardiff in 1091 and established a stronghold on the site of the old Roman fort.

The city as we see it today is largely a creation of the nineteenth century. Cardiff, a seaport ideally located to handle the iron and coal shipments of the region, saw in 1839 the construction of its first dock and, ten years later, its first railroad. Cardiff is accustomed to welcoming visitors and does it well. We're sure you will find yourself returning there again and again.

We suggest that you first visit the Cardiff information center on Bridge Street to get your bearings, pick up some brochures (including a map of the city), and then begin your sightseeing. If you are not certain of directions,

CARDIFF — *CAPITAL OF WALES*

A Day Excursion from London

DEPART FROM PADDINGTON STATION*	ARRIVE IN CARDIFF CENTRAL STATION	NOTES
0800	0950	(2)
0800	1026	(4)
0900	1056	(2)
0900	1127	(4)
1000	1150	(2)
1000	1226	(4)
1100	1256	(2)
1100	1322	(4)

(Plus other frequent service)

DEPART FROM CARDIFF CENTRAL STATION	ARRIVE IN PADDINGTON STATION	
1525	1722	(2)
1625	1828	(2)(4)
1725	1922	(2)(4)
1825	2023	(2)(4)
1925	2123	(2)(4)
2125	2341	(2)(4)

(Plus other frequent service)

Distance: 145 miles/233 km
References: Thomas Cook Table 531

* See Appendix, page 296, for London station plan.

(1) MON–FRI	(3) SAT
(2) MON–SAT	(4) SUN

Train Information: 0222–228000
InterCity Services: 071–262–6767
Cardiff Tourist Information Centre: 0222–227281

check in with British Rail's Travel Information Centre in Cardiff's Central Station. It's on your far right as you exit from the ticket checker's booth.

One block to the right of the station is St. Mary's Street. Walk through either the Royal or Wyndham arcade. You'll see a Toys 'R Us store; the tourist information center is located at 8–14 Bridge Street, under the multistory parking garage. It's open during the summer from Monday through Saturday, 0900–1800; Sunday, 1000–1600. Winter hours are Monday through Saturday, 0930–1800; closed Sunday. Sunday, by the way, is not the best day to visit Cardiff—the train service slows down, and many of the city's attractions are closed.

Lofty Cardiff Castle is a lavishly restored medieval fortress, and, like Mt. Everest, you can't overlook it. The castle provides the background for the Cardiff Spectacular, staged annually during the first week of August. The event involves members of the British armed forces in ceremonial uniform and guest units from other countries.

The shopping arcades are back on High Street and Queen Street. Many are pedestrian precincts—Cardiff claims to have had them long before the phrase was invented. The city map will help you in your orientation. We specifically recommend the *Cardiff Guide* booklet with the Cardiff Castle clock tower on its cover.

Cardiff's civic center lies beyond the castle, as does the National Museum of Wales. The civic center is one of the most impressive buildings in Europe. Separated by wide avenues and parks, the presence in the spring of cherry blossoms and tulip beds create a perfect setting for the white stone buildings. In the National Museum of Wales, you may view, among other art treasures, four recently discovered tapestry cartoons by Rubens. Rodin's bronze statuary, *The Kiss*, is also housed there. The museum is unusual in that it contains a variety of exhibits—from priceless works of art to a model of a coal mine. It is truly a place where there is something for everyone.

To sample some traditional Welsh dishes served by waitresses in traditional costume, try the Blas ar Gymru (A Taste of Wales) Restaurant at 48 Crwys Road, about a twenty-minute walk from Cardiff Castle. Proceed north through the Civic Centre to Corbett Road, turn right and over the bridge into Cathays Terrace, right onto Woodville Road, and left onto Crwys Road. Reservations advised—telephone (0222) 382132.

Trains depart Cardiff's Queen Street Station for Caerphilly hourly at twenty-three minutes past the hour. Trains returning to Cardiff depart Caerphilly hourly at six minutes past. Returning to Cardiff, ride through to the Central Station for connections with InterCity 125 trains back to London. Central Station is three minutes beyond the Queen Street Station.

The world-famous Rows, a double tier of shops with walkways at ground and first-floor levels, is Chester's most distinctive architectural feature. The Rows line streets originally laid down by Roman engineers almost 2,000 years ago. Extensive rebuilding followed the disastrous fire of 1278.

From London . . .

A DAY EXCURSION TO CHESTER
DISTANCE BY TRAIN: 178 miles (287 km)
AVERAGE TRAIN TIME: 2 hours, 30 minutes

"All's well" in Chester, but don't take our word for it. Check personally with Chester's town crier. He appears twice daily (Tuesday through Saturday, April through October) in the center of the city to announce that fact—first at noon and again at 1500. Chester is one of the few cities in England with its encircling walls completely intact. It is a splendid example of a fortified medieval town.

The center of Chester, known as the "Cross," takes its name from the stone "High Cross" standing in front of St. Peters Church. From this point you may view Chester's distinctive landmarks, the Rows—two tiers of shops (one at ground level, the other immediately above), each with its own walkway. The Rows are unique and justly world famous. The upper levels are great for people watchers who like to linger undisturbed while observing the stream of passers-by in the streets below. The true origin of the Rows has never been satisfactorily explained, but they far exceed any modern day shopping center in utility and beauty. One opinion is that they served as a means of defense against the incursions of the Welsh raiders, who came to plunder their richer English neighbors.

The Romans gave Chester its street plan. Walk today along the four main streets within the city's walls and you will follow the lines laid down by Roman engineers almost 2,000 years ago. Part of the Roman wall survives and is incorporated in the massive tenth-century fortifications enclosing the city. A walk on the walls provides an opportunity to enjoy the vista of the surrounding countryside. Restoration has thrived on a large scale in Chester. Entire blocks were renovated in massive programs. The city's famous "black and white" Tudor buildings survived the ravages of time but did not escape alterations to their facades by Victorian architects. In all, however, Chester has managed to preserve its pleasant medieval appearance.

The railway station in Chester is about a twenty-minute walk from the city's center. City Road, at the front of the station, will get you started in the right direction. Change at the pedestrian underpass onto Foregate Street, which turns into Eastgate Street and brings you to the center of the city's historic area. Or you can board a bus at the side of the Queen Hotel, just across the street from the station. The bus arrives at the town hall in approximately five minutes for a charge of sixteen pence. Taxi meters click off between £1.00 and £1.20 for the ride. Chester's street plan and

111

CHESTER — *MODERN "MEDIEVAL" CITY*

A Day Excursion from London

DEPART FROM EUSTON STATION*	ARRIVE IN CHESTER STATION	NOTES
0630	0957	(2)
0850	1152	(4)
0935	1217	(3)
0945	1217	(1)
1125	1407	(2)

DEPART FROM CHESTER STATION	ARRIVE IN EUSTON STATION	
1508	1800	(4)
1632	1932	(4)
1736	2033	(4)
1805	2050	(2)
1912	2249	(2)

Distance: 178 miles/287 km
References: Thomas Cook Table 555

* See Appendix, page 296, for London station plan.

(1) MON–FRI	(3) SAT
(2) MON–SAT	(4) SUN

Train Information
0244–40170
InterCity Services: 071–387–7070

Chester Tourist Information Centre
0244–324324
0244–313126 (24 hours/day)

directions to its tourist information center and visitor center are displayed graphically at the tourist information point at the entrance to the railway station.

Your first call should be at the Chester Visitor Centre, which is located on the Inner Ring Road, just outside the city walls in Vicars Lane. It is open from 0900 to 2100 seven days a week. The center operates an accommodations booking service, a licensed restaurant, and a reconstruction of a Chester street in Victorian times—complete with sights, sounds, and smells. In addition, the center has a video presentation of Chester's history and a money exchange. Regular guided walks of the city depart from the center from 1030 to 1930 daily. Special guided walks are also available: "Pastfinder" departs daily year-round at 1045 and 1430; "Ghosthunter" departs at 1930 from May through October; and "Roman Soldier Patrol" sets forth at 1130 and 1430 on Thursday and Saturday from June through September.

The tourist information center at the town hall is on Northgate Street across from the entrance to Abbey Square. It is open 0900–1730 Monday through Saturday from November through April; between May and October, weekday hours are 0900–1930 and Sunday 1000–1430. It offers a wide range of facilities, including guided walks, the first one departing daily at 1045. Opposite the town hall is Abbey Square, an island of quiet in the center of the city. By entering the square through its massive fourteenth-century gateway, you will find various buildings constructed anywhere from the sixteenth to the nineteenth century.

Chester also boasts a cathedral, which is within sight of the town hall. An abbey was founded on this site in the tenth century. It remained as a monastery until its dissolution in 1540, when the building was made a cathedral. The bell tower of the cathedral is a concrete structure that was finished in 1974, the first freestanding bell tower for a cathedral built since the fifteenth century.

An interesting observation point that provides a splendid view of the city, the River Dee, and the locks of the Chester canal is located at the north end of the city walls. A spur wall connects there with the water tower, which was built to protect the port of Chester. Another vantage point is from Bonewaldesthorne's tower, about one-hundred feet from the water tower. If you participate in the Roman Soldier Wall Patrol tour, you will be able to enjoy this view.

Also in view at a bend in the River Dee is Roodee, home of the Chester racecourse, one of the oldest in Britain. The main racing season is held in May and its richest prize, the Chester Cup, was first awarded 1824. As a matter of interest to sportive North Americans, the Roodee was, before horse racing, a football field. But due to the violent nature of the football matches, the city assembly members voted to terminate the sport in 1540.

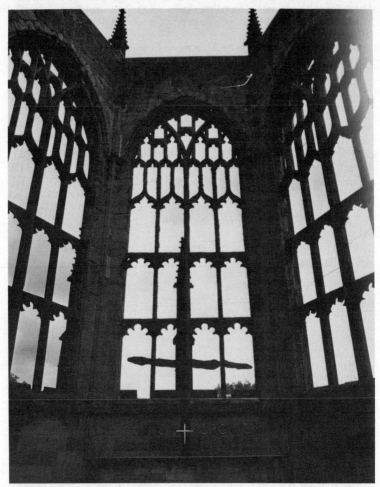

Stark ruins of Coventry's Cathedral of St. Michael stand alongside the city's fine new cathedral. Totally destroyed in a 1940 air raid, an altar of broken stones surmounted by a charred cross stands at the eastern end of the ruins, backed by the words, "Father, forgive."

A DAY EXCURSION TO COVENTRY
DISTANCE BY TRAIN: 100 miles (161 km)
AVERAGE TRAIN TIME: 1 hour, 10 minutes

Explore the legend of Lady Godiva! Did she actually put everything on a horse—or has this tale, retold through the ages, changed with the telling? Was there a "Peeping Tom?" Was he late for the show? Coventry holds the answers.

Coventry is best described as a modern city with ancient roots. Among its tall office buildings, new streets and attractive shops, there is a scattering of old homes and churches, Coventry's remnants of its far-reaching past. The city was devastated in 1940 by Nazi bombers, but after careful and patient rebuilding, a bright new city emerged.

Coventry's new cathedral, consecrated in 1962, stands as visible proof that today's craftsmen can, in fact, create memorable works of supreme beauty, as did their medieval counterparts. In the new cathedral you will see outstanding examples of the finest modern works of art, including the Baptistery Window, the largest piece of modern stained glass in the world. The tapestry *Christ in Glory* hangs behind the altar. Weighing nearly a ton, it is the largest tapestry in the world, ten men worked for three years to complete it. The cathedral, open from 0900–1930 in summer, closes at 1730 in winter.

Alongside the new stands the old Cathedral of St. Michael, reduced to ruins by one dreadful air raid in November 1940. An altar of broken stones surmounted by a charred cross stands at the eastern end of the ruins, backed by the words, "Father, forgive." In the nineteenth century John Ruskin wrote, "The sand of Coventry binds itself into stone which can be built half-way to the sky." Attesting to this, the tower and spire of the old cathedral survived intact after the bombing. Built in the fifteenth century, it is the third highest spire in England. A visit to both cathedrals should not be missed.

Coventry's rail station lies outside its "ringway," a circular super highway surrounding the city. At the bus stop, you'll find a city map and information regarding Coventry's information center. Buses marked "Pool Meadow" (No. 17 or 27) will take you to the center of town in five minutes along a route that requires at least twenty minutes to walk. Dismount at the shopping square by the Leofric Hotel. Lady Godiva's statue stands in a park immediately opposite the hotel, silhouetted against the spires of the cathedrals. Be certain to read the inscriptions on the east and west sides of the statue's pedestal. They were written by Alfred Tennyson, England's poet laureate.

COVENTRY — *LADY GODIVA LAND*

A Day Excursion from London

DEPART FROM EUSTON STATION*	ARRIVE IN COVENTRY STATION	NOTES
0710	0822	(1)
0740	0847	(2)
0810	0920	(2)
0840	0947	(2)
0910	1017	(1)
0940	1047	(2)
0940	1122	(4)
1010	1113	(1)

(Plus other frequent service)

DEPART FROM COVENTRY STATION	ARRIVE IN EUSTON STATION	
1540	1655	(1)
1604	1733	(4)
1610	1729	(2)
1710	1829	(2)(4)
1810	1929	(2)(4)
1940	2058	(1)
2010	2129	(2)
2111	2235	(4)
2140	2309	(2)

(Plus other frequent service)

Distance: 100 miles/161 km
References: Thomas Cook Table 540

* See Appendix, page 296, for London station plan.

(1) MON–FRI	(3) SAT
(2) MON–SAT	(4) SUN

Train Information
0203–555211
InterCity Services: 071–387–7070

Coventry Tourist Information Centre
0203–832312

The bus stop at the Leofric Hotel is Broadgate. The tourist information center is located at Central Library, Smithford Way, in the heart of the shopping precinct, and may be found via well-placed direction signs. The center operates Monday through Friday 0900–2000; Saturday, 0900–1630. Closed on Sunday, it remains open on bank holidays (except Christmas) from 1000–1600.

Among many informative publications, be sure to acquire the blue-and-white *City of Coventry* brochure. It contains a plan of the city's central area, along with a listing of restaurants and places of interest. Also described is "An Hour's Walk Around the City Center," which will lead you from Broadgate to a number of interesting places, including the two cathedrals. For the more ambitious visitor, a two-hour walking tour accompanied by a guide leaves the information center every Tuesday and Thursday at 1030 and 1430. The tour passes Fords Hospital, a fine example of sixteenth-century almshouses, several sections of the remaining city wall, and Cook Street Gate, one of the twelve ancient gates erected in the fourteenth century. You will also be able to see some of Coventry's new buildings, including the Retail Market and the Belgrade Theatre. The price of the tour is twenty-eight pence per person. When returning to the rail station, board the bus at the shelter directly in front of the Holy Trinity Church, opposite the hotel.

Lady Godiva was the wife of Leofric, the "grim" Lord of Coventry. Evidently, she bugged him about the heavy tax burdens he had levied on the townspeople. Legend says Leofric, weary of her nagging, agreed to decrease the tax rate if Her Ladyship would increase the town's morale by riding naked through its streets. Modern historians seriously doubt that Godiva made her gallop without benefit of even a riding crop. They believe her husband challenged her to ride *stripped of her finery and her jewels* and to ride humbly as one of his people and in full sight of them. Stripped of her rank—or just plain stripped—Her Ladyship *did* make the ride and taxes *were lowered*, but she commanded the people to remain indoors with windows barred. Legend says that one town resident called "Tom" unbarred his window to peep as she rode by. Before he could satisfy his gaze, he was struck blind, poor man!

In modern versions of the ride, Lady Godiva now rides her horse through Coventry wearing a body stocking—which is a considerable improvement of the event as conducted in Victorian days, when she was dressed up in petticoats.

Oddly enough, the Godiva story was told for some 500 years before the "Peeping Tom" version was added. In any case, a stunning bronze statue worthy of a *Playboy* centerfold perpetuates Her Ladyship's memory in Broadgate Park as Tom peeps out at her on the hour from the Broadgate clock. We can't help but wonder what effect Lady Godiva's ride would have on our modern-day Internal Revenue Service.

Famous white cliffs, probably Dover's best known landmark, attract thousands of sightseers. Dover Castle, standing guard atop the cliffs, boasts a fine keep, a lighthouse of Roman origin, and a church dating back to Saxon times. Dover's importance as a port began during the Roman invasion of England. Today, Dover is still the principal British maritime port for passenger traffic to and from Europe.

A DAY EXCURSION TO DOVER
DISTANCE BY TRAIN: 77 miles (124 km)
AVERAGE TRAIN TIME: 1 hour, 30 minutes

For centuries Dover has been one of Britain's major channel ports. In theory, this is where England ends and the Continent begins. Here is where countless Englishmen have been parted from, or united with, their homeland. Here stand the white cliffs of Dover. Below, on the beaches, the legions of the Roman Empire stormed ashore in 55 B.C., only to be repelled and to land again, successfully, at Deal.

Atop the cliffs broods Dover Castle. Initially constructed in the 1180s by Henry II to repel invaders, it has been reinforced at every threat to England's shores, including Hitler's in 1940. From its ramparts, on a clear day you can look across the twenty-one miles of the English Channel and see France. Approaching from the sea, a dramatic panorama unfolds as the white cliffs slowly rise from out of the horizon.

You cannot deny it—Dover is dramatic. Brooding hangs over it on a rainy, windswept day; grandeur surrounds it on a clear one when, for example, Boulogne in distant France becomes discernible. The deafening ramjets of the World War II German V-2 "buzz bombs" have been replaced by the humming vacuums of the hovercraft. But the screams of the gulls and the relentless crashing of the sea continue on, unchanged by time. If you are one to "stand in history," Dover becomes a must visit during your stay in Great Britain. Few other places on earth swell the imagination as do the "white cliffs of Dover."

Train service from London to Dover follows two routes. Departures from Victoria Station split destinations at Faversham. Part of the train goes to Dover, the other part to Margate and Ramsgate. As a precaution against "splitting," our schedule is based on direct train service to Dover from London's Charing Cross Station. Readers can, however, avail themselves of either rail route. As a suggestion, depart Charing Cross and return via Faversham to Victoria Station. This way, you will be "joined" by the Ramsgate train instead of being "split" by it.

Leave the train at Dover Priory Station. If you remain on the train, you could find yourself being loaded aboard a Sealink ferry for France, because the next (and last) station on the line is Dover Marine, where that sort of thing takes place. It's a short walk from Dover Priory to Townwall Street, where you will find the tourist information center next door to the Dover Moat House Motel. It's all downhill from the station and in the direction of the sea, so you may walk easily and arrive at the center in about twelve minutes.

DOVER — *ON THE WHITE CLIFFS*

A Day Excursion from London

DEPART FROM VICTORIA STATION*	ARRIVE IN DOVER PRIORY STATION†	NOTES
0723	0913	(2)(4)
0823	1013	(2)(4)
0923	1113	(2)(4)
1023	1213	(2)(4)
1123	1313	(2)(4)

(Plus other frequent service)

DEPART FROM DOVER PRIORY STATION	ARRIVE IN VICTORIA STATION	
1639	1833	(2)(4)
1739	1932	(2)(4)
1839	2055	(2)(4)
1939	2155	(2)(4)
2039	2255	(2)(4)
2139	2355	(2)(4)

(Plus other frequent service)

Distance: 77 miles/124 km
References: Thomas Cook Table 500

* See Appendix, page 296, for London station plan.
† Dover Priory is the last stop before the train arrives at the train-ferry docks for transport to Continental Europe. Hovercraft passengers also should leave the train at Dover Priory, connecting with bus service to the hoverport. See page 302 for Dover station plan.

(1) MON–FRI	(3) SAT
(2) MON–SAT	(4) SUN

Train Information
0304–201753
InterCity Services: 071–928–5100

Dover Tourist Information Centre
0304–205108

The information center is extensive, since Dover is a major debarkation point for visitors from the Continent. The center can provide information on all of Great Britain, as well as the local area. The center is open daily 0745–2200 from June through September. During the rest of the year, it's open weekdays 0900–1830 and Sundays 1000–1830.

Ask for information on Dover Castle and how to reach it. No doubt you will also be interested in visiting the Roman-painted house. It was discovered by an archaeological unit in 1971. Roman legions took over the structure about A.D. 300 for shore-defense purposes. It gains its name from the brilliantly painted plaster of its walls, the oldest and best preserved painted walls in Britain. Incredible as it seems, the Romans even installed an elaborate under-the-floor heating system in the house. The house is now a permanent museum, open every day, except Monday, from March through November.

Legend has it that if Romans are left alone long enough, they will build something. Apparently, this was the case in the second century, when the Roman legions constructed two lighthouse beacons on Dover's cliffs for the purpose of guiding their galleys into the sheltered anchorage below. The surviving lighthouse, reaching to a height of more than forty feet, is the tallest surviving Roman structure in Britain.

Dover can hardy be compared with the Continent's Riviera. Its beaches are small, tiny enclaves in the rugged face of the looming cliffs. And the height of the surf frequently becomes more than the average bather cares to contend with. Dover and its environs, however, lend themselves well to sunbathing, walking, and viewing. It is a point that more people pass through than pause to enjoy, but there is no other point in all of Britain more majestic than Dover. It is the very cornerstone of Britain.

During World War II, Dover was subjected to long-range artillery shelling from the Pas de Calais German gun emplacements. Dover's residents dug cellars deep into the cliffs as sanctuaries from the shelling. The surviving structures, most of which are small hotels, still maintain the shelters for use as wine cellars, bars, and boutiques.

Have you ever been to France? If not, now's your chance! You can whisk across the English Channel to Calais in about thirty-five hovercraft minutes; to Boulogne, in forty minutes. Day trips from Dover to the Continent are very popular. Stock up on wine and cheese, plus a yard or so of crusty French bread during your visit, and load up with duty-free tobacco and booze on the return journey. Plan ahead by asking any train information office for information on Sealink or hovercraft service.

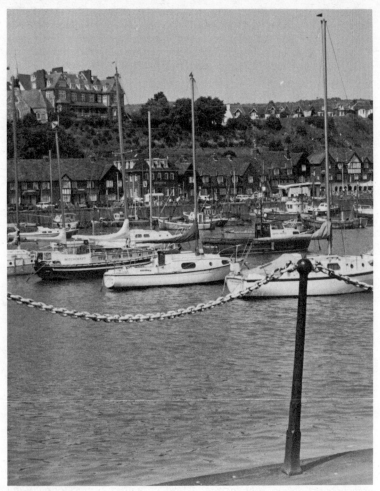

Small boat harbor provides protected haven for Folkestone's fleet of fishing and recreational craft. As a cross-channel port, Folkestone stands second only to Dover in passenger traffic aboard Sealink vessels, which call at the city's harbor–train station pier and the Continent.

A DAY EXCURSION TO FOLKESTONE
DISTANCE BY TRAIN: 70 miles (113 km)
AVERAGE TRAIN TIME: 1 hour, 20 minutes

Folkestone is a "triple treat" seaside resort. You may either stay within its confines for a delightful day of sightseeing and seafood, ply between Folkestone and Boulogne in France aboard Sealink, or elect to survey the thirteen-and-one-half miles of right of way on the world's smallest public railway—the Romney, Hythe and Dymchurch Light Railroad. Each of the three options should take a full day to enjoy, so perhaps you had better plan on making several trips out of London to Folkestone during your visit—or even stay over in Folkestone for a day or two.

Eurotunnel, the rail tunnel running under the English Channel, is scheduled to begin operation in June 1993. With the British terminal at nearby Cheriton, Folkestone now has yet another attraction to offer—the Eurotunnel Exhibition Centre. The progress of this exciting engineering project—one of the biggest in this century—can be followed at the center. Realistic displays show what the tunneling machinery looks like and how it operates. Video presentations give the latest information on the project. You can also see how the rail traffic through the tunnel will operate when opened. A scale model, one of the biggest N–gauge model-railway layouts ever constructed, shows the English and French terminals and the tunnel in-between in action. Check with the Folkestone tourist office or call the Eurotunnel Exhibition Centre (0303) 270111 for details. The center is closed on Monday.

With so many possibilities, we suggest that you make your way to Folkestone's tourist information center immediately on arrival. It can be reached by walking from the Folkestone Central Station down the pedestrian center to Old High Street. Sealink operates a free shuttle bus between Central Station and Harbor Station for the convenience of cross-channel passengers only. It leaves from the left of the Central Station entrance. A schedule is posted nearby explaining the shuttle-bus service, which operates 1000–2310 daily. The shuttle bus passes the information center but cannot stop until it reaches the Harbor Station, where passengers board the next outbound Sealink vessel.

The scenery along the seawall of Folkestone's outer harbor is enjoyable, to say the least. From there, you will have a commanding view of the harbor. The Sealink passage to Boulogne takes one hour and fifty minutes. So if you are tempted to set foot on French soil, the Sealink office will provide you with current fares and schedules. You can obtain tickets at the pier office or at the tourist information office. Fares are listed on page 65.

FOLKESTONE — *BEAUTIFUL KENT SEAPORT*

A Day Excursion from London

DEPART FROM CHARING CROSS STATION*	ARRIVE IN FOLKESTONE CENTRAL STATION†	NOTES
0700	0853	(2)
0800	0946	(4)
0830	1007	(1)
0900	1025	(2)
0956	1121	(1)
1000	1146	(4)

(Plus other frequent service)

DEPART FROM FOLKESTONE CENTRAL STATION	ARRIVE IN CHARING CROSS STATION	
1550	1720	(3)
1641	1818	(1)(4)
1741	1916	(1)(4)
1843	2016	(1)(4)
1943	2116	(1)(4)
1950	2120	(3)
2043	2216	(1)(4)
2050	2220	(3)
2143	2318	(1)(4)

(Plus other frequent service)

Distance: 70 miles/113 km
References: Thomas Cook Table 500

* See Appendix, page 296, for London station plan.
† See page 302 for Folkestone station plan.

(1) MON–FRI	(3) SAT
(2) MON–SAT	(4) SUN

Train Information: 0227–454411
InterCity Services: 071–928–5100

Folkestone Tourist Information Centre
0303–58594

Folkestone has a dual distinction. As a cross-channel port, it is second only to Dover in total passenger traffic. For beauty of location, it probably stands second to none. The Leas, Folkestone's famous cliff-top promenade, served as an inspiration for some of H. G. Wells's finest works. It surveys the town's beach from a vantage point more than 200 feet above. From there, one can view the landscape from Dover to Dungeness. Stretching behind the Leas are the spacious, well-planned business and residential quarters.

One side of the Leas promenade is lined with large hotels, the other with hanging gardens through which winding paths lead down to the beach. A route for the less hearty is the one-hundred-year-old "cliff lift," which plies between the Leas promenade and the picturesque harbor area.

Below the Leas, at harbor level, lie the city's marine gardens and the busy harbor pier, an endless source of interest to visitors.

The harbor area has been redeveloped extensively. Only a few of the quaint, old, narrow streets remain. Nevertheless, the area has a marked nautical flavor that sets it apart from the rest of the town. With the increased interest in sail boating, more of these small craft may be seen in the harbor.

Sandgate, on the western outskirts of Folkestone, has become one of the major antique centers of England. Numerous antique and curio shops, many of which retain their original bow-fronted windows, beckon to shoppers from Sandgate's narrow High Street. Also competing for shoppers' attention are several old-world inns and the Sandgate Castle.

Trains meeting the Sealink vessels at the Harbor Station proceed to London via Dover *and do not stop at Folkestone Central Station.* This, of course, makes possible a circuitous train trip back to London. But it could also lead to embarrassment if you boarded a London-bound train at the Folkestone Harbor Station but had friends or family waiting to join you at the Folkestone Central Station.

A bus from the city station will take you to the town of Hythe, west of Folkestone, in about twenty-two minutes. There, the young—and those not so young—may board the fascinating Romney, Hythe and Dymchurch Light Railroad for a delightful run by steam traction to New Romney, with stops in Dymchurch and St. Mary's Bay. Service is generally every hour, so you can stop en route at Dymchurch, England's "children's paradise," or at St. Mary's Bay, where boating and fishing are two highlights of that holiday center. The RH&D Railroad terminates its service at Dungeness, another five-and-a-half miles down the RH&D "road," where you'll find great contrast between its fishermen's shacks and its atomic plant.

Gloucester Cathedral, originally of Norman design (1089-1260), was remodeled (1331–1370) to house the tomb of King Edward II. The east window of the cathedral, one of the largest in England, was erected as a memorial to those who fought for England at Crécy in 1346.

A DAY EXCURSION TO GLOUCESTER
DISTANCE BY TRAIN: 114 miles (184 km)
AVERAGE TRAIN TIME: 1 hour, 50 minutes

Gloucester is steeped in history. First to arrive were the Romans, following their invasion of the British Isles. A legion fort was erected at the site of the present city center, and by A.D. 96–98, the Roman city of Glevum (now Gloucester) was established and flourishing. Little remains of the Roman presence in modern Gloucester. None of the Roman wall is now visible above ground, but its line is still followed by the principal streets of the city.

Although Gloucester is situated some distance from the open sea, by the construction of a ship canal in 1805, Queen Elizabeth I granted the city a charter and declared it a "port." Ocean-going ships of up to 5,000-ton capacity are able to dock at Sharpness, the terminal dock of the city's port system. The entire dock complex is being given a new "lease on life"; an ambitious redevelopment program is converting the site into a haven of recreation, education, and commerce.

The National Waterways Museum is the principal tourist attraction in the dock complex. Two hundred years of history, which shaped the fortunes of Britain, may be viewed there, housed in an imposing seven-story building. In the main basin of the dock area, you can inspect an authentic canal maintenance yard that has been re-created to display and demonstrate the traditional crafts and skills needed to operate the canals. Following this, you may ride in a horse-drawn wagon around the dockland area.

Gloucester's showplace is, of course, its cathedral. It consists of a Norman nucleus (1089–1260) with additions in every known style of Gothic architecture. Topped by a towering fifteenth-century pinnacle that rises 225 feet above ground level, Gloucester's cathedral is judged to be one of the six most beautiful buildings in Europe. If you have a limited amount of time to spend sightseeing in Gloucester, you will make the best use of it by concentrating on the cathedral and its surroundings.

The cathedral's origins began in 679, when the Saxons founded the monastery of St. Peter on the site. In the year 909, Alfred the Great's daughter gave relics to the priory, making it the Church of St. Oswald. The cathedral is the oldest building in Gloucester. It is a magnificent example of medieval architecture with its great Norman piers still in the cathedral nave. Since the fifteenth century, craftsmen have continued to work on the structure, gracing it with an elegant exterior of later architectural designs, but basically it remains a Norman edifice.

The city's tourist information center is located in St. Michael's Tower at

127

GLOUCESTER — *ON THE RIVER SEVERN*

A Day Excursion from London

DEPART FROM PADDINGTON STATION*	ARRIVE IN SWINDON STATION	NOTES	DEPART SWINDON STATION	Arrive GLOUCESTER STATION	NOTES
0745	0838	(1)	0845	0933	(1)
0830	0932	(1)	0937	1028	(1)
0915	1006	(2)	1055	1152	(1)
1000	—		—	1207	(4)
1105	—		—	1244	(1)

DEPART GLOUCESTER STATION	ARRIVE SWINDON STATION		DEPART SWINDON STATION	ARRIVE PADDINGTON STATION	
1551	—		—	1740	(1)
1631	—		—	1814	(4)
1748	1835	(1)	1853	1957	(1)
1830	—		—	2032	(4)
1930	2017	(1)	2029	2123	(2)

Distance: 114 miles/184 km
References: Thomas Cook Table 533

* See Appendix, page 296, for London station plan.

(1) MON–FRI	(3) SAT
(2) MON–SAT	(4) SUN

Train Information
0452–29501
InterCity Services: 071–387–7070

Gloucester Tourist Information Centre
0452–421188

the city's major intersection, "The Cross." Its hours of operation are 1000–1700 Monday through Saturday and 1400–1700 on Sunday. City bus transportation from Gloucester's Central Station to the tourist information center requires a transfer, and the taxi fare varies.

To reach the tourist center on foot, walk toward the cathedral from the Central Station until you reach Northgate Street. Then turn left to where it intersects Eastgate Street at The Cross. Northgate and Eastgate streets take their names from the ancient city routes through the Roman wall.

Sightseeing in Gloucester has been made easy by the "Via Sacra," a walkway around the city center that follows the lines of the original city wall. It is described in several publications that are available in the information center. It can be recognized by the pattern of dark paving placed in the sidewalk to keep visitors from going too far astray. The "Via Sacra" information sheet, the "Historic Gloucester" folder, and the *City of Gloucester* brochure all describe this suggested walk in good detail.

At the beginning of the walking tour, you can observe a considerable variety of early English architecture, ranging from fifteenth-century timber-frame structures to the Tudor facades of the present county offices. You will pass Blackfriars, the best preserved medieval Dominican friary in Britain. Although it is under restoration, a portion is open to the public. Greyfriars is also on the route. Unlike Blackfriars, however, most of it stands in ruins.

Stopping in the city museum and art gallery affords the opportunity to examine many archaeological items, including a part of the original Roman city wall. The museum is open 1000–1700 Monday through Saturday. It is also open 1000–1600 on Sunday from July through September.

The tour passes not only the old points of interest in Gloucester, but many of its new ones as well. Just beyond the city museum, for example, you will see the Eastgate Shopping Center, which provides traffic-free areas at ground level. The tour ends at the cathedral in St. Lucy's Garden, the approach to the college green.

Gloucester abounds with interesting eating establishments ranging from McDonald's to such ancient eateries as the New Inn on Northgate Street. But don't let the name fool you. The New Inn was built by St. Peter's Abbey to accommodate pilgrims in 1450. The inn courtyard was used for staging plays during the time of Queen Elizabeth I, and in the eighteenth century, the inn became renowned for its association with traveling menageries and exhibitions of "curiosities." It is said to be the finest medieval open-gallery inn in England, and the food served there today matches the excellence of its medieval decor.

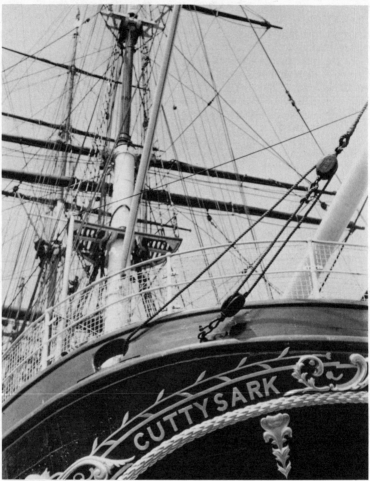

Cutty Sark, built for the China tea trade, rests in dry dock at Greenwich. One of the fastest of sailing ships, she once logged 363 nautical miles in twenty-four hours! Launched at Dumbarton, Scotland, November 1869, the dry-docked ship was opened to public view by Her Majesty Queen Elizabeth II in 1957 following refit.

From London . . .

A DAY EXCURSION TO GREENWICH
DISTANCE BY TRAIN: 7 miles (11 km)
AVERAGE TRAIN TIME: 12 minutes

Greenwich is the cradle of Britain's maritime history and the home of time. Henry VIII and Elizabeth I were born in the Royal Palace of Greenwich. It was here that Elizabeth greeted Sir Francis Drake upon his return from sailing around the world in 1580. Queen Elizabeth II knighted Sir Francis Chichester for his solo circumnavigation of the world at a public ceremony at the Royal Naval College, which now stands on the site of the Royal Palace.

The clipper *Cutty Sark*, one of the fastest of sailing ships, lies in dry dock at Greenwich. The world's largest maritime museum, the National Maritime Museum of Greenwich, has in its fascinating collection the paddle tug *Reliant*, often described as ''the world's largest ship in a bottle.'' At the Old Royal Observatory, visitors can stand astride the brass strip marking the Prime Meridian for Greenwich Mean Time (GMT), with one foot in an east longitude and the other one in west longitude. If time permits, you can walk *under* the Thames River to the Isle of Dogs and treat yourself to a panoramic view of Greenwich from that vantage point. Greenwich has much to offer.

Upon arrival in the Greenwich railway station, use the pedestrian subway (underpass) to the main station and the street. Turn left and walk down the hill into the town. Follow the signs guiding you to the National Maritime Museum and the *Cutty Sark*. Where they split, continue to follow the *Cutty Sark* signs until the ship's masts come into view. The local Greenwich information booth is just before the stern of the *Cutty Sark* at 46 Greenwich Church Street. The booth is open 1000–1800 daily from May through October and 1000–1700 November through April. Of the various publications available, we recommend the brochure, ''A Day in Greenwich.''

The *Cutty Sark* was launched in 1869 and served in the China tea trade, as well as the Australian wool trade. Her curious name, which means ''short chemise,'' originated in ''Tam o'Shanter,'' a poem by Robert Burns in which the witch Nanny appeared in a *cutty sark*. The ship's figurehead represents the witch Nanny.

A short distance away stands the fifty-three-foot ketch, *Gypsy Moth*, which Sir Francis Chichester sailed solo around the world. Sir Francis sailed from Plymouth on 27 August 1966. He completed his circumnavigation of the world on 28 May 1967, when he sailed into Plymouth harbor to a tumultuous welcome. In his voyage, he covered a distance of 28,500 miles.

GREENWICH — *ON THE PRIME MERIDIAN*

A Day Excursion from London

DEPART FROM CHARING CROSS STATION*	ARRIVE IN GREENWICH STATION	NOTES
0848	0901	(2)(4)
0918	0931	(2)(4)

Additional trains depart at eighteen and forty-eight minutes past the hour through 1948.

DEPART FROM GREENWICH STATION	ARRIVE IN CHARING CROSS STATION	
1542	1558	(2)(4)
1612	1628	(2)(4)

Additional trains depart at twelve and forty-two minutes past the hour through 2342.

Plus frequent service serving Waterloo (East), as well as Cannon Street station.

Distance: 7 miles/11 km
References: British Rail Table 201

* See Appendix, page 296, for London station plan.
(1) MON–FRI   (3) SAT
(2) MON–SAT   (4) SUN

For a circuitous rail trip to or from Greenwich, inquire regarding The Docklands Light Railway (DLR) running between its London terminal, Tower Gateway, and the Island Garden Station on the Isle of Dogs, with access to Greenwich via the foot tunnel under the Thames. Information is available by ringing up (071) 22–1234. *BritRail Pass not accepted.* One-way fare, Tower Gateway to Island Gardens, adults 90 pence; children under sixteen, 40 pence. The London Underground station, Tower Hill on the District Line, is within walking distance of the DLR's Tower Gate terminal.

Train Information
071–928–5100

Greenwich Tourist Information Centre
081–858–6376

While at Greenwich, you can take the opportunity of viewing it from the Island Gardens on the Isle of Dogs, located on the opposite bank of the River Thames. To get there, take the Greenwich foot tunnel under the river. It takes only about four minutes to walk through the tunnel to the opposite bank. From this vantage point, it is possible to photograph the entire Greenwich complex. The domed entrance to the tunnel lies in front of the *Cutty Sark*.

A few yards beyond the *Cutty Sark's* stern is the entrance to the Royal Naval College. Built on the original site of the old Tudor Palace at Greenwich during the seventeenth-century reign of William and Mary, the present buildings were used as a hospital for disabled and aged naval pensioners. In 1873, it became the Royal Naval College to provide for the higher education of naval officers.

Visitors are admitted to the Royal Naval College's Painted Hall and Chapel daily except Thursday from 1430 to 1700. (Admission is free.) The Painted Hall is now used as the officers' mess of the college. After the Battle of Trafalgar, the body of Lord Nelson lay in state in the Upper Hall. The interior decorating, by Sir James Thornhill, took nineteen years to complete. (You'll find out why when you see it.) Benjamin West's painting of the shipwrecked *St. Paul* in the college chapel is one of the highlights of that beautiful structure.

There is a small admission charge for the *Cutty Sark* and the National Maritime Museum. To reach the museum, turn left on King William walk, leaving the Naval College. Walk past the Seamen's Hospital to Romney Road. Cross it and turn left. The museum entrance is a few yards beyond. The National Maritime Museum tour leads you through its west wing where you can view the *Reliant* and the state barges once used on the River Thames. The central building houses an amazing display of old ship models, and the east wing features naval history of the nineteenth and twentieth centuries. Also included are two galleries of Victorian paintings and Arctic exploration exhibits.

Adjacent to the National Maritime Museum stands The Queen's House, a royal palace from the time of Charles I. Reopened by Queen Elizabeth II in May 1990, the palace has been restored to its former glory with sumptuous furnishings and rich silk hangings reflective of its heyday when Henrietta Maria, wife of Charles I, was in residence there. It is the earliest example of English Palladian architecture. The admission charge is £3.00.

In Greenwich Park, next to the museum, you may enter the Old Royal Observatory, an integral part of the museum. There is a small admission charge. The Prime Meridian marking the line of zero degrees longitude on which GMT (Greenwich mean time) is calculated is located in the courtyard of the observatory's meridian building.

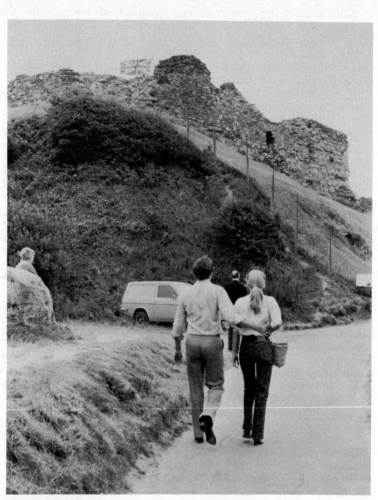

Hastings Castle beckons to visitors from atop the city's west hill, where it was built by William the Conqueror in 1067 following the Battle of Hastings the previous year. Among the castle ruins, you'll find an eleventh-century siege tent. Enter and you will be transported back to the most famous date in English history—1066! Below the fortress in the old city's narrow streets are many eighteenth-century houses.

A DAY EXCURSION TO HASTINGS
DISTANCE BY TRAIN: 63 miles (101 km)
AVERAGE TRAIN TIME: 1 hour, 30 minutes

Undoubtedly, 1066 is one of the most well-known dates in history. When dusk fell at the field of Senlac near Hastings on 14 October 1066, William the Conqueror, Duke of Normandy, had defeated the Saxon army of slain King Harold and had become the new king of England. Hastings holds the lore of the Battle of Hastings plus the lure of its ancient fishing village and Norman castle.

In addition to its rich historical heritage, Hastings has been an attractive seaside resort since the mid-eighteenth century, when London physicians began prescribing sea air and saltwater as a panacea for all their patients' ills. Three miles of promenades line its beaches, many of them two-tiered with sun-trapped shelters overlooking the English Channel. Sun is more sought after in Hastings than surf because the water is very cold. Examine any photo of an English seaside resort and you'll see that the majority of the bathers are on the beach, not in the sea!

There are four railway stations within the Borough of Hastings. Use the Hastings Central Station as a focal point. The tourist information center is at 4 Robertson Terrace. Leaving the Central Station, walk downhill to the seaside and orient yourself on Carlisle Parade. The Queens Hotel is plainly visible from here on the eastern edge of the Robertson Terrace ellipse. The information center is on the west end. The office operates Monday through Friday, 1000–1700; Saturday, 1000–1300. The sign on the center entrance reads "Tourist Information." During summer, the center is open longer hours during the week and on Sunday as well.

Contrary to popular belief, the Battle of Hastings was not fought in Hastings, nor was the Norman castle in Hastings involved. After landing, the Norman army marched northward about six miles, where they engaged the Saxons on the field of Senlac. The castle in Hastings, formerly a timber fort, was converted to stone in 1067, a year *after* the battle.

Harold's troops were not pushovers. Nineteen days prior to the Battle of Hastings, his men had put a Norse army to rout at Stamford Bridge near York. In the initial onslaught at Senlac, the Normans retreated with the Saxons in hot pursuit. In so doing, the Saxons had to break the tight formation of their Saxon wall of shields, and the Norman cavalry quickly took advantage of the hole opening up in the line and inflicted heavy losses upon the Saxons. This tactic was twice repeated and the conflict ended. Today's Super Bowl tactics may have developed in Hastings! To go sightseeing at the battleground, board any "Battle Abbey" bus.

HASTINGS — *FAMOUS BATTLE SITE*

A Day Excursion from London

DEPART FROM CHARING CROSS STATION*	ARRIVE IN HASTINGS STATION	NOTES
0815	0942	(1)
0820	0944	(3)
0900	1040	(4)
0915	1040	(1)
0920	1044	(3)
0950	1126	(2)
1000	1139	(4)
1020	1144	(2)
1050	1226	(2)

DEPART FROM HASTINGS STATION	ARRIVE IN CHARING CROSS STATION	
1600	1749	(1)(4)
1639	1804	(3)
1653	1832	(2)
1708	1848	(4)
1736	1904	(2)
1755	1933	(2)
1806	1948	(4)
1855	2034	(2)

Distance: 63 miles/101 km
References: Thomas Cook Table 500

* See Appendix, page 296, for London station plan.
(1) MON–FRI   (3) SAT
(2) MON–SAT   (4) SUN

Train Information
0424–429325
InterCity Services: 071–928–5100

Hastings Tourist Information Centre
0424–718888

During the Roman occupation, Hastings was one of the famous Cinque (five) Ports where the caesars moored their galleys. Later in history, however, the harbor was silted up by a series of violent storms, culminating with the great tempest in 1287. As a result, Hastings was reduced to the status of a small fishing community during the following four centuries.

The tourist information center has an excellent information sheet entitled "The Old Town Walk." With it in hand, you can easily visit the Norman castle via the west hill lift. After drinking in the panoramic sights from atop the hill, you can drift back toward the sea and Hastings' "Old Town." On Hill Street, observe the two cannonballs on either side of St. Clements Church belfry. The right one was shot into the tower by the French; the one on the left was added by the locals to balance things off.

The French artillery attack in 1337 also leveled the All Saints Church in the Old Town. Undaunted by the French shelling, the locals got busy and re-erected the church in 1436. The interior of the church contains a well-preserved fifteenth-century mural depicting the Last Judgment, with the devil casting souls into hell. The mural was intended for illiterate people of the Middle Ages to portray a lesson in morality. Today, television is utilized for the same purpose.

You'll pass many interesting points on your walk. Stop for a closer examination of the Old Town Hall on High Street. It is now a museum. Drop by the Stables Theatre opposite the Old Town Hall. It originally served as the stables for the Old Hastings House, which was spared demolition by being converted into a cultural center. Your next stop should be the Shovells, circa 1450, reputedly the oldest house in town. If you're desperate for a libation, you might try the Stag Inn opposite the Shovells, where remains of mummified cats and rats decorate the bar. Nearing the end of the Old Town walk, you will pass an unusual wedge-shaped house called the "piece of cheese," no doubt the funniest house in town.

Don't miss the 243-foot embroidery in Hastings' new town hall on Queens Road. It depicts eighty-one of the greatest events of British history since 1066, including the Battle of Hastings, the Boston Tea Party, and the first television broadcast.

The city of Hastings celebrates the famous battle every year by staging a program of events and attractions over a full week, encompassing the fourteenth day of October, to commemorate the battle day in 1066. Included are torchlight processions, art exhibitions, and open house at police, fire, and ambulance stations with combined demonstrations by these services. Sporting competitions including archery tournaments are staged, along with concerts and dances.

Station Hotel is a relatively new addition to Ipswich, considering the city was chartered in A.D. 1200. The hotel stands opposite the town's rail station, and its memorabilia of railroading provide a pleasant decor for luncheon, dinner, or a pint of ale while waiting for your train.

A DAY EXCURSION TO IPSWICH
DISTANCE BY TRAIN: 63 miles (101 km)
AVERAGE TRAIN TIME: 1 hour, 10 minutes

The architecture of Ipswich reflects its history. By-passed by the Romans, this town does not display the former grandeur of Rome. A seafaring community long before King John granted the town's first charter in 1200, Ipswich has always been engaged in commerce and has risen or declined along with the fortunes of its citizens' enterprises. The lack of Georgian buildings in Ipswich is evidence of the town's decline during that period, caused by the loss of its famous Suffolk cloth trade. A revitalization of its harbor by the mid-nineteenth century brought new prosperity to Ipswich and accounts for the number of splendid public buildings erected then, as well as the Victorian architecture of its homes.

Ipswich has withstood the onslaughts of the Vikings and other seaborne raiders down through the ages. Starting with World War I, the town's docks became the targets of a new type of raider coming from the sky rather than from the sea. From 1915 to the end of the conflict, there were a number of zeppelin attacks, but damage was light. During the years 1943–45, Ipswich was rimmed by no fewer than sixty-five air bases of the U.S. Eighth Air Force, from which were launched a staggering 3,000-plus bomber raids against the Third Reich.

Today, with a population of 120,000, Ipswich has a developing port and is an important industrial and commercial center with fine shopping, sports, and entertainment facilities. Ipswich considers its Tudor Christchurch Mansion, set in sixty-five acres of parkland, only a five-minute walk from the center of town, to be its finest attraction. The information office will gladly point out the way to you.

The tourist information center is easy to reach. It is located at the end of Princes Street at Cornhill, for centuries the focal point and principal meeting place of Ipswich townspeople. Princes Street begins (or ends, as the case may be) at the Ipswich train station. If the weather is inclement, you can board a "City Centre" bus or hail a taxi immediately in front of the station. The information center is located within the town hall, across the street from the post office. "You can't miss it," as the locals would say. Obtain a map at the information center before going off to explore the endless streets and enticing alleyways leading off Ipswich's Cornhill. Office hours are 0900–1700 Monday through Thursday, 0900–1630 on Friday, 1000–1600 on Saturday (April-August), and 0930–1230 Saturday (September-March). It is closed Sunday.

IPSWICH — *CHARTERED IN A.D. 1200*

A Day Excursion from London

DEPART FROM LIVERPOOL STREET STATION*	ARRIVE IN IPSWICH STATION	NOTES
0800	0858	(1)
0830	0935	(2)(4)
0930	0944	(2)
0930	1035	(2)
0935	1058	(4)
1030	1135	(2)
1030	1145	(4)

DEPART FROM IPSWICH STATION	ARRIVE IN LIVERPOOL STREET STATION	
1443	1550	(2)(4)
1543	1650	(2)(4)
1643	1750	(2)(4)
1743	1853	(2)(4)
1843	1950	(2)(4)
1943	2054	(2)(4)
2210	2347	(1)

Distance: 69 miles/111 km
References: Thomas Cook Table 580

* See Appendix, page 296, for London station plan.

(1) MON–FRI	(3) SAT
(2) MON–SAT	(4) SUN

Train Information
0473–690744
InterCity Services: 071–928–5100

Ipswich Tourist Information Centre
0473–258070

The town's Leisure Services Department has devised the excellent brochure *Tourist Town Trail*. The trail is signposted by black-and-white signs that are numbered to correspond with the descriptions in the brochure. No doubt the trail was laid out for British walkers, for it is much too ambitious a course for the average Yank to complete within the prescribed period of one hour—at least it was for us! The route is circular, so you can join (or leave) at any point.

Places along the Tourist Town Trail that may be of interest to you include the junction of Butter Market, St. Stephens Lane, and Dial Lane. As you can probably guess, the Butter Market was once a marketplace for many products, one of which was butter. If you enter the Ancient House in the Butter Market, you'll be reminded of its age (more than 500 years old), for its windows represent the known world during its time—and Australia is missing because it had not yet been discovered. A seventeenth-century merchant, Robert Sparrow, added the exquisite, ornate plasterwork to the exterior.

Dial Lane is a traffic-free pedestrian area that gets its name from a clock that was once on the St. Lawrence Church. Although most of the church dates back to the fifteenth and early sixteenth centuries, its tower was rebuilt in 1882 to reflect its original design.

By passing the church and turning left into St. Lawrence Street and then right into Tavern Street, you'll come upon the Great White Horse Hotel. It is the only surviving inn that can be traced in the city records before 1571. Its Georgian brick facade, completed in 1818, covers a basically timber-frame structure from the sixteenth century. A young London news reporter, sent to Ipswich to cover an election, stayed in the Great White Horse and later wrote his recollections in a comic novel that changed the course of his life. The reporter was Charles Dickens; the novel, *The Pickwick Papers*.

Near the end of your walking tour, take time to pause at the junction of Tavern Street and Dial Lane. The view down Dial Lane to the Ancient House is one of the most photographed areas in Ipswich. The Tudor-style buildings reflect the detail and attention of the city's craftsmen. From this point, a left turn will take you to the Cornhill, the end of your Tourist Town Trail walk.

As you stand at Cornhill, it may be sobering to consider that only 400 years ago, nine people were burned at the stake on this hill for heresy. Before becoming too sober, however, we suggest you visit one of the bars in the Great White Horse Hotel. Distinguished visitors of the past, who, besides Charles Dickens, included such notables as King George II, Louis XVIII, and Lord Nelson, have quaffed many a draft there. A toast to these gentlemen would seem only proper. So have a go at it, mate, if you can get there before they call "time!"

Thatched roofs of Shanklin, on the Isle of Wight, line visitor-crowded thoroughfares in the resort town where poet John Keats once resided.

Hovercraft skims between the mainland and the Isle of Wight, augmenting regular ferry service for residents and holiday makers on England's vacation isle.

From London . . .

A DAY EXCURSION TO THE ISLE OF WIGHT
DISTANCE BY TRAIN: 88 miles (142 km)
AVERAGE TRAIN TIME: 2 hours, 40 minutes

"Britain's miniature" is a term often employed to describe the Isle of Wight. Shaped like a diamond, the island is a veritable jewel of every feature of the mainland condensed into a mere 147 square miles. It is dotted with historic spots, sandy beaches, thatched villages, rolling countryside— and discotheques, too, if that's your pleasure. There is fun for everyone on the Isle of Wight, and getting there can be fun, too.

The majority of trains departing Waterloo Station in London for Portsmouth Harbor are InterCity trains. As they glide through the scenery of southern England bound for the coast, you'll be treated to a delightful kaleidoscope of England's landscape from the wide-vision train windows. Stay aboard when the train halts briefly in the Portsmouth and Southsea Station. Your destination is the Portsmouth Harbor Station, five minutes farther on.

Board the Portsmouth-Ryde catamaran at the end of the harbor station. Your BritRail Pass does not cover the passage. The fare is about $5.00 one way. The crossing takes only about fifteen minutes.

Docking at the Ryde pier head, you have three options of sightseeing on the island by train. The trains, by the way, run right onto the pier and look every bit like those of the Bakerloo Underground Line in London. All the coaches are one class, but try to select one with ventilators at the top of the windows. It can get a bit stuffy aboard the train in summer. The three options? They are Ryde, Sandown, or Shanklin. All three lie along the nine miles of track extending from the Ryde pier head to the terminal in Shanklin.

Ryde is the Isle of Wight's gateway. Set picturesquely on a hillside, it becomes a wonderful grandstand from which to watch the great ships of the world sailing by. The pier at Ryde is more than 2,300 feet long, so board the train after disembarking from the passenger ferry and ride the train to its first stop, Ryde Esplanade, where you will find a tourist information kiosk ready to assist you during summer season. The pier has a pedestrian walk, if you elect to make your way to the shore in a more leisurely manner. Ryde has six miles of sandy beach backed by pleasant, wooded gardens. The town is also noted for its Regency and Victorian buildings and for its Royal Victoria Arcade shopping center.

Sandown is the next railway stop after passing the Brading Station. It has all the facilities for a summer holiday, including a new pier complex that offers a modern theater, licensed bars, cafés, and a restaurant. The theater

ISLE OF WIGHT — *THE HOLIDAY ISLAND*

A Day Excursion from London†

DEPART FROM WATERLOO STATION*	ARRIVE IN SHANKLIN STATION	NOTES
0650	0927	(2)
0820	1106	(2)
0825	1106	(4)
0850	1106	(2)
0925	1206	(4)
0950	1206	(2)

DEPART FROM SHANKLIN STATION	ARRIVE IN WATERLOO STATION	
1551	1829	(2)
1611	1903	(4)
1651	1929	(2)
1711	2003	(4)
1751	2029	(2)
1811	2103	(4)
1851	2129	(2)
1934	2233	(2)
2019	2303	(4)

Distance: 88 miles/142 km

References: Thomas Cook Table 515

(Above service through September 25. Inquire in station for off-season schedules.)

* See Appendix, page 296, for London station plan.

† Via ferry service between Portsmouth-Ryde to Shanklin on the Isle of Wight. One-class service between Portsmouth Harbor and Shanklin. Buffet and bar service is available en route. BritRail Pass *not* accepted on ferry crossing. Purchase tickets at pier.

(1) MON–FRI	(3) SAT	
(2) MON–SAT	(4) SUN	

Catamaran service between Portsmouth/Southsea and Ryde runs frequently throughout the day. Purchase tickets at pier.

Shanklin Tourist Information Centre
0983–862942

offers a musical review, which opens in May and runs through the beginning of October. The sheltered Sandown Bay has more than five miles of attractive, sandy beaches where you may find such diversions as miniature golf and a canoe lake. Motor-launch trips are popular. Check at the pier or the tourist information center on the esplanade for details.

Sandown and Shanklin are considered the twin resorts on the Isle of Wight. Because the distance between the two rail stations is exactly two miles, you should select one or the other for your day excursion. There is much to see and do in either resort.

Shanklin frequently holds the British annual sunshine record. It is built on a cliff with a sheltered mile-long beach lying below. It is the end of the line for rail travel. It is easy, however, to transfer to the buses operated by the island's bus company, Southern Vectis, for farther points such as Ventnor, Newport, and Cowes. Check with the Southern Vectis Travel Office on Regent Street, two blocks from Shanklin's train station.

Our personal selection of the Isle's options would be Shanklin. It is certainly one of the prettiest towns in Britain. Shanklin's Old Village on Ventnor Road is world-famous for its quiet beauty. From there, you may descend to Shanklin's beach esplanade via a walk through Shanklin's Chine, a cleft in the town's cliff with overhanging trees, plants, ferns, and a cascading stream. Passage through the Chine costs seventy-five pence for adults; for children, forty pence. Check first with the town's information center at 67 High Street for all details.

One of the most gifted and appealing of England's nineteenth-century poets, John Keats, found Shanklin's climate congenial to his health and the town's scenic beauty so inspiring that he resided there for a long period of time. Keats Green, a spacious promenade on the cliff top of Shanklin, commemorates his loving association with the town.

Queen Victoria spent her holidays on the Isle of Wight and died there in Osborne House in 1901. This house, built by order of the queen in 1845, is maintained in good order with the queen's furniture still in place. In a shed on the Osborne House property, you can see the gardening tools of the royal children from more than a century ago. Each tool and wheelbarrow is marked with the small owners' initials. The Queen and Prince Albert used Osborne as a country residence, and it is said that the prince had a considerable influence on the design of the residence. The main rooms and many of the private apartments are open to the public between Easter Monday and early October. Situated at East Cowes, which is the northern one of the island's twin peaks, you can reach the Osborne House by bus from Ryde Esplanade Station.

Checker-work front graces the fifteenth-century Hall of the Trinity Guild, the town hall of King's Lynn, which was built in 1421. It houses an eighteenth-century card room and assembly rooms. The building was used as a theater during the eighteenth century.

From London . . .

A DAY EXCURSION TO KING'S LYNN
DISTANCE BY TRAIN: 97 miles (156 km)
AVERAGE TRAIN TIME: 2 hours, 5 minutes

King's Lynn, once "Bishops' Lynn" and renamed when Henry VIII took over the bishop's manor, is one of the most historic towns in England. The old section of town still seems medieval, complete with narrow streets, guild hall, and riverside quays, where the gulls reel and scream overhead. The town's former prosperity has left it with a rich heritage of architecture. Set along the east bank of the wide and muddy Ouse River, King's Lynn is the northern terminal of the London-Cambridge-Ely rail line.

King's Lynn came into being during the eleventh century on the middle of three islands, where four streams ran into the Ouse River. Water highways became vital to the commerce of the town. With these waterway connections to the English Midlands, the town of Lynn became an important trading port, bustling with the romance of foreign cargoes, sailing ships, and foreign accents. By the thirteenth century, the town found prosperity in the wool trade between England and the Continent. This aura of a wealthy medieval town still prevails. Today, the town is a thriving, modern port, an essential link between Britain and the rest of the Common Market.

Streets and alleyways in King's Lynn twist and wind about on a grand scale, so a town map will be an invaluable aid. We suggest you make your way immediately from the train station to the town hall, next to which you will find the town information center. To do so, walk directly away from the front of the train station (which faces the west) down Waterloo Street. The street undergoes a name change at every intersection—Market, Paradise, New Conduit, Purfleet—but if one continues walking toward the west, one will come to King Street. Turn left onto King Street, which immediately becomes Queen Street. But don't despair—the town hall is at the next intersection on the near left-hand corner.

You will be tempted to wander about in Queen Street with its lovely merchants' houses, each with a character all its own. Permit yourself a brief peek through the archway of No. 21 Queen Street at the Tudor warehouse with exposed beams, but further dalliance should be avoided. Proceed to the information center and equip yourself with a copy of the *King's Lynn Town Walk* booklet. With it, you'll know where you are. The information center operates on a variety of schedules. We suggest that you telephone ahead: (0553) 763044. Walking from the train station to the town hall takes about ten minutes.

The previously mentioned town-walk booklet is a masterpiece of simplic-

KING'S LYNN—*RICH IN ARCHITECTURE*

A Day Excursion from London

DEPART FROM LIVERPOOL STREET STATION*	DEPART FROM KING'S CROSS STATION	ARRIVE IN KING'S LYNN STATION	NOTES
0632(5)	—	0908	(2)
—	0650(5)	0922	(3)
—	0745(5)	1100	(4)
—	0840(5)	1058	(3)
—	0940(5)	1217	(2)

DEPART FROM KING'S LYNN STATION	ARRIVE IN LIVERPOOL STREET STATION	ARRIVE IN KING'S CROSS STATION	NOTES
1353(5)	—	1639	(2)
1530(5)	—	1818	(4)
1725(5)	—	1938	(3)(4)
1728(5)	2006	—	(1)
1812(5)	—	2022	(1)
1924(5)	2155	—	(2)
1925(5)	—	2138	(4)

Distance: 97 miles/156 km
References: Thomas Cook Table 585

* See Appendix, page 296, for London station plan.
(1) MON–FRI   (4) SUN
(2) MON–SAT   (5) Change trains in Cambridge
(3) SAT

Train Information
0553–772021
InterCity Services: 071–928–5100

King's Lynn Tourist Information Centre
0553–763044

ity. It is packed with facts about the town and its buildings. The trail follows a circular route, so you may start and finish wherever it is most convenient for you. We suggest starting at the town hall, which was rebuilt in 1421 after a fire. There is an admission charge to view its treasury. There you will see the magnificent King John Cup and the Red Register, purported to be one of the oldest books in the world.

A focal point in King's Lynn is the Tuesday Market Place, into which King Street leads. True to tradition, a country market is conducted there every Tuesday in the shadow of the Duke's Head Hotel, a most impressive seventeenth-century structure. The market is everything that one would expect it to be—stalls packed with the agricultural and manufacturing products of the area, augmented by absolutely free entertainment as the hucksters bid for attention.

If you miss the Tuesday market, there's another one on Saturday at a location appropriately named the Saturday Market Place. It is just opposite the town hall. A newer shopping center has been established in the center of town, on the site of the old cattle market, which was moved to one of the industrial estates outside of the town.

Visit the King's Lynn Centre for the Arts on King Street, previously St. George's Guild Hall. Built about 1410, it has been used as a theater, a court house, and an armory, and it is now a cultural center housing a theater and an art gallery.

King John, who ruled England between 1199 and 1216, granted the town its charter in 1204. The king came to the Lynn in October 1215 in pursuit of rebellious barons. One story relates that after he was wined and dined by the burghers of Lynn, the king and his entourage set off in hot pursuit of the baronial rebels. Heading west out of King's Lynn towards Newark, the king and his entourage crossed the Norfolk tidal flats, where the River Ouse empties into The Wash, a shallow bay known for the treachery of its sudden tides.

During the crossing, a high tide from The Wash wiped out the king's baggage train. King John reached the safety of higher shores, but he lost the crown jewels and everything else that went with such a collection in those days. King John was so distraught that he contracted dysentery (a bad "burger" perhaps?) and died a few days later. No one questioned the burghers as to exactly what they fed the king before he left Lynn. We have our suspicions, however, because reportedly all of the burghers felt fine the following morning.

The lost treasure has never been found. Somewhere near King's Lynn, buried under centuries of silt, lies King John's treasure. None of it has been recovered, and no one knows where to look for it. If you have any ideas, perhaps Geraldo Rivera would be interested.

Magnificent Lincoln Cathedral has withstood fire, earthquakes—even Cromwell's artillery. Each of its three towers had a lofty spire, but because one fell during a storm in 1547, the other two were removed in 1807. Its vault holds one of the four existing copies of the Magna Charta.

From London . . .

A DAY EXCURSION TO LINCOLN
DISTANCE BY TRAIN: 135 miles (217 km)
AVERAGE TRAIN TIME: 2 hours, 10 minutes

Lincoln's landmark is its cathedral. It stands on a ridge overlooking the city. Dominating the skyline, the cathedral appears as though it might be half church, half stronghold. There are actually two Lincolns—one, the cathedral and castle standing politely on the hilltop; the other, the city below girding the River Witham and buzzing with commerce. We suggest you scale the heights first and later return to the lower level by a dizzy descent down Steep Hill.

On arrival in Lincoln's Central Station, go to the city bus station, which is in front and to the right of the main station entrance (use the designated pedestrian walkways, because the vehicular traffic can be heavy at times). From the bus station, take city bus 1, 8, or 9 up the hill to the cathedral and ask the driver to let you off at the corner of Eastgate and Castle Square. The tourist information center is at No. 9 Castle Hill.

On the other hand, if you abound with energy, bear to the left when leaving the station and walk a short distance on Mary Street to where it intersects with High Street. Turn right at this point, and, keeping the cathedral in sight, start walking in its direction up High Street. Disregard the fact that the street changes names several times. When you reach an area where a ski lift or a cable car would be most welcome, you'll be on Steep Hill—and it's appropriately named. Now gain the high ground (and your breath), and you will find yourself in Castle Square. With a right turn at the Exchequer Gate, you may enter the cathedral grounds.

Walking up the Lincoln ridge from the railway station to the cathedral can give one a sense of accomplishment. It can also be hazardous to your health. Use discretion—take the bus or a taxi if there's any doubt in your mind about the climb.

Walking or riding up Steep Hill, you will pass the House of Aaron the Jew, a money lender from the twelfth century who reportedly became the richest man in England at that time. Halfway up Steep Hill, and turning off at Danesgate, your visit will be well rewarded by an inspection of the Usher Gallery. You can view an assortment of personal property belonging to England's poet laureate, Alfred, Lord Tennyson, born in a Lincoln suburb in 1809. The gallery also houses an extensive collection of paintings by Peter de Wint (1784–1849). Should you arrive at Castle Square in need of lunch or a libation, seek out the Wig & Mitre, a licensed restaurant with a Dickensian atmosphere.

LINCOLN—*HILLTOP CATHEDRAL*

A Day Excursion from London

DEPART KING'S CROSS*	ARRIVE NEWARK NORTHGATE	NOTES	DEPART NEWARK NORTHGATE	ARRIVE LINCOLN CENTRAL	NOTES
0700	0823	(2)	0853	0914	(1)
0820	0942	(1)	1027	1051	(2)
0930	1049	(1)	1118	1139	(2)
1010	1127	(1)	1212	1236	(2)

DEPART LINCOLN CENTRAL	ARRIVE NEWARK NORTHGATE		DEPART NEWARK NORTHGATE	ARRIVE KING'S CROSS	
1428	1511	(2)	1517	1645	(1)
1628	1652	(2)	1729	1857	(1)
1725	1754	(2)	1805	1936	(2)
1835	1859	(2)	1911	2047	(1)
			1917	2053	(3)

Distance: 135 miles/217 km
References: Thomas Cook Tables 570 and 574

* See Appendix, page 296, for London station plan.
Note: All trains are economy class only.
(1) MON–FRI
(2) MON–SAT
(3) SAT
(4) SUN

Train Information
0522–589502
InterCity Services: 071–387–7070

Lincoln Tourist Information Centre
0522–529828 and 512971

Earlier, we mentioned the "two Lincolns." As a matter of fact, each has a tourist information center. In lower Lincoln you will find the city information center located on Cornhill. To go there, turn right after passing the general post office on High Street. The tourist center atop Lincoln's ridge is between the castle and the cathedral. This office is open 0900–1730, except Friday, when it closes a half hour earlier. On Saturday and Sunday, it is open 1000–1600. There is a wealth of information available in both offices. The *Official Guide, City of Lincoln,* is published by the Lincoln Civic Trust and is worth its purchase price. There is an abundance of other saleable and free literature available as well.

The cathedral is the main point of interest in Lincoln. When you view its exterior and examine the spacious areas under its roof, it becomes rather difficult to comprehend that it was built by medieval craftsmen in only twenty years. The Normans began construction of the cathedral in 1072. In 1141 the roof was destroyed by a fire, and in 1185, the main structure crumbled into ruins as a result of an earthquake. But it survived.

Reconstruction, which began in 1186, returned the cathedral to its original conforms, and, through the ensuing centuries, it was altered frequently. The central tower was completed around 1311. In more modern times, Lincoln's greatest attraction has withstood Cromwell's artillery and Hitler's bombs. If you have but a short period of time to visit in Lincoln, the cathedral *must* take priority over all else.

Lincoln Castle was built by William the Conqueror in 1068. It became the Normans' military stronghold in the area. Its construction is unusual in that it has two mounds: one crowned by the twelfth century Tower of Lucy, the other with Norman structures on which in the nineteenth century an observatory tower was constructed. From either of these points of vantage, there are beautiful views of the cathedral and the surrounding countryside. Today the Lincoln Castle is a huge, walled enclosure of lawns and trees. The crown courts and the old county jail are located in the castle yard.

If you wish to visit the "other Lincoln," start by descending (or plunging down) Steep Hill with its bow-fronted shops until you again reach High Street. You will find interest in the twelfth-century High Bridge, which crosses the River Witham. It is the oldest one in Britain to still carry a building on its structure, in this case, a sixteenth-century timber-framed house. The route leading from the cathedral down Steep Hill is studded with other interesting structures such as numerous public houses and restaurants. Modern Lincoln blends easily with its historical counterparts.

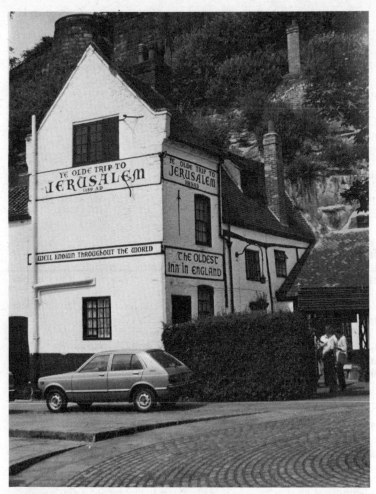

Ye Olde Trip to Jerusalem, one of Britain's oldest inns, crouches on the hillside below Nottingham Castle. It was so named because many crusaders stayed at the inn before setting off for the crusades. Its chimney, which runs about sixty feet through solid rock, is swept once every thirty years.

A DAY EXCURSION TO NOTTINGHAM
DISTANCE BY TRAIN: 127 miles (204 km)
AVERAGE TRAIN TIME: 2 hours

Nottingham is famous for many things, among them the legend of Robin Hood. Many tales of Robin and his band of merry men have been passed down through the ages by ballad and legend, though only scattered fragments remain of his origin. It appears that one Robert Fitzooth, reputed to be the Earl of Huntingdon, was born in 1160 during the reign of Henry II. Of noble birth, he squandered his inheritance at an early age; so either by necessity or by choice, he sought refuge in the forest. Here he was joined by men in similar circumstances, such as Little John, Will Scarlet, Friar Tuck, and—to add the love-interest angle to the legend—Maid Marian.

Robin Hood reigned in the forest, defying the powers of government, protecting the poor, and giving to the needy. The king's deer provided food and the king's forest provided fuel. Other necessities were obtained through barter. Taking the king's property was, of course, illegal and it drove the Sheriff of Nottingham "bananas," to the point where he offered a substantial reward for Robin's capture—dead or alive. Robin Hood eluded capture and supposedly lived to be eighty-seven years old. Records show his death occurred on 18 November 1247. This man, who lived in an age of feudal tyranny, endeared himself to countless generations and became the legendary hero of Nottingham. A fine statue to his memory stands in the courtyard of Nottingham Castle.

Nottingham is also famous for its lace. For centuries it has been the center for lace making in England. The ale that Robin Hood quaffed so copiously is still a local specialty. Why not quaff some yourself in England's oldest inn, Ye Olde Trip to Jerusalem? It has been in Nottingham since 1189 waiting for you. A portion of the inn was dug into the almost vertical rock formation supporting Nottingham Castle above. Legend has it that Robin Hood scaled this rock in his invasions of Nottingham Castle.

The castle was built as a fortress in 1068 by William the Conqueror. It was destroyed during the English civil war, rebuilt, and again destroyed by an angry mob in 1831. Following its second restoration, the castle was transformed into a museum and art gallery late in the nineteenth century. There are a series of underground passages beneath the castle. Naturally, there are many tales of intrigue relating to their purpose. The castle is open to the public daily; the underground passages can be seen only on conducted tours.

The train trip from London's St. Pancras Station passes through

A Day Excursion from London

DEPART FROM ST. PANCRAS STATION*	ARRIVE IN NOTTINGHAM STATION	NOTES
0730	0909	(2)
0830	1010	(1)
0930	1113	(2)
1030	1208	(2)(4)
1130	1304	(1)
1230	1413	(2)(4)

DEPART FROM NOTTINGHAM STATION	ARRIVE IN ST. PANCRAS STATION	
1437	1623	(2)
1537	1712	(1)(4)
1607	1751	(3)
1637	1815	(1)(4)
1737	1924	(2)(4)
1907	2057	(2)
2037	2221	(2)(4)

Distance: 127 miles/204 km
References: Thomas Cook Table 560

* See Appendix, page 296, for London station plan.
(1) MON–FRI
(2) MON–SAT
(3) SAT
(4) SUN

Train Information
0332–32051
InterCity Services: 071–387–7070

Nottingham Tourist Information Centre
0602–470661

England's Midlands en route to Nottingham, passing St. Albans, where Britain's first Christian martyr was executed, and Bedford, where John Bunyan wrote *Pilgrim's Progress*. For variety, you might want to return to London via Peterborough, transferring there to a train for King's Cross Station. Tables 571 and 581 in the *Thomas Cook European Timetable* will show you how, or you can consult with the train information office in Nottingham's station. It is located to your right as you exit from the trains. It is open Monday through Saturday 0800–1830 and Sunday 1000–1900.

The tourist information office in Nottingham is located at 14–16 Wheeler Gate, telephone 470661. The office is within walking distance of the train station. But if your time is limited, you can hail a cab at the station and save some time as well as your shoe leather. Otherwise, take Carrington Street on your right leaving the station to where it intersects Canal Street. A left turn at this point, followed by a right turn onto Maid Marian Way, will have you pointed in the right direction. When you reach Friar Lane, turn right again and walk to where Friar Lane meets Wheeler Gate. You can't miss it—but if you do, just inquire at one of the two taxi queues in that area.

Nottingham's tourist information center lies astride the city's two huge shopping centers—the Victoria and the Broad Marsh. Both are somewhat mind-boggling in size, and they are linked together by wide pedestrian avenues as well as a free bus service running between the two establishments every eight minutes throughout the day, Monday through Saturday.

If your time in Nottingham is limited, no doubt you should first see the historic castle area and return another day to see modern, downtown Nottingham. In the latter case, turn right as you exit the rail station onto Carrington Street. It intersects Canal Street. Turn left onto Canal Street, and three blocks farther along in the same direction, you will come to Castle Road running up the hill to your right. Following it a short distance brings you to Ye Olde Trip to Jerusalem pub, where we suggest you rest before continuing up Castle Road to the Nottingham Castle entrance, just off Castle Place. The pub's "grub" isn't bad—in fact, it's downright good—so you might want to arrive there about lunchtime. Books about Nottingham and the lore of Robin Hood are on sale in the Ye Olde Trip to Jerusalem pub and in Nottingham Castle.

Meanwhile, back at Victoria Center, the tourist information center is open Monday through Friday, 0830–1700; Saturday and Sunday, 0900–1700 (closed for lunch 1300–1400). It has a wide selection of literature, including a walking tour of Nottingham that takes you, among other places, along one of the city's main thoroughfares, Maid Marian Way.

Tom Tower of Christ Church dominates St. Aldate's Street in Oxford. The tower houses the Great Tom Bell, which traditionally tolls at five minutes past nine to signify the closing of the gates to its original 101 scholars. The student body now numbers about 13,500.

From London . . .

A DAY EXCURSION TO OXFORD
DISTANCE BY TRAIN: 64 miles (103 km)
AVERAGE TRAIN TIME: 1 hour

The first glimpse of Oxford as you approach it by train from London confirms its title, "the city of spires." Towers, domes, and pinnacles soar on its skyline. It is impressive. Oxford is one of the great architectural centers of the world, with the double distinction of being not only a university city but an industrial one as well. Oxford contains examples of practically every style of architecture since the time of the Saxons. In the less-than-one-half-square-mile area comprising the city center, you may see some of the finest ancient buildings in the world.

Oxford is the oldest university in Great Britain. It had its beginnings in the twelfth century. Between the thirteenth and fifteenth centuries, it became an established national institution. It has a history of 800 years of continual existence. Oxford's student body has doubled in the past thirty years to about 13,500 students, of which some 9,000 are undergraduates. There is no separate campus; the majority of its buildings lie within the center of the city. Basically, the university is a federation of independent colleges. Visitors coming to Oxford during the summer miss the normal sight of students passing between classes and the student sporting activities, but the buildings alone are worth the trip.

In addition to being a seat of learning, Oxford has a strong industrial segment. Unlike Cambridge, Oxford has made a compromise between scholarship and industry. Foremost in this area is car assembly for Austin Rover, the inheritors of the automobile empire founded by William Morris. Printing and paper making have become Oxford's second industry. Combining such a wide spectrum of academic and industrial endeavors together has created problems. Oxford seems to have worked out a reasonable solution, however, to its "town and gown" problems.

Like many other cities, Oxford's major problem since World War II has been traffic. Daily, thousands of automobiles pour into the city, clogging the streets and spoiling the view of its many fine buildings. Admittedly, transitions are rather abrupt when you step from a bustling byway into the tranquillity of a college quadrangle, but this typifies Oxford. The city fathers are urging everyone to return to the traditional Oxford method of propulsion—the bicycle. By the way, be on the lookout for bicycles propelled by gown-clad students pedaling themselves from one lecture to another. These wheeled hordes could be hazardous to your health!

OXFORD—*ANCIENT CITY CAMPUS*

A Day Excursion from London

DEPART FROM PADDINGTON STATION*	ARRIVE IN OXFORD STATION	NOTES
0810	0915	(4)
0820	0927	(2)
0920	1012	(2)
0950	1039	(1)
1020	1106	(2)

DEPART FROM OXFORD STATION	ARRIVE IN PADDINGTON STATION	
1600	1706	(2)
1637	1742	(4)
1700	1809	(2)(4)
1800	1902	(2)(4)
2000	2102	(1)
2224	2337	(2)

Distance: 63 miles/102 km
References: Thomas Cook Table 525

* See Appendix, page 296, for London station plan.
(1) MON–FRI
(2) MON–SAT
(3) SAT
(4) SUN

Train Information
0865–722333
InterCity Services: 071–928–5100

Oxford Tourist Information Centre
0865–726871

The Oxford tourist information center is on St. Aldate's Street, opposite the town hall and within a stone's throw of the most lavish of the Oxford colleges, Christ Church. The center is open year-round, Monday through Saturday, 0900–1730; Sunday and summer bank holidays, 1030–1600 (June-August). A fifteen-minute walk from the station up Park End-New Road-Queen Street (the street never changes, only its names) brings you to St. Aldate's. Or you can take any bus marked "City Centre" from the bus shelter at the train station. This mode will get you to the information-center vicinity in slightly less than ten minutes.

Beginning with Easter and throughout the summer, the information center conducts guided tours every day that it is open. These tours, which explore the heart of ancient Oxford, leave the center several times during the day and last about two hours. A daily coach tour from late May through September leaves the information center at 1430. It is a one-and-three-quarter-hour trip. The center also has a pamphlet that details a walking tour of Oxford's historic buildings, gardens, and rivers. The walking tour takes about two hours. With the apparent differences in the length of stride between the British and their cousins from "the Colonies," Americans should allow at least another half hour to complete the course.

On the tour, you may be taken by the formal wear of many Oxfordian students. In earlier chapters of this book, we emphasized the fact that Britain holds firmly to tradition. Oxford is a prime example. More than half of the students come to Oxford University from exclusive schools, such as Eton, founded by Henry VI in 1440. Carrying on with their Etonian traditions, students feel privileged to attend their classes in nineteenth-century-gentlemen's morning attire. Agreed, stiff collars and tailcoats are a far cry from T-shirts and jeans. But in one sense, "tradition" is being observed in both cases.

Apparently, there is no single explanation as to exactly how and when the university actually began. One theory claims that it was founded by English students who were expelled from the University of Paris in 1167. Others claim it came about from a gathering of various groups of students from monastic institutions in and around the growing city. From whatever origins, by the end of the twelfth century, Oxford was the established home of the first center of learning in England.

A renaissance of reconstruction and rebuilding in Oxford during the eighteenth century destroyed much of the old street system and the houses inhabited by many religious groups. From this, the city that emerged was more spacious than before. Notwithstanding this urban renewal program, Oxford still has a certain organized clutter about it that becomes readily discernible as you move from the rail station to the city center.

Penzance pirate is portrayed on the roof of the Admiral Benbow Inn on Chapel Street in Penzance. The interior of this 400-year-old tavern is decorated with genuine ship figureheads. Its nautical theme and low-beamed ceilings add to the inn's charm.

AN "OUT-AND-BACK" EXCURSION TO PENZANCE
DISTANCE BY TRAIN: 303 miles (488 km)
AVERAGE TRAIN TIME: 5 hours, 25 minutes

Penzance lends itself more to an "out-and-back" excursion than to a day excursion—although with British Rail's InterCity 125 trains, it is now possible to visit England's westernmost town in the course of a day and still be back in London that evening. An excellent way to visit Penzance is to board the sleeper that departs from London's Paddington Station at one minute before midnight. You can board about an hour before departure time, have the attendant make a nightcap for you, and be well into dreamland by the time the train rolls out of London's suburbs. At 0825 you arrive in Penzance Station after being awakened by the attendant bringing your morning tea or coffee and biscuits. After a full day's sightseeing in Penzance, you can board either the sleeper for your return to London or the InterCity 125 at 1625 and return to London by 2141 the same evening.

Penzance also offers a diversion. When you feel it's time to move on from London to the north and Edinburgh, check out of your London accommodations and take the sleeper to Penzance. Go sightseeing in Penzance, then arrive back in London as described above at 2141 and transfer leisurely to London's Euston Station to board the Night Scotsman at 2345. You'll arrive in Edinburgh the next morning at 0625. Passengers may remain aboard until 0800.

Sleeper reservations should be made well in advance—don't wait until the last minute or you may be disappointed, especially during holidays and peak summer travel periods. Don't forget to check the second-class-sleeper availability if first class is filled. Sometimes if you show up on the departure platform about half an hour before the train leaves, you can pick up a berth cancellation, but don't count on it.

When you arrive in Penzance, you are literally at "the end of the line" insofar as rail travel is concerned. Geographically speaking, you are also at the western end of England. A mere ten miles more would bring you to Land's End, where a road sign pointing to the west cryptically states, "America 4,000 miles." It is difficult to find a grander coastline. This is Land's End Peninsula—the sightseeing opportunities are endless. The tourist information center in Penzance is located on Station Road, immediately outside of the rail station. Upon arrival in the center, the first item of information you should collect is a Penzance & District map. This graphic presentation of the peninsula will help you put the area into the proper perspective for your visit.

PENZANCE—*WESTERN END OF THE LINE*

An "Out-and-Back" Excursion from London

DEPART FROM PADDINGTON STATION*	ARRIVE IN PENZANCE STATION	NOTES
0735	1242	(3)
0745	1315	(1)
0820	1359	(4)
0835	1427	(3)
1035	1528	(2)
1235	1757	(2)
1335	1929	(3)
1435	1938	(2)
2355 (sleeper)	0819 + 1	(2)(4)

DEPART FROM PENZANCE STATION	ARRIVE IN PADDINGTON STATION	
0835	1406	(3)(4)
0851	1333	(1)
0932	1509	(4)
0945	1452	(1)
1630	2205	(1)
1700	2213	(3)
1715	2249	(4)
2115 (sleeper)	0438 + 1	(3)
2215 (sleeper)	0530 + 1	(1)(4)

Distance: 305 miles/491 km

References: Thomas Cook Table 520

*   See Appendix, page 296, for London station plan.

(1)   MON–FRI

(2)   MON–SAT

(3)   SAT

(4)   SUN

Train Information: 0736–65831
InterCity Services: 071–262–6767

Penzance Tourist Information Centre: 0736–62207

Two additional publications which are available in the information center will prove to be extremely helpful to you as a visitor to Penzance. The first, *Penzance Town Trail,* will guide you on a grand tour of the town and its seacoast. It is available for a nominal fee. Another smaller one, *A Day in Chapel Street and Quay Penzance,* does exactly what you might think it would—hold you captive on these two streets for hours and hours. Because the latter publication lists numerous commercial enterprises (such as the Admiral Benbow Inn, where you will find "good food and drink at the sign"), it is provided free of charge.

When you leave the tourist information office fully armed with the publications needed to explore this most interesting area, we are certain that you will be immediately attracted to the harbor area lying to the left just beyond the rail terminal. We suggest that you make it your first "port of call," since it can readily put you in the proper adventurous mood to see the rest of the area.

At harbor side you will want to inspect the old warehouse and granary overlooking Battery Rocks. It has been converted to a craft center and art gallery and contains a saltwater aquarium specializing in local species of marine life. Next door is the Dolphin Inn, formerly a smugglers' hideaway and said to be haunted by an old sea captain's ghost. From there, a walk up Chapel Street away from the harbor brings you to a part of Old Penzance filled with Georgian town houses, fishermen's cottages, and the Museum of Nautical Art. This unusual museum, which takes the form of an eighteenth-century battleship with gun decks and life-size figures manning muzzle-loading guns, is filled with displays of actual navigational gear from former times. The museum is well worth a visit. It is a delight to young and old alike.

Termed the "Capital of the Cornish Riviera," Penzance occupies an unusually well-sheltered position on England's western coast. Because the town faces due south and is protected from all other points of the compass by a ring of hills, its climate is ideal year-round. Winter is mild and virtually without frost, followed by an early spring and a temperate summer. Botanically, Penzance is noted for its early flowers and produce.

You need not confine yourself to the limits of Penzance, although you'll find it almost impossible to get away from its magnetic attractions. Local bus service can take you to Land's End, and, as we have indicated on the schedule, rail connections can be made to other equally interesting points on the peninsula such as Falmouth, Newquay, and St. Ives. The tourist information center can give you the background on these interesting places, and you can ask the British Rail Travel Centre in the train station to work out the needed schedules.

Sir Francis Drake statue gazes seaward from atop Plymouth's Hoe, claimed to be the finest natural promenade in Europe. It was from this spot that Drake spied the Spanish Armada. Not overly impressed, he decided to continue his game of bowls—later defeating the Spanish in running naval engagements.

A DAY EXCURSION TO PLYMOUTH
DISTANCE BY TRAIN: 224 miles (361 km)
AVERAGE TRAIN TIME: 3 hours

Plymouth has one of the finest natural harbors in Europe. From Plymouth Hoe (a Saxon word meaning "high place"), there are magnificent views over Plymouth Sound and the harbor. Stand on this huge brow of a hill, which is claimed to be one of the world's finest natural promenades, and you stand in the midst of history. It was here that Sir Francis Drake continued his game of bowls before setting out to deal with the Spanish Armada in 1588. Earlier, in 1577, he set sail from the same harbor in the *Golden Hind* on a three-year voyage around the world. Here, too, in 1620 the Pilgrims embarked on the *Mayflower* for the New World. Too few remember that the first airplane to cross the Atlantic Ocean, the U.S. Navy seaplane NC4, touched down in Plymouth Sound. This spot is indeed steeped in historical heritage—much of it related to America. Stand here proudly!

Check in with the Plymouth tourist information office in Plymouth's Civic Centre. You can reach it on foot from the train station in about ten minutes through short underground passages and a pedestrianized area. There are streams, fountains, and gardens which form part of an outstanding display. You can also take a bus. Board any bus stopping at the shelter to the right of the station entrance. Pay your fare and ask to be "deposited" at the Civic Centre. Folks who are in a real hurry can hail a taxi for the trip. There is a taxi queue just outside of the rail station; the bus stop is a few steps beyond.

The Plymouth tourist information center is located in the main entrance hall of the fourteen-story Civic Centre. It is open Monday through Thursday, 0900–1700; Friday, 0900–1630; Saturday, 0900–1600 (May–September); and is closed Sunday. Train information is best obtained in the station's travel center, on the extreme right as you pass the ticket barrier. The travel center is open Monday through Friday, 0830–2000, and 0830–1800 on Sunday.

While at the tourist information office, you should ask for a copy of the pamphlet, "The Attractions of Plymouth." It contains an easy-to-read map of the attractions within and near Plymouth that are of interest to visitors. For an introduction to Plymouth, we suggest visiting the city's latest attraction, Plymouth Dome. Situated on Plymouth's famous Hoe, the dome is one of the most up-to-date centers of its kind in Britain. Here you can take a journey through time, use high-resolution cameras to zoom the shoreline, and do many other exciting things. We can guarantee that you won't run out of things to do while in Plymouth.

PLYMOUTH—*PILGRIM'S PROGRESS PORT*

A Day Excursion from London

DEPART FROM PADDINGTON STATION*	ARRIVE IN PLYMOUTH STATION	NOTES
0735	1046	(3)
0745	1129	(1)
0820	1208	(4)
0836	1226	(3)
0935	1258	(1)
1020	1354	(4)
1035	1334	(2)

DEPART FROM PLYMOUTH STATION	ARRIVE IN PADDINGTON STATION	
1524	1852	(1)
1632	1939	(2)
1655	2049	(4)
1805	2136	(3)
1835	2205	(1)
1905	2213	(3)(4)

Distance: 226 miles/363 km
References: Thomas Cook Table 520

*   See Appendix, page 296, for London station plan.
(1)   MON–FRI
(2)   MON–SAT
(3)   SAT
(4)   SUN

Train Information: 0752–221300
InterCity Services: 071–262–6767

Plymouth Tourist Information Centre: 0752–264849

The Plymouth of today is a city of two distinct parts—the original Elizabethan section called the "Barbican" and the modern city center that has risen from the devastation and debris of the last world war. If your time in Plymouth is limited, we suggest you concentrate on visiting the Barbican area of the city.

The harbor area, where the old town of Plymouth nestled, derived its title, Barbican, from the fact that at the entrance to the harbor stood an outpost of the ancient Plymouth Castle. According to castle phraseology, such outer fortifications were called *barbicans*. The Barbican was spared much of the damage that Plymouth suffered during the bombardments of World War II. Consequently, there are still many old buildings and narrow streets in this area that recapture the Elizabethan atmosphere.

One Barbican landmark of particular interest to Americans is a memorial stone that marks the place on the harbor pier from which the *Mayflower* sailed. The Barbican's historic Elizabethan buildings include the Black Friars Distillery, home of Plymouth Gin since 1793. The distillery is still operating in buildings formerly used as a monastery and dating back to 1425. Visitors are welcome. The Merchants House on St. Andrews Street is the largest and finest structure remaining from the sixteenth and seventeenth centuries. Restored recently, it features displays of Plymouth's history with the theme, "Tinker, Tailor, Soldier, Sailor . . ." It is open daily, except Mondays and there is an admission charge.

Towering over the Barbican, the Royal Citadel, built in the 1660s by Charles II, was erected as a warning to the citizens of Plymouth. Many of the fortress cannon still point toward the town and not out to sea, as one would normally expect them to do.

If you have ever sung a chorus or two of "The Eddystone Light," you are a likely customer for the engrossing book *The Four Eddystone Lighthouses* by Robert Sanderson. Additional information on the lighthouses may also be found in the booklet *Smeaton's Tower and the Plymouth Breakwater*. The first Eddystone lighthouse was blown down in a storm. The second lighthouse withstood the elements but was destroyed by fire. Smeaton's Tower stood on the Eddystone Reef from 1759 to 1884 and subsequently was reerected on Plymouth Hoe. The tower is open to the public daily, from the end of April to the beginning of October, from 1030 to one hour before sunset.

If your urge "to go down to the sea in ships" overwhelms you, take a boat trip on Plymouth Sound. The information center has the details, including how to view the nearby Royal Naval Base at Devonport. If your call to the sea is more limited, browsing in the Barbican area will suffice if you throw an occasional glance seaward to impress the locals.

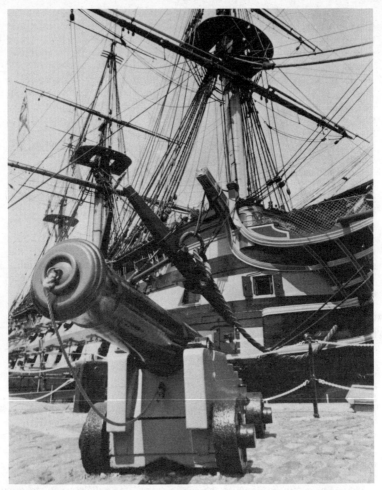

HMS _Victory_, Lord Nelson's flagship at Trafalgar in 1805, has been described as "the proudest sight in Britain." She lies, meticulously preserved, at the Portsmouth Naval Base. One of the ship's cannon partially shields the _Victory_'s starboard sheet anchor.

A DAY EXCURSION TO PORTSMOUTH
DISTANCE BY TRAIN: 74 miles (119 km)
AVERAGE TRAIN TIME: 1 hour, 30 minutes

A visit to Portsmouth requires priorities—priorities involving the choice of what to see there. The city abounds in vast quantities of history, architecture, amusements, and literature. Portsmouth has variety, contrasts, and veneration. Here are a few choices.

If the sea is ''your thing,'' Portsmouth is flanked by natural harbors, east and west. It is the home of one of the world's greatest naval bases, and its resort area, Southsea, offers the largest amusement complex on England's south coast plus four miles of beaches, promenades, and gardens.

Old Portsmouth is for those who relish fine buildings. Lombard Street boasts a host of splendid seventeenth- and eighteenth-century houses, many with distinctive Dutch gables. On adjoining High Street, the motif is primarily eighteenth century, but this gives way as you approach the ultramodern, ''new'' Portsmouth with its traffic-free shopping precinct on Arundel and Commercial streets.

The literary greats of Portsmouth—Charles Dickens, H. G. Wells, Conan Doyle, Rudyard Kipling, and Neville Shute, to name a few—have left their mark on the city in birthplaces, residences, and museums. Resting in the world's oldest dry dock in Portsmouth's naval yard is Lord Horatio Nelson's flagship, HMS *Victory*. Alongside the ship stands the Royal Naval Museum with relics of England's naval hero, ship models, and an outstanding collection of marine paintings. For priority, our first selection is HMS *Victory*. It has been described as ''the proudest sight in Britain,'' and well it is! Meticulously preserved, it stirs the imagination as you relive the events of the Battle of Trafalgar that ''made all England weep.''

Portsmouth has a total of four tourist information centers. The one you should contact first is located on the main street, The Hard, right next to the Portsmouth Naval Base and the Harbor Rail Station. Trains call first at the Portsmouth and Southsea Station, so stay aboard to the end of the line. Then, instead of moving straight ahead to the ferry dock, exit the station on the right-hand side of the platform to The Hard, from where you will be able to see the gate of the naval base to your left. The tourist information center on The Hard is open daily throughout the year (except December 25 and 26) from 0930 to 1730 (telephone 826722). The other centers are located at the Pyramids Resort Centre, the Continental Ferryport, and the Civic Offices. The Harbor Centre can direct you should you need their services.

In addition to visiting the HMS *Victory* in the Portsmouth naval yard, you

171

PORTSMOUTH—*BRITAIN'S NAVAL PORT*

A Day Excursion from London

DEPART FROM WATERLOO STATION*	ARRIVE IN PORTSMOUTH HARBOR STATION†	NOTES
0730	0845	(1)
0750	0909	(3)
0755	0941	(4)
0820	1001	(2)
0825	0958	(4)
0850	1009	(2)

DEPART FROM PORTSMOUTH HARBOR STATION	ARRIVE IN WATERLOO STATION	
1610	1729	(2)(4)
1710	1829	(2)(4)
1810	1929	(2)(4)
1910	2029	(2)(4)
2106	2233	(2)(4)

Distance: 74 miles/119 km
References: Thomas Cook Table 515

*   See Appendix, page 296, for London station plan.
†   Portsmouth has two railway stations—Portsmouth Harbor and Portsmouth & Southsea. Portsmouth Harbor should be used for departures to the Isle of Wight as well as visits to Portsmouth Royal Navy Base. Consult British Rail Table 156 or make inquiries with train information personnel for Portsmouth & Southsea train service.
(1)   MON–FRI
(2)   MON–SAT
(3)   SAT
(4)   SUN

Train Information
0705–825771
InterCity Services: 071–928–5100

Portsmouth Tourist Information Centre
0705–832464

may also inspect the hull of Henry VIII's *Mary Rose*, which is undergoing restoration in a special dry-dock workshop. Launched in 1510, *Mary Rose* went down while sailing against a French invasion fleet in 1545; the remains were raised in 1982. The story of the *Mary Rose*—her loss and her dramatic recovery—is related in an audiovisual presentation, and the objects salvaged from the ship are on exhibit.

Some vital statistics in history regarding HMS *Victory* may be beneficial while you are waiting to go aboard. The ship was launched on 7 May 1765. (Lord Nelson was a mere child of six on that date.) She is a vessel of 3,500 tons with an overall length of 226.5 feet. All totaled, *Victory* carried 104 guns and a complement of 850 officers and men. In 1801, the ship was rebuilt extensively and given the appearance she has today. Recommissioned in April 1803, she became Nelson's flagship. On 21 October 1805, the English fleet under Nelson's command vanquished the combined fleets of France and Spain off Cape Trafalgar. Lord Nelson was killed aboard *Victory* in the final moments of what has been termed "the most decisive battle ever fought at sea."

Newcomer to the scene at the Portsmouth Naval Base is the Victorian ironclad, HMS *Warrior*. Launched in 1860, she was the largest, fastest, and best-armored warship of her time. She is currently being restored throughout to her appearance during her first commission of 1861–64; when you step aboard you can catch a unique glimpse of life as it was experienced on a nineteenth-century British warship.

The Royal Navy Museum supports these famous ships with displays that set them in their historic context and continues the story of the British Navy into the twentieth century, up to the Falklands Campaign of 1982.

In the resort department, Portsmouth offers the Pyramids, a giant leisure attraction built by the sea next to King Henry XIII's Southsea Castle. A true tropical paradise, where the temperature never drops below 84 degrees Fahrenheit, the center features four areas of entertainment, ranging from swimming pools, top-name entertainment, and a patio bar to a supervised "Fun Factory" where Mom and Dad can park the kids.

Close by the Southsea Castle and the Pyramids, Portsmouth's D-Day Museum tells the story of that historic event through pictures, plans, and the re-creation of wartime scenes, along with exhibits of various weapons and vehicles. A special audiovisual presentation relates the events leading to the recapture of Normandy. More history unfolds in the castle where an exhibition traces the development of "Fortress Portsmouth."

Portsmouth bears the title "The South's Historic Maritime Resort City." We are certain that you will agree with this entitlement.

Foy Boat Inn and hotel stands behind cannon on the site where a watch house stood in eighteenth-century Ramsgate. In the days of sails, foy boats took provisions to ships anchored off Ramsgate. The original inn was destroyed in World War II.

A DAY EXCURSION TO RAMSGATE
DISTANCE BY TRAIN: 79 miles (127 km)
AVERAGE TRAIN TIME: 1 hour, 50 minutes

This day excursion to Ramsgate encompasses the northeast tip of England's Kent County, which is called the Isle of Thanet. Although the sea inlets have all been drained, it still bears the semblance of an island with clusters of seaside towns known as Kent's Leisure Coast, each with its own character. Londoners were attracted to Thanet early in the nineteenth century, and it has been a thriving resort area ever since. The attraction of sandy beaches, safe bathing, and entertainment are the assets the area has to offer.

Ramsgate has been selected as the primary point for the day excursion, for it is the terminal stop for trains departing London's Victoria Station on the North Kent line. En route stops at other Isle of Thanet towns are made on this rail line at Margate and Broadstairs. More comments about them follow. It should be noted that it is possible to return to Victoria Station via another rail route from Ramsgate through Ashford, or yet another route calling at Dover and Folkestone. With so many possibilities, you should consult the timetables posted in all three of the previously mentioned Thanet towns for possible variations of your own itinerary. The train schedule shown on the following page gives details for the London Victoria Station–Faversham–Margate–Ramsgate–North Kent rail line only.

This frequent train service departs from the first bay (platforms 1–8) of London's Victoria Station. *A word of caution:* The first cars (usually four) closest to the ticket barrier will go to Dover. The balance of the cars (usually eight) at the head of the train will terminate in Ramsgate. The train "splits" at Faversham. You will be reminded of this again by a train announcement when the train stops briefly in the Bromley South Station after leaving Victoria Station and crossing the Thames. Stay alert and board one of the proper cars.

There are tourist information centers in all three Thanet towns touched by rail service—Margate, Broadstairs, and Ramsgate. The Margate information center is on Marine Terrace, east of the railway station near the Bembom Brothers Whiteknuckle Theme Park. In Broadstairs, its center is relatively near the station in Pierremont Hall. A left turn on High Street out of the railway station will bring you to Pierremont Park and the information center. Ramsgate's information center is in the district-council offices on Queen Street, some distance from the railway station, which lies west of the town's center. Buses from the station will take you there, or you can hail a taxi.

175

RAMSGATE—*SEASIDE RESORT*

A Day Excursion from London

DEPART FROM VICTORIA STATION*	ARRIVE IN RAMSGATE STATION†	NOTES
0750	0940	(2)
0850	1039	(2)(4)
0950	1139	(2)(4)
1050	1239	(2)(4)

(Plus other frequent service)

DEPART FROM RAMSGATE STATION	ARRIVE IN VICTORIA STATION	
1612	1803	(2)
1642	1855	(4)
1712	1903	(2)
1742	1932	(4)
1842	2035	(2)(4)
1942	2135	(2)(4)

(Plus other frequent service)

Distance: 79 miles/127 km
References: Thomas Cook Table 501

*   See Appendix, page 296, for London station plan.
†   See page 302 for Ramsgate station plan.
(1)   MON-FRI
(2)   MON-SAT
(3)   SAT
(4)   SUN

Train Information
0227–454411
InterCity Services: 071–928–5100

Ramsgate Tourist Information Centre
0843–591086

All three centers operate on approximately the same schedule: Monday through Thursday, 0900–1730; Friday, 0900–1700. During summer periods, they also are open on Saturday, 1000–1300 and 1400–1600, and Sunday 1000–1300.

Margate is the Thanet town that has been conjuring up visions of holidays for years. Its biggest drawing card is the famous amusement park, Dreamland Pleasure Park, set on a twenty-acre complex. The municipality of Margate owns nine miles of seafront with sandy beaches and promenades running practically its full distance. The atmosphere of the area differs somewhat from that of England's south coast in that it is more sedate in mood and tempo. Perhaps the presence of the North Sea is one of the contributing factors.

Arriving at Margate Station, the first sight to greet you is the golden sand of the beach. The promenade paralleling the beach is a length of souvenir shops, restaurants, confectioneries, and amusement halls, terminating at the gates of Bembom's Theme Park. Beyond the park lies Margate's main shopping center, where courteous Kentish clerks are most eager to assist you in your shopping. Extending from the promenade, Margate's Old Town of narrow streets and houses clusters around the town's harbor.

Broadstairs has a Victorian atmosphere about it and became a fashionable "watering hole" during the regency of King George IV. Victorians, one of the most eminent being Charles Dickens, favored holidays in Broadstairs. A leaflet from the information center will permit you to follow in his footsteps and see many interesting points within the town. Every June, townspeople remember Dickens by appearing in costume while attending a series of plays, readings, parades, and parties set against the backdrop of Victorian Broadstairs.

Ramsgate, being strong on regency flavor, centers its activities around its royal harbor and marina. The harbor is a source of constant interest, as is the model village at West Cliff, a charming miniature of England's Tudor countryside. Permanently moored on the clifftops at Pegwell Bay in Ramsgate is a Viking ship commemorating the original Viking landing in 449. Ramsgate harbor has seen Wellington's troops embark for the Continent, where they continued on to defeat Napoleon at Waterloo. The harbor also received thousands of battered British troops during the evacuation from Dunkerque in 1940.

Many recall memories of their travels through their senses of sight and sound. In the case of Ramsgate, we recall our visits there by our sense of taste. While dining at the Foy Boat Inn, we were urged by our server to try the seafood specialty of the house—plaice, a delicate, mildly flavored local fish rivaling Dover sole. We did, and we can't wait until our next trip when, without doubt, we will order it again.

Fifteenth-century clock tower standing in St. Albans's French Row was originally a curfew tower, the bell dating back to 1335. To the left of the tower stands the Fleur-de-Lys Inn on a site where King John of France was held prisoner after the Battle of Poitiers in 1356.

A DAY EXCURSION TO ST. ALBANS
DISTANCE BY TRAIN: 20 miles (32 km)
AVERAGE TRAIN TIME: 25 minutes

St. Albans takes its name from Britain's first Christian martyr, a Romano-British citizen who was beheaded for his faith on a hilltop outside Verulamium, one of the most important towns at that time in the western Roman Empire. A magnificent fifteenth-century Norman cathedral now stands on the hilltop, and Verulamium has become a parkland on the western side of the city.

St. Albans has much to offer its visitors. Tucked away in various corners of the city are old coach inns, many with a fascinating history. The White Hart Inn, built in the fifteenth century, was restored in 1930. The Fleur-de-Lys Inn on French Row was erected between 1420 and 1440 on the site where King John of France was held prisoner after the Battle of Poitiers. Another inn, the Fighting Cocks, claims to be the oldest licensed house in England. It derived its name from the cock fights that were held there for many years. All three of these ancient "watering holes" are open to the public during licensed hours. St. Albans has always had an open mind concerning alcoholic beverages—Elizabeth I granted the city permission to issue wine licenses in 1560.

French Row in St. Albans, a narrow street of medieval appearance, is fronted by a clock tower built between 1402 and 1411 from the flint and rubble of Verulamium. Its original curfew bell was cast in 1335. Across from the bell tower stands the Wax House Gate, where once candles and tapers were made and sold to pilgrims visiting the shrine of St. Albans. The path through the gate is still the shortest route for pedestrians en route to the cathedral, proving that the ancients had a sharp eye for customer traffic flow. The St. Albans Cathedral contains traces of an eighth-century Saxon church. It has one of the largest Gothic naves in Europe. The cathedral tower was built largely of stone from Verulamium.

Arriving in St. Albans, leave the train station by walking uphill towards the city center on Victoria Street. At the junction of St. Peters and Chequer streets, the tourist information center can be seen opposite, in the town hall. Office hours are 1000–1700 Monday through Friday and 1000–1600 on Saturday. The uphill walk takes about fifteen minutes. The alternative is city bus transportation, which departs from a bus shelter in the station area. The bus stop for returning to the station is at the top of Victoria Street.

179

ST. ALBANS—*FROM ROMANS TO ROSES*

A Day Excursion from London

DEPART FROM KING'S CROSS STATION*	ARRIVE IN ST. ALBANS STATION	NOTES
0800	0820	(2)
0805	0824	(4)
0901	0920	(2)
0905	0924	(4)
1000	1020	(2)
1005	1024	(4)
1100	1119	(2)
1105	1124	(4)

(Plus other frequent service)

DEPART FROM ST. ALBANS STATION	ARRIVE IN KING'S CROSS STATION	
1427	1454	(4)
1452	1514	(2)
1527	1554	(4)
1553	1614	(2)
1627	1654	(4)
1653	1714	(2)
1733	1752	(4)
1752	1813	(2)

(Plus other frequent service)

Distance: 20 miles/32 km
References: British Rail Table 52

*   See Appendix, page 296, for London station plan.
(1) MON–FRI
(2) MON–SAT
(3) SAT
(4) SUN

Train Information: 071–387–7070

St. Albans Tourist Information Centre: 0727–64511

Many of the points of interest in St. Albans must be reached on foot. The information center has a pamphlet describing a walking tour, "St. Alban's Town Trail," which includes the cathedral and the abbey. The tour (two and one-half miles) may prove a bit too ambitious for the less-experienced, less-conditioned walker, but both lead past one or more of the previously described inns, where a libation will probably instill a desire to press on—or stay at the inn until "time" is called.

Helpful publications to take on the trails are *A Historical Map* of St. Albans and *City Guide*. The center has them available for a small fee. The information center is close to the marketplace. Markets are held in St. Albans every Wednesday and Saturday. If you are in town on these days, be sure to "go to market" and enjoy the opportunity of watching the locals barter back and forth with the tradesmen. Everything from apples to zinnias, including the weather and current prices, will become subjects of discussion.

The Roman city of Verulamium is engrossing. You can spend an entire day at the site visiting its 200-acre grounds, which include a temple, forum, museum, hypocaust, and theater. The museum houses an impressive collection of Roman antiquities. From the center of St. Albans, you can reach Verulamium in about twenty minutes on foot, or you can opt for a local bus. The tourist information office will give you the directions.

At the Verulamium Museum, artifacts taken from the ruins are displayed in an environment of natural surroundings. The small items from the houses and shops range from iron hinges, latches, and locks to personal ornaments worn by the inhabitants. A full range of pottery and glassware, both for table and kitchen use, are on exhibit.

Exploratory excavations of the site have taken place from time to time, but experts estimate that only one-third of the area within the Roman town walls has been uncovered. Modern techniques such as aerial photography continue to reveal additional features.

The gardens of the Royal National Rose Society are in St. Albans. The British Rose Festival is staged there annually during a weekend in early July. The rose trial grounds is the place to see the future "greats" of the rose world. The society made its first award for a new rose in 1883 and subsequently established its own trial grounds. New varieties from all over the world are sent to St. Albans to undergo a comprehensive, three-year assessment. The twelve acres of gardens, a spectacle for the casual visitor, are a total fascination to rose enthusiasts. Open from June through October, the gardens are accessible to the public 1000–1800 daily.

The range of history in St. Albans extends from A.D 43 and the first evidences of the Roman enclosure at Verulamium to the moment you arrive to enjoy the vitality of this timeless city.

181

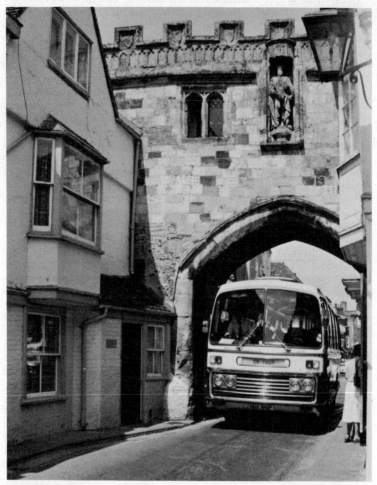

Tight squeeze hinders a tour bus negotiating the High Street Gate in Salisbury. The gate marks the boundary between the two distinct areas of Salisbury—the ''close'' around the cathedral and the city's marketplace. Traditionally, the gate is closed and locked every night.

A DAY EXCURSION TO SALISBURY
DISTANCE BY TRAIN: 84 miles (135 km)
AVERAGE TRAIN TIME: 1 hour, 25 minutes

Salisbury holds the distinction of being one of the few English cities *not* originally founded by the Romans. The old town, Old Sarum, had been in existence since the Iron Age. The Romans fortified it, and the Saxons later developed it into an industrial town. All went well in Old Sarum until arguments between the occupants of the church and the castle caused a new church to be built in the valley below the original town site. This new location proved to be more popular than the old. Consequently, although known as Salisbury, the town's official name is New Sarum.

The center of Salisbury has traditionally been divided into two distinct areas, the cathedral and the marketplace. This tradition still exists, and the gates leading to the cathedral and the buildings in the "close" surrounding it are locked every night. Beautiful houses of medieval and Georgian architecture overlook the green.

The marketplace has a history all its own. In the original Charter of 1227, the town was authorized to hold a Tuesday market. This got out of hand and grew into almost a daily market until protests from nearby towns resulted in a reduction of market days in Salisbury to Tuesdays and Saturdays only. Today, Salisbury maintains those traditional market days. The cattle market, once an integral part of the market, was a cause of some congestion in the city center. It is now housed at its new site off Ashley Road. Perhaps moving the cattle market was a step in the right direction, since tourists and cow slips don't go well together.

Salisbury boasts a brace of historic inns that have given rest and refreshment to travelers down through the centuries. The fireplaces in the King's Arms Inn have the same stone as that used in the construction of the cathedral. The Haunch of Venison, an old English chop house, was built about 1320. The Red Lion Hotel, dating back to the same era, was the starting point for the Salisbury Flying Machine, the nightly horse-drawn coach to London.

In Salisbury, you will find many impressive examples of architectural styles, ranging from the town's thirteenth-century cathedral to a modern pedestrian shopping district known as the Old George Mall. The most unexpected structure is the foyer of the movie theater on New Canal Street. Once the banqueting hall of the merchant John Halle, four-time Mayor of Salisbury, it is now a splendid example of fifteenth-century black-and-white timbering.

A Day Excursion from London

DEPART FROM WATERLOO STATION*	ARRIVE IN SALISBURY STATION	NOTES
0750	0919	(2)
0840	1041	(4)
0915	1041	(2)
1000	1208	(4)
1015	1143	(2)
1040	1239	(4)
1115	1239	(2)

DEPART FROM SALISBURY STATION	ARRIVE IN WATERLOO STATION	
1424	1549 (1622 SUN)	(2)(4)
1624	1749 (1822 SUN)	(2)(4)
1824	1950 (2016 SUN)	(2)(4)
2000	2125	(1)
2039	2216	(4)
2145	2310	(1)

Distance: 84 miles/135 km
References: Thomas Cook Table 521

*   See Appendix, page 296, for London station plan.
(1) MON-FRI
(2) MON-SAT
(3) SAT
(4) SUN

Train Information
0722–27591
InterCity Services: 071–928–5100

Salisbury Tourist Information Centre
0722–334956

Salisbury's tourist information center is situated at the rear of the Town Guildhall where Market Square corners on Fish Row. Telephone ahead from the rail station (334956) for directions, or proceed on foot down Fisherton Street, which you will find to your far left as you exit the station. After crossing the River Avon, the street will narrow and change names several times until it becomes Fish Row.

The center is open seven days a week during the tourist season; otherwise, it's open Monday through Saturday. Summer hours are 0900–1900; 0900–1700 throughout the balance of the year. The center operates a booking service for local hotel accommodations as well as the popular "Book-A-Bed-Ahead" program.

From mid-April through September, you can join a daily (except Sunday) guided walking tour of Salisbury at 1000, 1200, or 1400 from in front of the tourist information center on Fish Row. The tour lasts one and a half hours.

The cathedral has a unity of design that no doubt is attributable to the fact that, unlike most other cathedrals, which took centuries to complete, the Salisbury Cathedral was constructed in only thirty-eight years. In other words, it wasn't affected by several different periods of architecture. Its foundation stones were laid in 1220, during the heyday of Gothic design. One of its greatest treasures is its ancient clock mechanism, which dates from 1386 and is one of the oldest pieces of operating machinery in the world. It originally stood in a detached belfry.

The cathedral contains a library founded in 1089. Seventy of the books installed in the library at that time are still there. The great treasure of the library is the *Magna Charta,* written at Runnymede on 15 June 1215. It was brought to Salisbury by William, Earl of Salisbury, who placed it in the cathedral for safekeeping. It remained there until 1940, when it was hidden for five years in a quarry. Among its many historical achievements, Salisbury made its mark in the annals of medical care. Of the four hospitals currently in or near the city, the Trinity Hospital, on Trinity Street, has a rather interesting story concerning its founding in 1379 by Agnes Botten-ham. Chronicles relate that Ms. Agnes ran a "house of ill repute" on the site, and when it prospered, she built a hospital and almshouse there as an act of penitence.

Visitors interested in seeing Old Sarum, one and a half miles north of the new town, can do so by city bus or taxi. Excavations and reconstruction have been under way for some time. Oddly enough, even after the old city was abandoned, the owner of the estate continued to send two members to the Parliament, despite the fact that the city had no inhabitants. It was a case of representation without taxation.

Sheffield's Town Hall on the left and its modern extension (right) aptly depict the changing attitudes of the city. The original building was opened (by Queen Victoria) in 1897; the latter, in 1977. Both buildings were constructed from stone taken from the same quarry in an attempt to blend the two contrasting architectural styles. Another extension to the Town Hall (not visible) was opened by the Prince of Wales in 1923. It bears a strong resemblance to a French chateau.

A DAY EXCURSION TO SHEFFIELD
DISTANCE BY TRAIN: 165 miles (265 km)
AVERAGE TRAIN TIME: 2 hours, 10 minutes

The name of England's cutlery city, Sheffield, is synonymous with quality. Sheffield also has the reputation of being a typical industrial center, dotted with smoke-belching chimneys and all the atmospheric nightmares that go with that sort of environment. *Not so.* Visitors to Sheffield will be surprised to find the city quite different from its reputation. Today, though the city is proud to be one of the world's largest industrial complexes, Sheffield's environment has changed entirely—only the "Made in Sheffield, England" quality remains. Initiated in 1959 and completed in 1972, the city's clean-air programs have paid magnificent dividends. Sheffield now is virtually smokeless and is probably the cleanest industrial city in Europe.

The art of metal working began more than eight centuries ago in the Sheffield area when monks built furnaces there for the purpose of making iron implements. By the fourteenth century, a Sheffield *thwitel* (knife) was so well known that Chaucer referred to one in his Canterbury tales. Formed in 1642, the Company of Cutlers has guarded the reputation of its craftsmen and maintained the high standards necessary to allow cutlery to bear the trademark "Sheffield."

Sheffield's history is not devoted entirely to the development of her major industries. A chapter in royal intrigue records that Mary Queen of Scots was held captive in the Sheffield Castle for fourteen years by the Earl of Shrewsbury.

Charles Dickens probably would never recognize the town he visited to gather material for his novel *Hard Times*. He found Sheffield's fog thick enough to compare with thick soup. Nor when the fog cleared would he recognize Sheffield's skyline. Slums have been swept away, and some of the boldest architecture in Britain has emerged since the city's ambitious building programs and town planning took shape at the end of World War II. A striking example is the award-winning Castle Square in the city center, which blends a vehicular round-about (traffic circle) with a pedestrian underpass and a shopping center.

For a quick look at "new" Sheffield, you can ride the "city clipper," which is a minibus that cuts a circular swath through the center of Sheffield. Serving the railway station, as well as other central points, the city-clipper service runs on weekdays 0930–1730. The bus-service cost is nominal, so just hop aboard, pay up, then lean back and enjoy Sheffield's scenery.

Sheffield's tourist information center invites visitors to use its many

187

SHEFFIELD—*TRADEMARK OF QUALITY*

A Day Excursion from London

DEPART FROM ST. PANCRAS STATION*	ARRIVE IN SHEFFIELD STATION	NOTES
0800	1022	(1)
0830	1049 (1150 SUN)	(3)(4)
0900	1119	(1)
1000	1217	(2)

DEPART FROM SHEFFIELD STATION	ARRIVE IN ST. PANCRAS STATION	
1523	1753	(1)
1554	1824	(3)
1620	1853	(4)
1623	1848	(1)
1723	1946	(2)
2054	2328	(2)

Distance: 165 miles/265 km
References: Thomas Cook Table 560

*   See Appendix, page 296, for London station plan.
(1) MON–FRI   (3) SAT
(2) MON–SAT   (4) SUN

Train Information
0742–726411
InterCity Services: 071–278–2477

Sheffield Tourist Information Centre
0742–734671/2

services during their stay. The office is open Monday through Friday, 0930–1715, and Saturday, 0930–1615. The office is located in the city's Town Hall Extension Building, accessible on foot from the train station. Use the pedestrian subway (underpass) directly in front of the station and walk until you reach the far end. Exit the subway by using the stairs leading off to the right. Back at ground level, walk straight ahead, following the tourist information and town hall directional signs.

If you need more explicit directions, you may inquire at the travel center (train information office) in the station. It is located on the far left of the station hall as you exit from the trains. Hours of operation are 0930–2000 daily. The personnel there will be glad to point the way. Taxi service is also available from the station to the tourist information center. Ask to be taken to the Town Hall Extension Building, Union Street entrance.

The free city map that you may obtain from the information center in Sheffield is nicely augmented by *Walk About,* which sells for a small fee. The aim of the publication is to act as a guide to visitors for a walking tour of central Sheffield. Taking just over an hour to complete, the walk is designed to show some of Sheffield's past as well as the improvements that have taken place more recently. The tour begins in front of the town hall, a short distance from the Town Hall Extension Building. The town hall was officially opened by Queen Victoria on 21 May 1897.

For an expanded overview of Sheffield and its environs, ask for a copy of the color brochure, *Sheffield Visitor.* It is packed with photos and facts that touch on the city's history, entertainment, sports, shopping, and a number of places to visit. Churches, parks, and homes also are included in this descriptive publication.

Although Sheffield is an industrial city, it is of great interest to tourists. Sheffield boasts extensive recreation facilities in fifty-four parks and open spaces within the city. More than sixty different kinds of recreational pursuits are made available to all who choose to participate.

A stone's throw from the town hall on Church Street you will find Cutlers' Hall. Erected in 1832, the hall houses the Cutlers' Company silver collection and is the scene for the annual Cutlers' Feast. Arrangements to view the silver collection can be made through the city's tourist information center. The City Museum in Weston Park houses the world's largest collection of Sheffield Plate. Another section of the museum is devoted to a collection of fine cutlery.

Southampton's Bargate, one of four medieval gates in the wall surrounding the original city, has not lost its character despite numerous alterations. Constructed in the twelfth century, it now houses a museum that previously was a guild hall. Its most recent alteration included a new roof and heating system.

A DAY EXCURSION TO SOUTHAMPTON
DISTANCE BY TRAIN: 79 miles (127 km)
AVERAGE TRAIN TIME: 1 hour, 10 minutes

In the minds of many, Southampton conjures visions of the great transatlantic ocean liners, for it is Britain's prime ocean-passenger port and home of many of the world's greatest passenger ships, including Britain's flagship, the *Queen Elizabeth II* (*QE2*). Many visitors, however, know little about Southampton's span of centuries, which has given it a rich heritage in the history of England and of Europe. Southampton's museums, classic buildings, and ancient ruins help reveal this rich and interesting heritage.

Southampton is best seen on foot, with the possible assist from a city bus now and then. From the railway station, you can board any "City Centre" bound bus and ask the driver to "deposit" you at the Above Bar Shopping Precinct, where you will find the city tourist information center. The center is open for business Monday through Saturday 0900–1700 throughout the year. It is closed on Sunday.

The center can make hotel and bed-and-breakfast reservations in Southampton and its surroundings. Written and telephone requests for reservations may also be made. Write to the Southampton Tourism Unit, Civic Centre, Southampton S09 4XF, England, or telephone (0703) 832712 or 832330.

There is a map outside the Southampton railway station showing the route to the center. Consider purchasing the official *Southampton Handbook*. It contains suggestions for sightseeing and also has an engrossing history of the Southampton area. Visitors from the United States will take special interest in the sailing of the *Mayflower* from Southampton in 1620. Persons proving descent from original *Mayflower* passengers can have their names entered on the memorial.

As mentioned in the official handbook, there are many places of interest within easy walking distance of the city information center. A visit to them will gradually unfold a picture of Southampton's past. To catch Southampton's seagoing flavor, a visit to the Ocean Village or the Town Quay Marina would be in order. Similar to the harbor renovation of Baltimore, Maryland, Southampton's Ocean Village has transformed some of its old docks into a cosmopolitan playground with a bevy of specialty shops and eateries overlooking a yacht basin. The Town Quay Marina plays host to the cream of the yacht-racing world. Both areas are close to the terminal used by HMS *Queen Elizabeth II* (*QE2*). Check with the information center concerning walking directions and the possibility of the *QE2* being in the harbor.

SOUTHAMPTON—*AN IMPOSING HERITAGE*

A Day Excursion from London

DEPART FROM WATERLOO STATION*	ARRIVE IN SOUTHAMPTON STATION	NOTES
0815	0924	(1)
0845	1007	(2)
0930	1100	(4)
0932	1037	(2)
1030	1200	(4)
1032	1137	(2)

DEPART FROM SOUTHAMPTON STATION	ARRIVE IN WATERLOO STATION	
1610	1748	(4)
1617	1724	(2)
1717	1824	(2)
1810	1950	(4)
1817	1924	(2)
1917	2023	(2)
2010	2148	(4)

Distance: 79 miles/127 km
References: Thomas Cook Table 510

*   See Appendix, page 296, for London station plan.
(1)   MON–FRI
(2)   MON–SAT
(3)   SAT
(4)   SUN

Train Information
0703–229393

Southampton Tourist Information Centre
0703–832712 or 832330

Next in line is the Tudor House Museum, where the costumes, paintings, and furniture of centuries past are displayed against the oak beams and stone carvings of Tudor House itself. The Tudor House is one of the few surviving examples in Southampton of a large town house from the early Tudor period. It contains a banquet hall and is surrounded by an authentic Elizabethan herb garden. Don't miss the tunnel entrance to the remains of a twelfth-century merchant's home. The kids will love it.

Next on the agenda is Wool House, once a medieval warehouse and now a showplace for the city's involvement with the sea. Since early times, Southampton has been an important port of call. Its docks have been piled high with luxuries from the Mediterranean and the East, brought there by Genoan and Venetian fleets. If you are not fortunate enough to see the *QE2* during your Southampton visit, Wool House will make up for it with its history of the "Queens," highlighted by a scale model of the *Queen Mary* from the boardroom of the Cunard Shipping Company.

If you never expected to see a marine museum in a wool house, you'll be equally surprised to find an archaeological collection in a museum bearing the name God's House Tower. It started out as a gunnery store, changed its use many times, and finally opened as a museum in 1950. It currently houses the most extensive collection of post-Roman European pottery to be found in Europe.

Also in Southampton's repertoire is the Hall of Aviation on Albert Road. The museum is a memorial to R. J. Mitchell, Southampton's famous aircraft designer of the Spitfire, the fighter that valiantly defended the country during the Battle of Britain. The exhibits include a Spitfire Mark 24, possibly one of the last of 24,500 Spitfires produced by the Supermarine Aircraft Company in nearby Woolston, a quarter mile from the museum. The museum's collection also includes a Sandringham Flying Boat as well as hundreds of photographs, plans, and models connected with inventor R. J. Mitchell and the Supermarine factory.

The route between the museums, by the way, is dotted with historic buildings, such as the Duke of Wellington Pub and the Red Lion Pub. Pausing for a pint may provide a pleasant period for pondering Southampton's past and present.

Free guided walks through medieval Southampton depart from the Bargate at 1030 Sunday all year round. From July through September, the guided walks depart at 1030 and 1430 on Friday, Saturday, and Sunday. Check for details at the tourist information center.

Quay side at Southampton's port, you stand in history. Four-hundred years before the pilgrim fathers departed on their journey to the new world, Richard the Lion-Hearted embarked on the Third Crusade.

A unique wonder of the world, Stonehenge is viewed annually by more than a million visitors. The monument stands on a bed of solid chalk. Because it has been constantly robbed of stone and defaced throughout the centuries, visitors are no longer permitted to enter the stone circle.

A DAY EXCURSION TO STONEHENGE
DISTANCE BY TRAIN: 84 miles (135 km)
AVERAGE TRAIN TIME: 1 hour, 45 minutes

"Observatory, altar, temple, tomb, erected none knows when by none knows whom, to serve strange gods or watch familiar stars . . ." wrote the poet Sir John Squire about Stonehenge. Stonehenge is unmatched—truly one of the wonders of the world. There are many opinions regarding the use and purpose of the monument. Whatever the reason for its existence, however, Stonehenge remains an awe-inspiring reminder of the past.

The landscape for a few miles around the Stonehenge monument reportedly contains more prehistoric remains than any other area of the same size in Britain. There are earthworks, burial sites, erected stones, and hill carvings. Because they belong to the prehistoric period, long before any written records were made, there are many questions about them all that we shall never to be able to answer. Through technology, modern man has been able to tell *how* they were made and, in some cases, *when* and *by whom*. The unanswered question is *why*.

Stonehenge sits on the Salisbury plain, an almost treeless, windswept plateau. With its origins dating from 2700 B.C. to about 1400 B.C., Stonehenge comprises a circular group of stones roughly 110 feet in diameter that stand in an area surrounded by a low earthen rampart and ditch approximately 200 feet in diameter. The largest stones, some weighing as much as fifty tons, were brought to the site from quarries some twenty miles distant. The stones are placed accurately to record the position of the sun on the four main dates of the seasons, possibly for an agricultural or a religious purpose.

The monument stands on 300 feet of solid chalk, of which only twelve inches have eroded in the past 4,000 years. Unfortunately, Stonehenge has been robbed constantly of its stone throughout the centuries. In Victorian times, it was common practice for visitors to bring hammers and chisels to chip off souvenir sections of the temple stones.

Deodorus Ciculus, historian to Julius Caesar, described Stonehenge as a temple to the sun god Apollo. Modern Britons have marked the area with small clumps of trees to commemorate the Battle of Trafalgar in 1805. The Order of Druids gathers annually at Stonehenge on the longest day of the year to celebrate the sun's zenith and watch it rise over the heel stone of the temple. One theory relates that Stonehenge was built by the Druids as colleges of philosophy, theology, and science. The theory has been discredited by the revelation that the original Druids arrived in Britain long after Stonehenge was built.

STONEHENGE—*MYSTERIOUS PAGAN SHRINE*

A Day Excursion from London

DEPART FROM WATERLOO STATION*	ARRIVE IN SALISBURY STATION	NOTES
0750	0919	(2)
0840	1041	(4)
0915	1041	(2)
1000	1208	(4)
1015	1143	(2)
1040	1239	(4)
1115	1239	(2)

DEPART FROM SALISBURY STATION	ARRIVE IN WATERLOO STATION	
1424	1549 (1622 SUN)	(1)(4)
1624	1749 (1822 SUN)	(2)(4)
1824	1950 (2016 SUN)	(2)(4)
2000	2125	(1)
2039	2216	(4)
2145	2310	(1)

Distance: 84 miles/135 km
References: Thomas Cook Table 521

*   See Appendix, page 296, for London station plan.
(1)   MON–FRI
(2)   MON–SAT
(3)   SAT
(4)   SUN

Train Information
0722–27591
InterCity Services: 071–928–5100

Salisbury Tourist Information Centre
0722–334956

The 0915 train from Waterloo Station in London is met by a special Stonehenge excursion bus at the Salisbury rail station. The bus is the traditional, British red double-decker and easy to spot. It stands in front of the station slightly to the left of the main entrance. You should board it immediately because the premium seats on the upper deck fill up fast. The round-trip fare to Stonehenge and return is £2.45. It's a travel bargain that you won't regret. Admission to the Stonehenge site is not included in the fare.

The Stonehenge excursion bus leaves the Salisbury Station at 1045 for a short run to the city bus terminal in Salisbury. If there are standees (the double-decker bus seats seventy), they are transferred to another bus at the terminal. Departure for Stonehenge, eleven miles away, is scheduled for 11:10 A.M. The trip, including a stop in Amesbury, takes about thirty minutes.

Plan to depart from Stonehenge on the 1420 bus, which arrives at the Salisbury rail station at 1444, or the 1650 bus, which will deposit you at the rail station by 1717. Either bus will place you back in Salisbury in ample time to make your train to London.

Time permitting, upon arriving back in Salisbury, you may want to explore the city prior to boarding your London-bound train. If so, stay aboard the bus returning from Stonehenge until it arrives at the Salisbury bus terminal approximately five minutes after its arrival at the rail station. You will note on both the Stonehenge and Salisbury rail schedules that three later train departures to London will still be available to you.

We recommend that you use the special excursion bus. Otherwise, you would be obliged to use the regular bus service between Salisbury and Amesbury, then walk or take a taxi for two miles to the Stonehenge site. Another excursion bus meets the train arriving in Salisbury from London at 1234 and provides the same service to the Stonehenge site.

The site opens daily throughout the year at 0930, except for Christmas Eve, Christmas Day, Boxing Day (the first weekday after Christmas), and New Year's Day. From May through September, the site closes at 1830; in October, at 1730; and November through February, at 1600. Snack-bar service and a book shop are available at the entrance.

A sad note: Because of damage to the monument, visitors are no longer permitted to enter the stone circle but can view it only from a distance. Now, except for special events, visitors are required to remain behind a fence built around the Stonehenge temple to protect it. "Time," as the announcement observes, "is taking its toll."

The Royal Shakespeare Theatre, built in 1932 to replace the original theater destroyed by fire in 1926, employs both decorative and structural brickwork.

Anne Hathaway's Cottage, two miles from the center of Stratford, attracts tens of thousands of visitors annually during visits to Shakespeare country.

From London . . .

A DAY EXCURSION TO STRATFORD-UPON-AVON
DISTANCE BY TRAIN: 121 miles (195 km)
AVERAGE TRAIN TIME: 2 hours, 30 minutes

Visitors—"pilgrims," as many term themselves—began trickling into Stratford-upon-Avon soon after the first folio of Shakespeare's plays was published in 1623. That "trickle" has increased through the centuries. Today, it is a torrent. Swept up in the bardolatry, admirers of William Shakespeare make the pilgrimage to Stratford-upon-Avon regardless of the consequences. It is said that half a million visitors pass through the narrow corridors and down the twisting staircases of his birthplace every year. Sometimes, it seems like they are all there at the same time that you are. Stratford-upon Avon is crowded, commercialized, stereotyped, and yet inevitable. Despite all that, we know you'll go there.

BritRail Pass holders may travel from Paddington Station in London to Stratford-upon-Avon via Leamington Spa, where it is necessary to change trains on all services. The Paddington–Leamington Spa–Stratford train service has two drawbacks: Service on Sundays is limited to summer months only (usually May to September), and weekday schedules on this route do not permit both attendance at the evening theater performances in Stratford and a return to London the same evening.

Trains arriving in Leamington Spa from Paddington Station stop on platform 2, which adjoins platform 1. From platform 1, you board the single-class train for Stratford-upon-Avon. Returning to Leamington Spa, the train halts at platform 4, where you connect immediately with trains returning to Paddington Station from platform 3. Remember, there is no through-train service on this route. You *must change trains* at Leamington Spa.

Another route is available between London's Euston Station to Coventry, where you connect with a special motor coach service to and from Stratford-upon-Avon. BritRail Pass holders may use this service by paying a supplementary charge to the motor-coach driver for the road portion of the journey. Without a BritRail Pass, travelers pay £4.50 for a single journey and £6.00 for a round-trip.

The British Rail link through Coventry makes it possible to attend an evening performance at the Royal Shakespeare Theatre in Stratford-upon-Avon and return to London the same evening, except on Sunday. Check British Rail's brochure, *The Shakespeare Connection,* for complete details. You can pick up a copy in London's Euston Station. Many hotels have the same brochure available at the porter's desk.

STRATFORD-UPON-AVON—*SHAKESPEARE COUNTRY*
A Day Excursion from London

DEPART FROM PADDINGTON	ARRIVE IN STRATFORD-UPON-AVON	NOTES
0810	1206	(4)
0920	1151	(2)
1020	1350	(3)
1040	1350	(1)
1050	1406	(4)
1215	1529	(1)
1400	1650	(3)
1420	1650	(1)
1450	1806	(4)
1520	1830	(3)
1545	1829	(1)
1730	2018	(3)
1750	2018	(1)
1830	2138	(3)
1915	2138	(1)

DEPART FROM STRATFORD-UPON-AVON	ARRIVE IN PADDINGTON	
0805	1042	(2)
0938	1222	(1)
0938	1240	(3)
1200	1448	(1)
1215	1547	(4)
1400	1635	(2)
1405	1659	(4)
1538	1848	(2)
1707	1935	(2)
1838	2217	(4)
2105	2337	(2)

Distance: 121 miles/195 km
References: Thomas Cook Tables 525, 528

* See Appendix, page 296, for London station plan.
  Note: Transfer at Leamington Spa for all trains to and from Stratford-upon-Avon.

(1) MON–FRI   (3) SAT
(2) MON–SAT   (4) SUN

Train Information
021–643–2711
Stratford-Upon-Avon Tourist Information Centre
0789–293127

Passengers arriving in Coventry from Euston Station should look for the special motor-coach connections to Stratford-upon-Avon in the bus lanes on the right-hand side of the station. The 0840 train from London arrives in Coventry at 0951, connecting with the coach that departs at 1000 and arrives in Stratford-upon-Avon at 1035. To assure coach-train connections returning to London, take either the 1715 or the 2315 coach. Check with the travel centers (train information office) in the stations for full details and schedules.

Stratford's tourist information center is in Judith Shakespeare's House at 1 High Street. It's open 0900–1730 Monday through Saturday and 1400–1700 on Sunday.

Our advice is to take a guided tour of Stratford-upon-Avon. A popular one is the "Stratford and Shakespeare Story Tour," operated by Guide Friday Limited, located in Stratford Civic Hall. On this tour, you are transported by open-top, double-decker buses along a thirteen-mile route and visit all five of the Shakespeare properties: Shakespeare's birthplace on Henley Street; the Nash's House, in which Shakespeare spent his retirement years before his death in 1616; the Hall's Croft Home of Shakespeare's daughter Susanna; Shakespeare's mother's house; and Anne Hathaway's Cottage.

William Shakespeare, the superb English poet and playwright recognized universally as the greatest of all dramatists, was born in Stratford-upon-Avon in 1564. His mother was the daughter of a local farmer; his father was a wool merchant who entered politics to become mayor of Stratford. Although Shakespeare lived throughout his professional career in London, he kept his home ties with Stratford. In 1597 he purchased New Place, one of Stratford's largest houses. He died there in 1616 and was buried in Stratford's parish church.

A visit to the Royal Shakespeare Theatre is a must. It is advisable to reserve theater seats as far in advance as possible. Telephone (0789) 69191 for twenty-four-hour information on program and seat availability. To book seats, telephone the theater box office direct at (0789) 295623. The theater has several restaurant/bar facilities. Telephone (0789) 293226 for more information and reservations. The Box Tree is a luxuriously appointed restaurant overlooking the Avon River and serving classical cuisine (closed Sundays), and the River Terrace is a modern restaurant/coffee shop/wine bar serving light international dishes. You can even "Pick-up-a-Picnic" by placing your order with the cashier at the River Terrace Restaurant two hours in advance.

Royal Guard stands at castle-hill entrance to Windsor Castle grounds. Changing of the guard ceremony takes place mid-morning daily.

Royal Oak Restaurant, on Datchet Road immediately opposite the Windsor Riverside train station, is a delightful rally point following a castle tour.

From London . . .

A DAY EXCURSION TO WINDSOR
DISTANCE BY TRAIN: 25 miles (41 km)
AVERAGE TRAIN TIME: 50 minutes

Historic Windsor Castle is the official home of English royalty. William the Conqueror built the first structure on this site, a wooden fort that doubled as a royal hunting lodge. Other English kings added to the castle during their reigns, but despite the multiplicity of royalty and architects, the castle has managed to retain a unity of style all its own. It's the largest inhabited castle in the world.

The present queen, Elizabeth II, uses the castle far more than any of her predecessors. For this reason, it is wise to inquire if the queen is in official residence before going to Windsor. When she is, which is usually during the month of April and for periods during March, May, June, and December, the state apartments will be closed to the public. There will still be many areas of Windsor Castle open to the public; however, you will miss seeing the splendor of the various rooms contained within the state apartments. Chances of seeing Her Majesty, should she be in residence, will be rather slim. Nevertheless, during that time you may find Prince Philip watching his son Charles, the Prince of Wales, and his polo team bashing about in the Great Windsor Park. Again, it may be difficult to find the princes, for although the castle itself occupies a mere thirteen acres, the park stretches over 4,000 acres below the battlements of the castle.

For full appreciation of Windsor, we definitely recommend a guided tour. It takes two hours and it is well worth every penny. The tour cost includes the admission charge to St. George's Chapel and the castle precincts. The tours start daily at 1015, 1130, and 1330 from the Windsor tourist information center in Windsor's central rail station. The guides are required to pass a demanding examination set by the Regional Tourist Board.

You have a choice of two rail routes from London to Windsor. For the schedule given here, we have selected the route from Waterloo Station in London to Windsor Riverside Station. This line does not require changing trains en route. The alternate route, which departs Paddington Station in London, requires a change at Slough to a shuttle train before arriving at Windsor Central Station. If you take the Paddington-Slough route, the shuttle train arrives and departs in Slough from track 1. Either route gives you a magnificent view approaching Windsor Castle. On either train, sit on the left-hand side (outbound) to take full advantage of the scenery.

The tourist information center is in the Windsor Central Station. Signs

WINDSOR—*THE ROYAL CASTLE*

A Day Excursion from London

DEPART FROM WATERLOO STATION*	ARRIVE IN WINDSOR RIVERSIDE STATION	NOTES
0813	0903	(2)
0843	0933	(2)
0850	0940	(4)
0913	1003	(2)
0943	1033	(2)
0950	1040	(4)

(Plus other frequent service)

DEPART FROM WINDSOR RIVERSIDE STATION	ARRIVE IN WATERLOO STATION	
1205	1255	(4)
1208	1258	(2)
1238	1328	(2)
1305	1355	(4)
1308	1358	(2)
1338	1428	(2)

(Plus other frequent service)

Distance: 25 miles/41 km
References: Thomas Cook Table 513

* See Appendix, page 296, for London station plan.
(1) MON–FRI
(2) MON–SAT
(3) SAT
(4) SUN

Train Information
071–928–5100

Windsor Tourist Information Centre
0753–852010

with the traditional "i" will lead the way from either arrival point. The grounds of Windsor Castle are immediately across the street from the tourist information center. The center operates 0930–1800 in summer and 0930–1730 in winter. Be sure to purchase an illustrated guidebook on Windsor Castle even though you plan to take the guided tour. It will become a fond reminder of your visit.

Rare state occasions such as the investiture of the Garter, when the queen proceeds down the walks of Windsor Castle accompanied by a full entourage of castle guards and Knights of the Garter, are difficult for the general public to view. The changing of the castle guard, however, is a daily event conducted in a manner in which the general public can participate. The new guard leaves the Victoria Barracks precisely at 1015, then marches along High Street to the castle. The guard changing takes place at 1025 and the old guard returns by the same route at 1100. By positioning yourself along High Street or Castle Hill, you will have a good view of the pageantry as it unfolds.

From the battlements of Windsor Castle, you may look down and across the stately River Thames onto the playing fields of Eton College, where "how the game is played" has always been more important than the final score. The importance of Eton lies less in what it is than in what it stands for. The school yard and cloisters are open 1400–1700 throughout the year except during school holidays, when they are open 1030–1700.

Your initial entry into the town of Eton may be a bit frightening at first, for you will probably find yourself surrounded by a group of young gentlemen uniformed in pin-striped trousers, white bow ties, and formal black coats with tails. You have not been thrust among a flock of penguins. What you are surrounded by are the students of Eton College, one of Britain's most exclusive educational institutions and a strong reminder that the British on occasion can cling fiercely to their traditions.

A respite from pageantry and tradition during your visit to Windsor may be taken by cruising on the River Thames. At the bottom of High Street, at its intersection with Barry Avenue, the Windsor Boat Pier offers two cruises. The first is a thirty-five-minute trip upstream and the other is a full two-hour trip with light refreshments and a licensed bar aboard.

If you have not yet been introduced to the British public house, there is no better time than now. The Royal Oak, directly across the street from Windsor Riverside Station, is highly recommended. No more prim a pub can you find in all of England. Its impeccable oaken interior matches the high quality of its food and service. The inn was constructed as an ale house in 1736 and restored in 1937. Should we meet you there, we'll buy the first round!

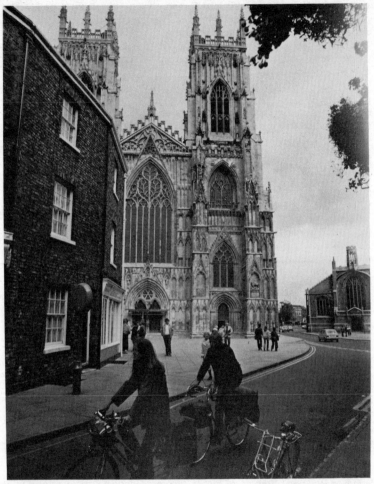

York Minster, largest Gothic church in Britain, stands on a site previously occupied by a Roman military headquarters and a former Norman cathedral. The earlier remains are still visible. Construction of the Minster, begun in 1220, required approximately 250 years.

From London . . .

A DAY EXCURSION TO YORK
DISTANCE BY TRAIN: 188 miles (302 km)
AVERAGE TRAIN TIME: 2 hours, 10 minutes

"The history of York," according to King George VI, "is the history of England." The Romans took it from a Celtic tribe, the Brigantes, in A.D. 71. According to legend, King Arthur captured the city sometime after the Roman legions retreated in A.D. 406. The Saxons took charge of York in the seventh century. The Danes ran the Saxons off the property in 867, only to get their comeuppance from the Anglo-Saxons when Edmund tamed them in 944. In 1066, York saw the fastest turnaround ever when King Harold of England defeated the King of Norway at Stamford Bridge, six miles from York. Nineteen days later, York's management (and all of England, as a matter of fact) passed to the Normans when Harold was killed in the Battle of Hastings.

William the Conqueror, following his victory at Hastings, came north to quell a rebellion, which he did by his version of urban renewal, known in those days as the "scorched-earth" policy. The ruins and rubble of the Romans, the Saxons, the Vikings, and the Anglo-Saxons, however, never was cleaned out thoroughly. Much of it is still there, layer upon layer, and is now being unearthed in York for you to view upon arrival.

Charles I, fleeing the fermenting civil war, left London in 1639 to take residence in York. Cromwell's troops finally took York in July 1644. A condition of surrender was that there would be no pillaging; thus, the fine medieval stained glass of York Minster was saved. It is estimated that the Minster contains more than one-half of all the medieval stained glass in England.

York, similar to Chester, has retained most of its fourteenth-century city walls. You will see a part of them as you exit from York's railway station. The city of York is best explored on foot. You can do it on your own or take a conducted tour. A two-mile walk around the walls provides a panorama of the city.

Following a relaxing ride aboard an InterCity 125 train from King's Cross Station in London, we suggest that you check in with the York tourist information center in the rail station. Once you are armed with a map, we suggest that you proceed on foot into the city. Although it's a ten-to-fifteen-minute walk, you will see a lot of history en route. Turn left leaving the station and proceed along the city wall toward the tower of the York Minster. After crossing the River Ouse, at the intersection of Duncome Place and St. Leonard's Place, you will see the Minster straight ahead. York's main tourist office is nearby in Exhibition Square.

YORK—*FINE MEDIEVAL CITY*

A Day Excursion from London

DEPART FROM KING'S CROSS STATION*	ARRIVE IN YORK STATION	NOTES
0730	0932 (0937 SAT)	(2)
0800	1007	(2)
0830	1033 (1141 SUN)	(3)(4)
0900	1058 (1207 SUN)	(2)(4)
0930	1142 (1225 SUN)	(2)(4)
1000	1151 (1257 SUN)	(2)(4)
1100	1258 (1355 SUN)	(2)(4)

DEPART FROM YORK STATION	ARRIVE IN KING'S CROSS STATION	
1511	1739	(4)
1537	1747	(1)
1552	1804	(3)
1637	1857	(1)
1700	1917	(4)
1701	1911	(1)
1741	1954 (2007 SUN)	(1)(4)
1907	2124	(1)
1919	2143	(4)
1922	2138	(3)

Distance: 188 miles/302 km
References: Thomas Cook Table 570

* See Appendix, page 296, for London station plan.

(1) MON–FRI   (3) SAT
(2) MON–SAT   (4) SUN

Train Information
0904–642155
InterCity Services: 071–278–2477

York Tourist Information Centre
0904–621756 or 643700

This center is open June-September, 0900–2000 Monday through Saturday and 1400–1700 on Sunday. October-May, the center is closed on Sunday and operates 0900–1700 Monday through Saturday. City tours leave from the fountain opposite the center. Summer tour hours are 1015, 1415, and 1900 daily. The announcement describing the availability of the tours states: "The tour, which is on foot, will help you to discover the wealth of interest the city offers to its visitors and learn something of its history. There is no charge—our reward is your appreciation of this ancient and historic city." A warmer, more sincere welcome would be hard to find.

York is a compact city, easy to stroll around. Among its points of interest, York Minster draws first choice. Built between 1220 and 1472, the Minster is England's largest Gothic cathedral. As the mother church of the Church of England's northern province, it is outranked in religious importance only by Canterbury Cathedral. York uses the archaic term *minster,* meaning a center of Christian teaching or ministering, for its cathedral.

We suggest that you also visit the National Railway Museum on Leeman Road, a ten-minute walk from the York railway station. It will stand comparison with any railway museum in the world. Star of the show is a 190-ton British-built steam locomotive that was returned home after forty-five years of service in the mountains of China. The rolling stock of diesel, electric, and steam locomotives are arranged around two original turntables so that visitors may view a changing display covering more than 150 years of British railway history.

Another important attraction is the Castle Museum, one of the most interesting folk museums in the world. Famous streets of York have been reconstructed in the museum and depict the daily life and occupations of various periods from Tudor to Edwardian times. The museum also contains an eighteenth-century water mill that operates throughout the summer. Other sections of the museum are devoted to Yorkshire crafts, costumes, and military history.

While walking, no doubt, you will find the narrow, winding streets of York the most fascinating of all the city's attractions. The streets developed from the original Roman street plans. In turn, each century has added a bit more color—and perhaps confusion. The Vikings left their mark in the use of street names ending in "gate," such as *Stonegate* and *Petergate*. The medieval citizens following the Vikings gave York its winding streets. One of these streets, The Shambles, is reputed to be one of the best preserved medieval streets in Europe. Originally the street was crammed with butcher shops in half-timbered, overhanging buildings. The east-west line of the street kept the meat in cool shade for most of the day. It now houses an assortment of interesting stores and book shops, where the meat hooks still hang.

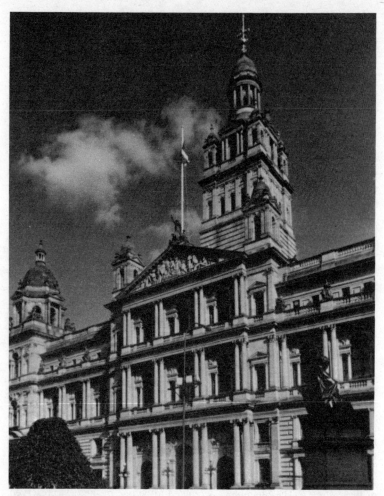

City Chambers, headquarters of the Glasgow District Council, occupies the entire east side of George Square, the city's picturesque ''breathing place.'' Designed by William Young, the building is an impressive treatment of Italian Renaissance architecture. The loggia balcony, marble staircase, and banqueting hall of the building are particularly impressive.

11 GLASGOW

In succession to Athens, Florence, Amsterdam, Berlin, and Paris, Glasgow was selected as the Cultural Capital of Europe 1990. Over the past decade, the city has undergone a sweeping renaissance, shaking off the grim, depressed industrial image of the Industrial Revolution to emerge as one of Europe's foremost cities of culture and ambiance.

Now, out from under a century or so of accumulated grime, the cleaning-up process has highlighted, in gleaming gold and red sandstone, some of Europe's finest Victorian architecture. Bustling city streets lined with imposing hand-carved facades pay homage to the optimism of the Victorian city fathers, as do the stunning marble staircases of the opulent City Chambers in central George Square. Glaswegians have reason to be proud of their city and cordially invite you to enjoy it with them.

Direct transatlantic flights into the Glasgow Airport, only fifteen minutes from the city center, as well as regular train services from London and the south, make Glasgow an ideal "base city" site for Scotland. It is conveniently located, as is Edinburgh, for access to our Scottish day excursions. For this reason we are introducing the "Glasgow Connection," wherein the choice of base cities—Edinburgh or Glasgow—becomes a matter of individual selection. The excellent train service between the two cities permits visitors to move with ease between them.

Glasgow is Scotland's largest metropolis, with a population approaching one million. It is the gateway to Loch Lomond and the western Highlands. Glasgow's River Clyde flows into the Firth of Clyde, thus opening its western waterways to a myriad of islands and the Irish Sea. At the height of its shipbuilding boom, Glasgow was launching more than one-third of the world's shipping tonnage. The *Queen Mary,* the *Queen Elizabeth I,* and the *Queen Elizabeth II* were built there. With the industry now only a shadow of its former self, the River Clyde has become a scenic waterway where you can cruise aboard luxury riverboats or the paddle-wheel steamer *Waverly.*

Glasgow abounds with sights to see and things to do, ranging from its great twelfth-century cathedral to a variety of museums and universities. It is said that Glasgow has more parks than any other European city of its size. One in particular, George Square, opposite the Queen Street railway station, projects a panorama of Scottish and British history in its statuary of those individuals who forged the British Commonwealth through their science, leadership, and literature.

Among the many superb galleries and museums throughout Glasgow, you shouldn't miss the renowned Burrell Collection in the Pollok Country Park, a unique collection of more than 8,000 objets d'art donated to the city by one man, Sir William Burrell.

Glasgow's Railway Stations—Central Station & Queen Street Station

Glasgow has two main railway stations. Trains arriving from southwestern Scotland and England terminate in the Glasgow Central Station. For train travel north and east out of Glasgow to Edinburgh, Perth, and Inverness or west to Oban and Fort William, the Glasgow Queen Street Station becomes the departure point. A convenient city bus service links the two rail stations. The fifteen-minute walk between them, however, runs through some of the city's finer shopping areas, thereby offering the opportunity to walk off a few British "pounds."

If you choose to walk from the Queen Street Station to the Central Station, walk past George Square to St. Vincent Street. At this point, turn right and walk one block farther to Buchanan Street, a pedestrian shopping precinct. Turn left onto Buchanan Street and walk until your path intersects with Gordon Street. The intersection is easy to locate because this section of Gordon Street is reserved for pedestrians (and shops). Turning right at this point and continuing along Gordon Street for two blocks will bring you to the Glasgow Central Station, on your left.

From the Central Station to the Queen Street Station, merely reverse your line of march. Those who wish to avoid running the shopper's gauntlet on Buchanan Street may proceed between the two stations by traversing Queen and Argyle streets. We suggest that you consult a map of central Glasgow, which is available at the tourist information center in St. Vincent Place.

The city bus (No. 98) service linking the two rail stations is strictly for transferring passengers between the stations with no stops en route. The buses run Monday through Friday, 0700–2300; Saturday, 0800–2300; and Sunday, 1400–2300. Departures are approximately every fifteen minutes.

Don't look for a kiosk or a newsstand where you can purchase tickets—you pay your fare when you get on the bus. BritRail Passes are *not* accepted for the bus transfer between rail stations. The time en route varies between five and ten minutes, depending upon traffic conditions. For those in a hurry or those who are heavily ladened with luggage, taxis are standing by in queues at both stations.

If you are arriving in one of Glasgow's rail stations to transfer to the Glasgow Airport at Abbotsinch or to Prestwick Airport near Ayr, a frequent bus service is operated for this purpose out of Anderston Cross Bus Station. The bus terminal is three blocks west of the Central Station, just off Argyle Street. It's quite a distance from the Queen Street Station to the terminal—a taxi is recommended.

Glasgow Central Station, transformed radically in the past few years, caters to those needs of the train traveler ranging from rest rooms with bathing facilities to a grand Victorian hostelry—the Central Hotel. What is more, the station's old ticket office has been transformed into a delightful array of quality shops, bars, and restaurants.

The Glasgow Central Station provides InterCity electric services for English destinations, including Liverpool, Manchester, Birmingham, and London (Euston Station). Also provided are connections for Wales, the west of England, and destinations in south and west Scotland, which include Ayr and Stranraer (for connections to Northern Ireland via Larne). Commuter-train service to Gourock and Wemyss Bay for connections with steamer services on the River Clyde also operate from the Central Station.

Money exchange is available only within the station during times when the banks are closed. An office of the Royal Bank of Scotland is directly across from the main entrance of the station. After banking hours, ticket window No. 9 in the Central Station will exchange foreign currency and cash traveler's checks up to a $50 limit. The American Express office is to the left of the station entrance at 115 Hope Street. The Thomas Cook office is just one block to the right of the station entrance at 15-17 Gordon Street.

Hotel reservations may be arranged at the tourist information center located at 35 St. Vincent Place.

Tourist information is available in Glasgow's information center at 35 St. Vincent Place, telephone (041) 204-4400.

Train information is displayed in the Central Station by means of a huge, digital departures-and-arrivals board located between tracks 2 and 5. For expanded train information, visit the Inquiries and Reservations Office (travel center) on the right side of the main hall at the end of platforms 1, 2, and 3.

Train reservations may be arranged in the travel center. For sleeping-car reservations, you will be directed to the InterCity Sleeper Centre at the entrance to platform 1.

Queen Street Station is the terminal for trains operating on the scenic West Highland Line to Oban, Fort William, and Mallaig, where steamer connections can be made to the Scottish islands. From the Queen Street Station, InterCity express trains depart for Edinburgh and connect with destinations in England including York, Doncaster, and London (King's Cross Station).

Services for north and east Scotland, including Stirling, Perth, Dundee, Aberdeen, Inverness, and the Kyle of Lochalsh, depart from the Queen Street Station. Electric trains to Dumbarton and Balloch (for Loch Lomond cruises) also operate from this station.

Tolbooth steeple, erected in 1626, is all that remains at the intersection of High Street and Trongate in Glasgow of a once sprawling complex including the town hall and jail. Other interesting landmarks in this vicinity include the Tron Steeple (1637) and the Mercat Cross (replica–1979).

Money-exchange services are not available within the Queen Street Station. There are several banks in the general area, including an office of the Royal Bank of Scotland adjacent to the main entrance of the Central Station. After banking hours, however, the only money-exchange facility available in the area is ticket window No. 9 in the Central Station.

Hotel reservations for Glasgow and for all of Scotland may be arranged through the "Book-A-Bed-Ahead" service with the Greater Glasgow Tourist Information Centre located at 35 St. Vincent Place.

Tourist information in Glasgow is available at the Greater Glasgow Tourist Information Centre. Hours of operation June through September are 0900–2100 Monday through Saturday and 1400–2100 Sunday. From October through May, the center is open Monday through Saturday from 0900 to 1700, closed Sunday until Easter, then open on Sunday through May between 0900 and 1800.

The center has a wealth of Glasgow tourist information on hand. Call there to request a copy of the "Greater Glasgow" booklet. In addition to a listing of city attractions, the booklet's centerfold contains a map that you will find very helpful for getting around Glasgow. There is a Bureau de Change in operation in the center as well as an office for theater and sporting events tickets.

Train information is available in the British Rail Travel Centre located on the left-hand side of the station as you face the train platforms.

Train reservations can be made in the travel center. For sleeper reservations, however, use the "InterCity Sleeper Centre" in the Central Station.

Glasgow Gazette

Glasgow's modern subway system is a circular line with trains running in both directions beneath the center of the city. It provides a three-minute service from each of its fifteen stations, achieving a circular journey in about twenty-two minutes. A separate subway, the Argyle Line, links the British Rail suburban networks. The main link with British Rail services, however, is the subway station at Buchanan Street, connecting with the Queen Street Station by a moving pedestrian platform similar to those found in airports.

For readers going on the day excursion to Loch Lomond, the rail route departing Glasgow is an electric-train service that departs from subterranean platform 8 in the Queen Street Station. To reach it, after entering the main hall of the station, turn left and exit the station by the side entrance, where you turn right to follow the well-marked "Platform 8" signs.

In the Queen Street Station's British Rail Travel Centre, you may obtain full information and tickets for cruising on the Clyde River aboard the Caledonia MacBrayne vessel *Glen Sannox*. Connecting rail services to the ship's pier originate in the Queen Street Station. The third Clyde steamship

215

to be given the name *Glen Sannox,* the vessel offers a number of interesting cruises on the Clyde River and the Firth of Clyde. On Saturdays during the summer, a special upriver cruise is conducted. Advance bookings for the cruise are recommended.

Throughout the summer, a two-hour bus tour of Glasgow aboard specially converted double-deck buses will take you around some of the best known places—and some of the more out-of-the-way places—in the city. For bus tour schedules and rates, check with the Greater Glasgow Tourist Information Centre.

Every visitor to Glasgow, and model railroad buffs in particular, will not want to miss Glasgow's Museum of Transport in Kelvin Hall on Argyle Street. The museum is located in the west end of Glasgow only ten minutes from the city center by bus or subway. It's open Monday through Saturday from 1000 to 1700 and Sunday between 1400 and 1700. Displays include ship models, Glasgow trams and buses, locomotives of Scottish origins, Scottish-built motorcars, fire engines, and a reconstructed subway station. There is also a section in the museum known as "The Clyde Room," where meticulously detailed models illustrate the story of shipbuilding and shipping on the River Clyde. An operating model railroad is one of the museum's highlights.

Glasgow's Art Gallery and Museum is immediately opposite Kelvin Hall. Home of Britain's finest civic collection of British and European paintings, the museum also features displays of natural history, archaeology, and collections of silver, pottery, arms, and armor. In the performing arts sector, Glasgow's Mayfest (which, of course, occurs in the merry month of May) is a key international festival for theater, dance, music, and related performing arts in Europe.

Previously, we identified that area of the city between the two rail stations as an ideal place to "walk off a few British 'pounds.' " It is. Glasgow is a shoppers' paradise, with more than ample opportunity to find that special souvenir or gift for friends back home—and pick up something for yourself, too. Department stores line the great pedestrianized shopping districts of Argyle and Buchanan streets. Adjacent to them, Princes Square provides some of Europe's top specialty shops blended into an exciting array of restaurants and bars. Slightly farther than a stone's throw from the square, St. Enochs indoor shopping mall offers a wide variety of stores beneath the same roof, and Argyle's Victorian Arcade is the place to look for jewelry and fine gifts.

Farther out, but well worth it if you are visiting Glasgow over a weekend, is the city's famous "Barras Street Market." It's a bargain collector's delight with goods ranging from Victorian bric-a-brac to high fashion—all flavored by the antics of the stall holders.

The "Glasgow Connection"

All day excursions described in chapter 12 that depart from Edinburgh also may be taken from Glasgow. In fact, three of the day excursions—Ayr, Loch Lomond, and Stranraer—require passing through Glasgow. For these excursions readers residing in Glasgow need only refer to the appropriate day-excursion schedule in chapter 12 for the "Glasgow Connection."

Two of the day excursions—Dunbar and Dunfermline—can be reached conveniently only through Edinburgh. Consequently, readers need only refer to the Glasgow-Edinburgh shuttle-service schedule to determine the "Glasgow Connection" for these day excursions.

Five day excursions—Aberdeen, Dundee, Montrose, St. Andrews, and Stirling—are so situated on Scotland's rail lines that they may be reached either by direct connection from the Queen Street Station in Glasgow or through Edinburgh. A condensation of the "Glasgow Connections" for direct service appears on page 218.

Three other day excursions—Inverness, Kyle of Lochalsh, and Perth—are reached more conveniently from Glasgow by direct train service from the Queen Street Station rather than through Edinburgh. For a condensation of the "Glasgow Connections," you are referred again to page 218 for details.

The "Glasgow Connection" for express trains to London is given on page 219 of this chapter. All services shown are subject to alteration. Readers are advised to consult with the schedules posted in the train stations or with a British Rail Travel Centre for train information before commencing each journey. The publishers cannot be held responsible for changes or inaccuracies in the schedules.

Regardless of which city you select as your "base," don't forget that the frequent train service between Glasgow and Edinburgh enables you to make a "day excursion" to the one you didn't select as your base. For what to see and do in Edinburgh, consult the following chapter on Scotland's capital for details.

There are times throughout the year when one of the two cities, either Glasgow or Edinburgh, may be "fully booked." This can take place in Glasgow during May when the city hosts a Mayfest—a festival focusing attention on Glasgow's many activities within its cultural sphere. On the other hand, Edinburgh can be filled to overflowing when visitors attend its world famous "Edinburgh Tattoo." When this happens, and your reservationist gives up on the city of your choice—try the other. Your chances of finding accommodations there are very good, and the ease of rail travel between Glasgow and Edinburgh will make it an "easy commute," far better than anything that the Long Island Railroad could come up with!

"GLASGOW CONNECTIONS"

Excursion Destination	Depart Glasgow	Destination Arrive	Destination Depart	Return Glasgow	Notes
Aberdeen	0715	1005	1527	1813	weekdays
	0822	1102	1742	2035	"
	0922	1208	1925	2214	"
	0922	1242	1908	2212	Sundays
Dundee	0715	0845	1637	1813	weekdays
	0822	0950	1742	1914	"
	0922	1050	2041	2214	"
	0922	1110	1822	2007	Sundays
Inverness	0755	1137	1318	1703	weekdays
	0955	1325	1633	2010	"
Montrose	0715	0919	1709	1914	weekdays
	0922	1126	2008	2214	"
	0922	1146	1749	2007	Sundays
Perth	0715	0819	1605	1710	weekdays
	0822	0923	1808	1914	"
	0922	1023	2007	2112	"
	0922	1032	1822	2007	Sundays
Stirling	0922	0950	1739	1813	weekdays
	1022	1050	2038	2112	"
	0922	1006	1917	2007	Sundays

St. Andrews Train from Glasgow Queen Street Station to Dundee. Transfer to St. Andrews bus, departing every hour on the half-hour.

Glasgow-Edinburgh Shuttle Service

Weekday Service: Departs Glasgow Queen Street Station for Edinburgh at 0622, 0700, 0730, and every half-hour thereafter until 2300. Departs Edinburgh at 0700 and every half-hour thereafter until 2330. Journey fifty to seventy minutes.

Sunday Service: Departs Glasgow Queen Street Station for Edinburgh at 0800 and on the hour thereafter until 2300; also at 1830, 1930, 2030, and 2130. Departs Edinburgh at 0830 and on the half-hour thereafter until 2330; also at 0820, 1040, 1800, 1900, 2000, 2100, 2200, and 2300. Journey takes fifty-five minutes.

GLASGOW-LONDON TRAIN SERVICE

(First- and second-class accommodations for all services listed)

DEPART FROM
GLASGOW CENTRAL   **ARRIVE IN EUSTON STATION***
STATION

DEPART FROM GLASGOW CENTRAL STATION	ARRIVE IN EUSTON STATION* Monday-Saturday	Sunday	NOTES
0700	1218 (1228 SAT)	—	(1)
0815	1314 (1324 SAT)	—	(1)
0900	1432	—	(1)
1010	—	1814	(1)
1015	1505 (1515 SAT)	—	(1)
1200	1734 (1744 SAT)	—	(1)
1325	—	1938	(1)
1405	1932	—	(1)
1500	—	2058	(1)
1610	—	2212	(1)
1705	2235 (2245 SAT)	2251	(1)
2350 (sleeper)	0604 + 1	0604 + 1	(2)

Distance: 402 miles/647 km
References: Thomas Cook Table 550
*   See Appendix, page 296, for London station plan
(1) High-speed train, food service available.
(2) Sleeping cars only. Passengers may remain aboard until 0730.

Train Information
041–204–2844
InterCity Services: 071–387–7070

Glasgow Tourist Information Centre
041–204–4400

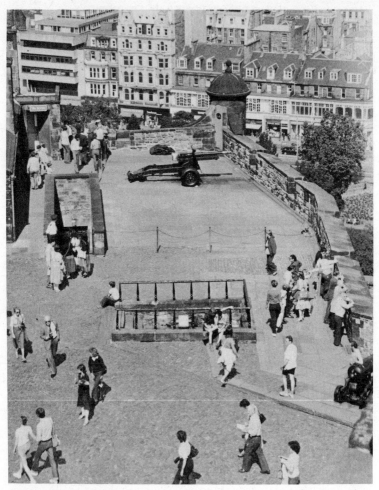

The one o'clock gun at Edinburgh Castle is fired every day except Sunday to provide an unusual time check for the city. Visiting shoppers on Princes Street (visible at the lower level in the background), unaware of the firing, may be seen doing their own version of the ''One O'clock Jump'' at precisely the same moment.

12 EDINBURGH

"This profusion of eccentricities, this dream in masonry and living rock," wrote Robert Louis Stevenson of Edinburgh, "is not a drop-scene in a theater, but a city in a world of everyday reality!" There is an understandable feeling of rocklike perpetuity enveloping Edinburgh. Formed by volcanic heat, scoured and shaped by ice-age glaciers in a valley punctuating its skyline with upward- thrusting crags, Scotland's capital city of Edinburgh is nothing short of dramatic in its setting.

Edinburgh's exact origins are lost in antiquity. Although dissenting opinions exist, it appears that the historical jigzaw of Edinburgh was pieced together in the following pattern. A primitive fortress was established around A.D. 452 by the Picts on the sloping ground leading from the great Castle Rock on which Edinburgh Castle stands today. There have been fortresses on Castle Rock since that time, each in turn razed by a challenger, rebuilt by the challenger, only to be razed again by another challenger. By the time of the eleventh century, however, Edinburgh began to calm down and get on with the task of becoming a civilized and prosperous town.

From its earliest days, Edinburgh's stern, almost aloof countenance has retained and fostered those enduring qualities that have inspired great men to great achievements. Edinburgh is actually two cities. The Old Town, built on a rocky ledge running from Edinburgh Castle to the Royal Palace of Holyroodhouse, is steeped in ancient history. It huddled on high ground in typical medieval fear of attack.

The New Town, which took form on the lower side of North Loch, a lake created from a swamp and eventually drained in 1816, spread serenely in a succession of streets and avenues reflecting the optimism of the latter centuries. The New Town was conceived in 1767 when the Scottish Parliament approved an extension of the city and the Town Council lost no time in proceeding with the work. The city planning that followed made possible Edinburgh's present wide streets and spacious squares.

Its contrasts of two cities within a city are further reflected, on the one hand, by Edinburgh's reserved exterior and, on the other, by its ability to expressing great warmth and, upon occasion, a high degree of gaiety. Edinburgh has been termed one of the most attractive capital cities in the world. As Oliver Wendell Holmes aptly put it, "Edinburgh is a city of incomparable loveliness."

From the beauty of its setting, enhanced by its architecture, to the turbulence of its history and the quality of its citizens, Edinburgh is a city of inexhaustible delight. Edinburgh Castle, Holyroodhouse, the Royal Mile, and Princes Street await you. Welcome to Scotland's capital!

Day Excursions

A "baker's dozen," thirteen exciting day excursions, have been selected for our readers. All were chosen so that those who prefer staying in Glasgow rather than in Edinburgh can enjoy them as well. (See "Glasgow Connections" in chapter 11.)

Scotland is known as "the land that likes to be visited." To ensure that your opportunity to visit this marvelous country by rail includes seeing as many of its features as possible, we have divided the selected day excursions into Scotland's four geographic areas: the east coast, central region, west coast, and Highlands.

East Coast. Along the east coast of Scotland, starting at the North Sea fishing port of Dunbar near the English border, we then swing north from Edinburgh through the trio cities of Dundee, Montrose, and Aberdeen—not overlooking a stop en route at the golf capital of the world, St. Andrews.

Central Region. In the central part of the country, we have selected excursions to two of Scotland's most historic cities—Perth and Stirling—plus a visit to Andrew Carnegie's birthplace, Dunfermline, and a cruise on one of the world's most famous lakes, Loch Lomond.

West Coast. For our forays to the western coast, we delve deep into the heart of Robert Burns's country by a visit to Ayr, the poet's favorite town. Further west on the Firth of Clyde, we call at Stranraer, the gateway to the Irish Sea and the "Emerald Isle" of Ireland.

Highlands. North in the Highlands, Inverness serves as a gateway to explorations of Loch Ness, with its legendary monster, "Nessie," and as a "base city" for a dash to the west to Kyle of Lochalsh and the Isle of Skye.

Scotland has often been compared to an iceberg—in that there is much more than first meets the eye. Come to Scotland with an open mind, a keen eye, and a sense of adventure.

Arriving And Departing

By Air. Prestwick, Scotland's international airport located twenty-nine miles southwest of Glasgow, is a convenient port of entry for overseas visitors arriving in Great Britain. It is the most fog-free airport on the British Isles. Prestwick enlarged its airport facilities and became an international air terminal during World War II due to its location in western Scotland. It was on the extreme edge of the German air force's long-range-bomber capabilities and, therefore, relatively immune to air attack.

Many of the regularly scheduled international air carriers have service to Prestwick. They thus provide British Rail travelers with an unusual opportunity to take advantage of "open-jaw" airline ticketing—arriving or departing on one leg of their transatlantic flight in Scotland, rather than flying both in and out of the London complex of Gatwick and Heathrow.

You can check with Air Canada, British Airways, Icelandair, KLM, Lufthansa, Northwest, and SAS.

Direct rail service connecting with Glasgow is available from the train station in the town of Prestwick. The most convenient mode of transport between the train station and the airport is by taxi. There is a taxi queue at the airport arrival- hall exit, and if a taxi is not standing at the Prestwick train station when you arrive, you may ask the stationmaster to summon one for you.

Travel time between Prestwick and Glasgow is less than one hour, and trains depart every half-hour on weekdays and every hour on Sunday. Trains arrive in Glasgow Central Station, where you must transfer to the Queen Street Station for train connections to Edinburgh (see page 218). Airport buses run from Prestwick to Edinburgh daily at 0740 and 0930, from Edinburgh to Prestwick daily at 0910 and 1140. The fare is £10.00. The bus fare from Prestwick to Glasgow is £3.00—all flights are met by this bus service to Glasgow.

By Train. There is only one major train station in Edinburgh—Waverley Station. Some InterCity trains from London go on to Aberdeen after a brief station stop in Edinburgh. If you are aboard one of these trains, be prepared to "set down" in the Waverley Station as quickly as possible following your arrival. Edinburgh does have a suburban station, Haymarket, where all trains halt en route to Glasgow or Aberdeen. Trains arriving from England via Newcastle and York, however, bypass Haymarket Station.

Edinburgh's Railway Station—Waverley

The train terminal in Edinburgh appears to be completely immersed in an open ravine. The area was once a swamp that was converted into a lake as a northern defense for Edinburgh Castle during the reign of King James II (1437–1460). The lake was drained in 1816 to become the site of the Princes Street Gardens separating the Old Town and New Town in Edinburgh.

In 1847, rail lines were laid through the middle of the Princes Street Gardens to the east end, where Waverley Station was constructed. The tracks are now all but concealed by landscaping. Today's Waverley Station complex is the second largest in Britain.

Waverley Station is equipped with twenty-one tracks strewn about in a labyrinth of steps and passageways that could easily drive a laboratory white rat berserk. But a plenitude of signs and the helpful presence of Edinburghers (who appear to be specially trained to assist visitors) will help you put it all together.

Basically, there are three accesses to Waverley Station. The first is a set of rather steep steps connecting the north side of the station (the trackage

Floral clock attracts Edinburgh's citizens and visitors alike. Built in 1903 in the city's West Princes Gardens, it is the oldest floral clock in the world. A cuckoo pops out to herald every quarter hour, and the flowers are changed frequently for important events.

runs east and west) with Princes Street, the city's main artery. The second and third approaches are ramps leading from the main floor of the station to the Waverley Bridge, which runs between the Old Town and the New Town. Both ramps have pedestrian walkways. The northern ramp serves incoming vehicles; the one to the south is for outgoing vehicles.

Many of the facilities sought by incoming passengers, such as banking, city information, and hotel accommodations, are located nearby in the combined offices of the Scottish Tourist Board and Edinburgh City Information Centre beyond the north end of Waverley Bridge at the corner of Waverley and Princes streets. To reach the center, use the pedestrian ramp on the north side of the station, turning right as you reach the Waverley Bridge level. There are several "Tourist Information" signs to help guide the way.

Tracks 12 to 18 form the backbone, or center, of the Waverley Station. At the entrance to these tracks is a digital-display bulletin board for train arrivals, departures, and special announcements. If your train is departing from tracks other than 12 to 18, ask the railroad personnel at the ticket barriers for directions; otherwise, you may end up in some dark corner like a berserk white rat.

Pay special attention to multiple train departures from the same track. In other words, a line of coaches on a single train track can actually be two trains departing for two separate destinations. They are announced with red-bannered "Front Train" or "Rear Train" signs. It pays to ask questions however—one advantage you have over the rat!

The British Rail Travel Centre (train information center) is located in the waiting-room area of the station. Covered by a huge glass dome, the waiting area also contains digital arrival/departure information and a series of facilities, including rest rooms, a magazine kiosk, and the Talisman Bar and the Talisman Buffet. The principal entrance to this area is located across the main-station concourse from the stub ends of tracks 16 and 17.

The North British Hotel, topped by a mammoth 200-foot Gothic clock tower, is located between Waverley Station and Princes Street. The hotel is commended as an excellent accommodation in Edinburgh and a "must" place to visit. Erected during the Age of Steam, the hotel's spacious foyer and well-appointed lounges must be seen to be appreciated. The hotel is Victoriana throughout and recently underwent an extensive restoration program. For convenience to the rail station, you couldn't pick a better hotel.

Guests of the North British Hotel may utilize the lift (elevator) services between the hotel's lobby on Princes Street and the station level. The lift entrance in the station is under a lighted "Hotel" sign opposite the end of track 17, next to the station's waiting-area entrance. Use the lift to the service passageway, where signs will lead you to the regular hotel elevators.

Adjoining the North British Hotel is the Waverley Bridge Bus Station and Airport Bus Terminal. In addition to the previously mentioned airports of Glasgow and Prestwick, Edinburgh utilizes the Turnhouse Airport, six miles west of the city. Airport ground transportation to all three facilities is available from this location. City tours also depart from the Waverley Bridge Bus Station.

Money exchange (Bureau de Change) is available from the Clydesdale Bank, located in the Edinburgh tourist information center. Hours of operation are 0830–2030 Monday through Saturday and 1100–1500 on Sunday (July to September 9). During May, June, and September 10-30, the hours are 0830–1930 Monday through Saturday and 1100–1500 on Sunday. October-April, it is open 0900–1730 Monday through Friday, 0900–1230 Saturday, and is closed on Sunday.

Hotel accommodations are provided by the Edinburgh tourist information center. Hours are: (July-September 8) Monday through Saturday, 0830–2100, and Sunday, 1100–2100; (May-June and September 9–30) Monday through Saturday, 0830-2000, and Sunday, 1100–2000; (October-April) Monday through Friday, 0900–1800, Saturday, 0900–1300. The hotel-accommodations reservation fee is twenty-five pence per booking.

Tourist information is available at two locations within Edinburgh's information center, both operating at the same hours as the "Hotel Accommodations" section mentioned above. The first section has information on all of Scotland; it is to your left as you enter the center. The other section specializes in information regarding the city of Edinburgh. You will find it on your right as you enter, along with a self-service area for purchasing Scottish books, maps, and posters.

For bus tours of Edinburgh, you will be referred to the Regional Transportation Organization, whose offices are located on the opposite end of Waverley Bridge in the Waverley Bridge Bus Station. A half-day tour is conducted from April to November at 0930 and 1330 daily.

Train information is available at the British Rail Travel Centre in the waiting- room area of Waverley Station. City information is *not* available in this office. Operating hours are 0830–2100 daily.

Train reservations may be made in the travel center at any one of the counters in operation during the time of your visit.

Shopping in Edinburgh

The city of Edinburgh is well known for its fine boutiques, shops, and department stores. You can still find bargains in the famous Harris tweeds, Fair Isle sweaters, and Tartan plaids. Princes Street is lined with shops displaying a variety of Scottish wares from argyles and bagpipes to whiskey. And when you run out of stores and shops to visit on Princes Street, turn north two blocks to George Street and continue your shopping there. (You may need to stop by the bank on the way.)

Shoppers' havens on Princes Street include large department stores such as Jenners and C. & A., opposite the Scott Monument in the Waverley Street Station area. If you've not been in a store 180 years old, try Romanes & Paterson, Ltd. at 62 Princes Street. You will find traditional Scottish tweed, exquisite Edinburgh crystal, Caithness glass, knitwear from the borders, and, of course, tartans.

Still not tired of shopping? The Scotch House next door contains more than 300 tartans available by the meter, along with Shetland knitwear and original gifts. If you know a wee person, check out Hop Scotch, The Scotch House's special department for children.

With all that shopping, you may be ready for a libation and a snack. You don't have far to go—between, and parallel to, Princes Street and George Street is Rose Street, which probably has more convivial pubs to the meter than any other street in the world.

Greyfriars Bobby

On Candlemaker Row, a short distance from Edinburgh's Royal Mile, stands a statue in tribute to a small dog's affection and fidelity to his master. In 1858, a wee Skye terrier followed the remains of his master, Auld Jock, to Greyfriars churchyard, where the dog lingered and slept on his master's grave for fourteen years until his death in 1872.

People tried to take Bobby away. They even found a home for him in the country. Still, Bobby returned to the churchyard, where friends began bringing food to sustain him during his vigil. The story of Greyfriars Bobby spread throughout Edinburgh, and soon Bobby's tale of devotion reached Queen Victoria in London. She sent a special envoy, Lady Burdett-Coutts, to investigate this unusual story.

Bobby, in the meantime, had made friends with a number of children in a nearby orphanage. The terrier brought joy and love to the children, particularly to Tammy, a crippled boy with whom Bobby would play by the hour. Bobby lived his own life, however, and returned nightly to his master's grave—at first secretly, for the presence of a dog in a churchyard was unthinkable in those times. But as Bobby won hearts, he gained privileges, too. He even won the heart of the Lord Provost of Edinburgh, who had a collar made for the dog in 1867 and paid Bobby's licensing fee. (The collar can be seen today in the Huntley House Museum on Canongate Street.)

Bobby never went to London to see the queen, but royal annals reflect

Greyfriars Bobby, a small Skye terrier whose devotion to his master in both life and death captured hearts throughout Edinburgh, is commemorated there by a fountain with his statue on it. A film by Walt Disney has made Bobby world-famous. The Bobby Bar may be seen in the background.

that the queen actually was planning to pay *him* a visit at Greyfriars. Bobby died, however, before that honor became a reality.

The dog's body was buried alongside that of his master's. Although Bobby is no longer visible, his presence is felt so strongly by the residents of the area that they frankly admit to opening their doors briefly before retiring at night—just in case. Perhaps, when the door to heaven is opened for them, they will see Bobby again, running on the green pastures at the heels of his master, beside the still waters. Bobby is there. If there wasn't room enough in God's heaven for the love of this dog for his master, Bobby would not have kept the vigil at his master's grave—he would just have gone away.

A fountain with Bobby's statue on it stands close to the iron gates of Greyfriars churchyard, where Auld Jock and his faithful dog are interred. The story of Greyfriars Bobby was filmed by Walt Disney. We think it's worth your while to visit Greyfriars, just as we do each time we return to Edinburgh.

Enticing Edinburgh

Amid the contrasting charms of its Old Town and New Town, Edinburgh takes its place among an elite group of European cities conspicuous for their romance and physical attributes. As more and more enclosures were built during the post-medieval period, the term *close* came into existence in old Edinburgh to describe the narrow passageways giving access or right of way to the buildings in the rear of others. There are well over one hundred closes in Old Town, many of which have brass tablets at their entrances to explain their historical significance.

There are many aspects of Edinburgh to see on conducted tours, but the city's real beauty is best seen by exploring it on foot at your own pace. Walk the Royal Mile in Old Town from Edinburgh Castle to the Palace of Holyroodhouse. En route, you'll pass a fantastic assembly of picturesque old buildings, such as Brodie's Close, the Cannonball House, Anchor Close, and the Canongate Tollbooth.

Brodie's Close housed Deacon Brodie, a respectable town councilor by day and a burglar by night. Brodie's life-style supposedly provided the basis for Robert Louis Stevenson's *Dr. Jekyll and Mr. Hyde*. The Cannonball House, dating from 1630, got its name from a cannonball lodged in its gable, ostensibly fired from the castle by an errant cannoneer during the blockade of 1745. Anchor Close is the site where the first edition of the *Encyclopedia Britannica* was printed. The Edinburgh edition of Robert Burns's poems was also printed there. Reportedly, Burns himself read the proofs on the premises. Last renovated in 1591, the Cannongate Tollbooth has been used as the Town Council House and a prison for the ancient village of Cannongate, now incorporated into the city of Edinburgh.

Although the Palace of Holyroodhouse originated as a guest house for the Abbey of Holyrood, most of the palace we see today was built for Charles II in 1671. The most famous figure associated with the palace, however, was Mary Queen of Scots, who spent six years of her tragic reign there. On the palace grounds, you can view Queen Mary's Bath House where, according to today's Scottish tour guides, Mary Queen of Scots bathed daily. The guides also explain that her cousin, Queen Elizabeth I, bathed once a month—whether she needed it or not.

The Royal Mile was for many centuries the center of Edinburgh life. Its citizens lived and conducted their affairs on this busy, crowded street. At the point where High Street changes into Cannongate, you will find a line of the letter "S" embedded in the pavement. Until 1880, it marked the limits of sanctuary extended by Holyrood Abbey. It is said that debtors were often seen running toward the line with creditors in hot pursuit and bystanders wagering on the outcome.

EDINBURGH-LONDON TRAIN SERVICE

(First- and second-class accommodations for all services listed)

DEPART FROM WAVERLEY STATION	ARRIVE KING'S CROSS STATION* Monday-Saturday	Sunday	NOTES
0650	1150	—	(1)
0730	1215	—	(1)
0830	1310	—	(1)
0930	1404	1505	(1)
1030	1457 (1503 SAT)	1605	(1)
1100	1553	1627	(1)
1200	1653 (1703 SAT)	—	(1)
1230	1702 (1716 SAT)	1801	(1)
1330	1811 (1827 SAT)	1856	(1)
1430	1911 (1923 SAT)	1925	(1)
1530	2020 (2028 SAT)	2042	(1)
1630	2124 (2138 SAT)	2143	(1)
1835	2342	—	(1)
0015	0655 + 1	0659 + 1	(2)

Distance: 393 miles/632 km
References: Thomas Cook Table 570

*   See Appendix, page 296, for London station plan.
(1) High-speed train, food service available
(2) Sleeping cars only

Tourist Information
British Tourist Authority: 071–499–9325
Edinburgh: 031–557–1700

Train Information
Edinburgh: 031–556–2451
InterCity Services: 071–278–2477

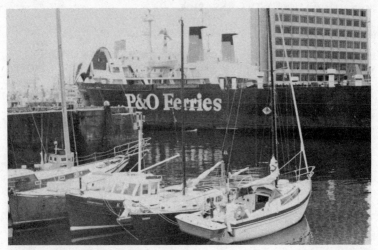

Aberdeen's many faces (above) are depicted in its harbor and academic countenances. Its harbor bustles with commercial fishing craft, outlying-island ferries, and vessels resupplying offshore oil rigs. Kings College (below) provides tranquillity with its seventeenth-century crown tower.

A DAY EXCURSION TO ABERDEEN
DISTANCE BY TRAIN: 131 miles (211 km)
AVERAGE TRAIN TIME: 2 hours, 30 minutes

Since the discovery of oil in the North Sea, Aberdeen has earned the title of ''Europe's offshore oil capital.'' The city, however, has not been spoiled by this new industry. Oil does not come ashore in Aberdeen; moreover, only occasionally can an oil rig be seen on the horizon—under tow to a new location or at anchor awaiting a new contract.

The development of North Sea oil plus the gathering strength of northeast Scotland's agriculture, fishing, and manufacturing industries have combined to give Aberdeen the highest growth rate of any city in Great Britain. Therefore, you will find Aberdeen a city of many moods. It is steeped in history. It is an ancient university town and a thriving seaport as well. It has grown very cosmopolitan, yet it remains old in grace. Above all else, the Aberdonians always have time—time to help, time to be interested, and time to talk.

Aberdeen lies between the rivers Dee and Don with two miles of golden sand connecting them. But don't think of Aberdeen merely as a large city with a beach. Union Street bisects the city and provides a mile-long shopping center lined with excellent shops. If you can make it out of bed and down to the docks no later than 0730, you'll see one of the city's biggest attractions, the fish market, in full operation.

Aberdeen University comprises Kings College and Marischal College. Both are architecturally attractive yet totally different. Marischal College is one of the largest granite buildings in the world. It was founded in 1593 and united with Kings College in 1860 to form the University of Aberdeen. King's College, in Old Aberdeen, was founded in 1495. The ivy-covered building with its distinctive crown tower has stood for centuries as a symbol of Aberdeen.

Standing like a sentinel, the gleaming white Girdleness Lighthouse guarding Aberdeen's harbor will be the first welcoming sign you'll see in Scotland's third largest city. It becomes visible on the right as the train curves away to the left from Nigg Bay to cross the River Dee, then glides to a halt in Aberdeen's rail station.

The port of Aberdeen is the jumping-off place for adventurers bound for the Orkney Islands and Shetland Islands to the north. Don't be surprised if you see a cruise ship or two in Aberdeen's harbor. Aberdeen has attracted the cruise ships by constructing a passenger landing stage in its Victoria Dock area. It appears that everyone wants to visit Europe's offshore capital, Aberdeen. Enjoy your visit.

ABERDEEN—*THE GRANITE CITY*

A Day Excursion from Edinburgh

DEPART FROM EDINBURGH STATION	ARRIVE IN ABERDEEN STATION	NOTES
0640	0910	(2)
0840	1115	(2)
0855	1147	(4)
1020	1249	(2)
1042	1315	(3)

DEPART FROM ABERDEEN STATION	ARRIVE IN EDINBURGH STATION	
1545	1815	(4)
1555	1828	(2)
1815	2045	(2)
1850	2120	(4)
1950	2255	(3)
2050	2323	(2)(4)

Distance: 131 miles/211 km
References: Thomas Cook Table 595

(1)	MON–FRI
(2)	MON–SAT
(3)	SAT
(4)	SUN

Train Information
0224–594222
InterCity Services: 071–278–2477

Aberdeen Tourist Information Centre
0224–632727

Aberdeen Whats on Line—24-Hour Service
0224–636363

Aberdeen maintains tourist information in the form of a well-stocked literature stand alongside the Travel Centre information counter in the rail station. There's also a 24-hour "EMU" service—a very user-friendly computerized inquiry unit.

The main tourist information center is in St. Nicholas House on Broad Street. When leaving the station, turn right onto Guild Street and walk until you arrive at Market Street, where the docks come into view. A left turn onto Market Street followed by a right turn onto Union Street will keep you on course (mind the shops!) until you spy Aberdeen's Town House at the head of Broad Street leading to your left. The center is a short distance up Broad Street on the left-hand side, opposite Marischal College and its award-winning Museum of Human History.

This information center is open daily throughout the year except on Sundays from October through May. During summer (June through September), the center is open Monday through Saturday, 0900–1800 and Sunday, 1000–1600 (closes two hours later July and August). From October to May, it is open Monday through Friday, 0900–1700, and Saturday, 1000–1400. On public and local holidays, with the exception of Christmas and New Year's Day, the center is normally open 0900–1700.

The Aberdeen information center has a wide variety of booklets, leaflets, posters, and slides of Aberdeen and the surrounding area. Also available are the publications of the Scottish Tourist Board covering the entire country. The center is divided into three operating sections: inquiries, accommodations, and tickets. Walking-tour and bus-tour information is also available here.

Clustered around the tourist information center on Broad Street, many of Aberdeen's places of interest are only a short walk away. In the restored Provost Skene's House on Broad Street, the oldest domestic dwelling in Aberdeen, dating from 1545, you will find rooms furnished in styles covering different periods in Aberdeen's history.

The Aberdeen Maritime Museum is housed in Provost Ross's House overlooking the city's harbor. Here, attractive displays not only depict Aberdeen's maritime heritage of fishing, shipbuilding, and trade, but also its offshore oil industry (with scale-model oil rigs). Provost Ross's House, a restored sixteenth-century dwelling, also houses a visitor's center featuring audiovisual displays of National Trust for Scotland properties, a fascinating collection of more than 100 properties representing a rich variety of castles, gardens, scenic areas, islands, and historic sights.

Tam o'Shanter Museum on High Street in Ayr is loaded with lore of Scotland's bard, Robert Burns. The city of Ayr is a principal point for starting out on the Burns Heritage Trail, developed by the Scottish Tourist Board. The trail tours places linked to the history of Scotland's greatest poet.

A DAY EXCURSION TO AYR
DISTANCE BY TRAIN: 88 miles (142 km)
AVERAGE TRAIN TIME: 1 hour, 40 minutes

What William Shakespeare is to England, Robert Burns is to Scotland. Ayr is the acknowledged center of the celebrated ''Burns Country.'' The town is rich in the history of Scotland's bard. Many famous landmarks remain in Ayr today to tell the Burnsian stories.

The Tam o'Shanter Inn on High Street, where Tam began his celebrated ride, is now a Burns museum. The Auld Brig (old bridge) that for 500 years was the only bridge in town still offers a delightful passage across the River Ayr. In a conspicuous location outside the Ayr train station, a statue of Robert Burns waits to greet travelers.

In Alloway, a pleasant southern suburb of Ayr, you will find the Land O'Burns Interpretation Centre, where visual displays introduce you to the life of Robert Burns and acquaint you with locations in and around Ayr that you may later want to visit. A brief walk from the Interpretation Centre will bring you to Burns's Cottage, where the poet was born on 25 January 1759. More than 100,000 visitors pass through the center and the cottage annually. The ruins of the Alloway Auld Kirk (old church), also close to the center, were the inspiration for Burns's narrative poem ''Tam o'Shanter.''

It was from the ruins of the Auld Kirk that witches pursued Tam, but he escaped over the Auld Brig O'Doon—the bridge over the River Doon—and eluded his pursuers, because according to legend witches were unable to cross running water. Maggie, the mare that Tam rode, was less fortunate: ''Ae spring brought off her master hale,/But left behind her ain gray tail:/The carlin claught her by the rump,/And left poor Maggie scarce a stump.''

Ayr was a seaside resort long before the term was invented. Well-heeled Glasgow merchants came to Ayr for short vacations, liked what they saw, and built houses there. In addition to providing Scottish gentry with suburban abodes, Ayr is also an industrial town, a market center, and a fishing port—for good measure. With all these assets, Ayr is assured of retaining its prosperous, bustling atmosphere even after the summer visitors have gone.

Throughout the year on Tuesdays and Thursdays, the farmers bring their cattle to market in Ayr. Year-round, the town's harbor provides the locale for those who enjoy watching the fishermen bringing in their catch. As the shopping center for the district, Ayr surprises visitors with the range and size of its stores and shops.

A Day Excursion from Edinburgh

DEPART FROM EDINBURGH WAVERLEY STATION	ARRIVE IN GLASGOW QUEEN STREET STATION	NOTES
0700 or 0900	0750 or 0950	(2)
0820	0925	(4)

Transfer to Glasgow Central Station (See chapter 11)

DEPART FROM GLASGOW CENTRAL STATION	ARRIVE IN AYR STATION	
0830 or 1030	0924 or 1122	(2)
0840 or 1000	0928 or 1052	(4)

(Plus other frequent service)

DEPART FROM AYR STATION	ARRIVE IN GLASGOW CENTRAL STATION	
1556	1645	(2)(4)
1615 or 1815	1709 or 1907	(2)

Transfer to Glasgow Queen Street Station (See chapter 11)
(Plus other frequent service)

DEPART FROM GLASGOW QUEEN STREET STATION	ARRIVE IN EDINBURGH WAVERLEY STATION	
1700 or 1930	1750 or 2020	(2)
1700	1755	(4)

Distance: 88 miles/142 km
References: Thomas Cook Tables 590, 591

(1)	MON–FRI	(3) SAT
(2)	MON–SAT	(4) SUN

Train Information: 041–204–2844
InterCity Services: 071–387–7070

Ayr Tourist Information Centre: 0292–284196

238

After arriving in Ayr, head for the town's tourist information center at 39 Sandgate. After admiring Burns's statue in front of the railway station, follow the road down the right-hand side of the square and down High Street, then turn left at Newmarket Street. It is not more than a ten-minute walk—unless you stop to admire the flowers along the way. From Easter to the end of May, the office is open Monday through Friday, 0845–1645, and Saturday and Sunday, 1000–1800. June-September, hours are Monday through Friday, 0845–1900, and Saturday and Sunday, 1000–1900. October to Easter, it is open Monday through Friday 0845–1645.

Literature on Ayr, the district surrounding it, and Scotland's famous poet, Robert Burns, abounds by the pound in the information center. You will want to collect such informative booklets as the one published by the district that's crammed with facts and photos. In addition, ask for a copy of the historical guide *Ayr, Prestwick and District*. It is the best authority for a tour of Ayr on foot that we have found.

You will hear mention of the Burns Heritage Trail during your visit in Ayr. If you are interested in taking it or a bus to "Burns Country," you should gather all the details from the information center. The Burns Heritage Trail has been developed by the Scottish Tourist Board. It is a tour of the places linked with Scotland's poet. On the trail, you can see many places that have been developed to tell the story of Burns and his lifetime. The trail tour includes a visit to Tarbolton and the Lochlea Farm, where the Burns family lived from 1777 to 1784, and a stop at Mauchline, where it is said the Robert Burns met his wife to be, Jean Armour.

With more than two miles of golden, sandy beach, Ayr gets more than its fair share of the summer Scottish sun. Golf, bowling, and tennis are among the many sports activities which can be enjoyed there. The town has three golf courses, forming part of the famous fifteen-mile stretch of "golfing coast" you'll see from the train approaching Ayr. All the traditional seaside amusements can be enjoyed in Ayr, as well as horse racing, held at the Ayr Racecourse throughout the year.

Away from the beaches, there are many beautiful parks and gardens, notably Belleisle, Craigie, and Rozelle. Rozelle is also the home of Ayr's Art Gallery and displays one of the very few Henry Moore sculptures to be seen in Scotland. Ayr's beauty has frequently brought it the coveted titles, "Britain's Floral Town" and "Scotland's Floral Town." If you delight in old houses, Ayr has many, including one that was built in 1470— twenty-two years before Columbus discovered America!

Following your visit to Ayr, you probably will be in accord with "Robbie" Burns when he wrote, "Auld Ayr, wham ne'er a town surpasses/For honest men and bonnie lasses."

RNLB *Margaret*, a Royal National Life Boat, stands ready for rescue duty in Dunbar's Victoria Harbor. The ruins of Dunbar Castle mark the narrow passageway leading from the harbor into the North Sea. The old lifeboat house on the harbor's quay is now a museum.

A DAY EXCURSION TO DUNBAR
DISTANCE BY TRAIN: 29 miles (46 km)
AVERAGE TRAIN TIME: 30 minutes

Put on your walking shoes—we're going to Dunbar. The town offers two wonderful walking opportunities: one through the historic center of old Dunbar to appreciate the great and varied wealth of its traditional Scottish buildings, the other along the cliffs brooding over the North Sea in the John Muir Country Park. Those unaccustomed to walking or slower of pace can take solace in Dunbar's harbor area by watching fishermen and their customers on the quay buying and selling freshly caught fish as their colorful fishing boats bob about on the tide. Further assurance of a pleasant outing for all is the presence of several public houses in the harbor area. Among them is the Volunteer Arms, which houses the Volunteer Bar and the Haven Lounge, where one can either seek haven or volunteer.

Dunbar is situated amid some of the most beautiful countryside and coastline in Scotland. There are few other places where it is possible to witness the full range of history of a Scottish east-coast fishing port and market center. Dunbar has always played an important part in Scotland's history. Due to its strategic location, the town has been a stronghold down through centuries. Dunbar, Gaelic for "the fort on the point," had a castle fortress at least as early as 856. The remains of the castle stand on the promontory overlooking Dunbar's Victoria Harbor.

The Dunbar Castle was the place where Bothwell brought Mary Queen of Scots when he abducted her in 1567. That same year, the Scottish Parliament ordered that Dunbar Castle should be demolished. When the Victoria Harbor was constructed in the nineteenth century, the channel leading into the harbor was cut through the rocky palisade where the ruins of the castle lay. The remains that you may inspect during your visit to Dunbar are only a fragment of the original great castle.

There are two harbors: the old harbor, extended by Oliver Cromwell, and Victoria Harbor. Construction on the old harbor began in 1655, and it was improved and extended in the eighteenth century. This harbor, now nearly deserted, still retains the old paving stones as well as a fishermen's barometer that was erected in 1856. As part of the redevelopment, the harbor areas have had cottage-type houses built since 1951 to the special design of Sir Basil Spence, the architect of the new Coventry Cathedral. Perhaps the best evidence of Dunbar's beauty is the large number of visitors walking about simply admiring the scenery.

An interesting part of Victoria harbor is Dunbar's RNLB (Royal National

DUNBAR—*"FORT ON THE POINT"*

A Day Excursion from Edinburgh

DEPART FROM EDINBURGH WAVERLEY STATION	ARRIVE IN DUNBAR STATION	NOTES
0650	0708	(2)
0930	0948	(4)
1000	1018	(2)

DEPART FROM DUNBAR STATION	ARRIVE IN EDINBURGH WAVERLEY STATION	
1415	1432	(1)
1419	1447	(3)
1625	1703	(4)
1706	1738	(1)
1723	1755	(3)
2004	2036	(1)
2018	2050	(3)
2217	2249	(1)

Distance: 29 miles/46 km
References: Thomas Cook Table 570

(1)   MON–FRI
(2)   MON–SAT
(3)   SAT
(4)   SUN

Train Information
031–556–2451
InterCity Services: 071–278–2477

Dunbar Tourist Information Centre
0368–63353

Life Boat) *Margaret*. Opposite its mooring is the Lifeboat Museum, which is well worth a visit. Lifeboats out of Dunbar have saved more than 200 lives since beginning operation in 1808.

The Dunbar tourist information center is in the Town House on High Street. Part of the building, incidentally, is a tolbooth (toll gate) dating back to the seventeenth century, when a toll road between Edinburgh and Newcastle ran through Dunbar. The center is a short walk from the railway station. Station Road runs from the front of the station to where it crosses Countess Road and becomes Abbey Road. When you reach the general post office on your left, the thoroughfare has another name change to High Street and remains so until you reach the information center on the right-hand side.

The information center is open during summer 0900–1900 Monday through Saturday and 1100–1300 on Sunday. During the balance of the year, it is open Monday through Friday, 0900–1700, and closed Saturday and Sunday. Note the sundial on the tolbooth tower as you enter the information center. You can still set your watch by it—provided, of course, that the sun is shining during your visit.

For the town tour we mentioned, ask for a copy of *A Walk Around the Old Burgh of Dunbar*. A guidebook for the self-guided trail laid out along the cliffs running out of Dunbar is also available. This cliff-top trail is prominently marked on the previously mentioned street plan, as are other features of the town, including the two harbors.

If you brought your walking shoes with you, the place to try them out is the John Muir Country Park, which begins at Dunbar harbor and extends to the Ravensheugh sands to the west, on the south approaches to the Firth of Forth. The cliff-top trail has controlled public accesses to the beaches below. Throughout the summer, a ranger is normally on duty in the park, usually on horseback, and is available to answer your questions and provide directions. You may join the ranger on a ramble along the cliff-top trail starting at the Dunbar harbor at 1400. There are several horse riding routes within the park. If interested, ask the tourist information center for a copy of *Horse Riding Guide*.

If you are a golf nut and have not been able to obtain a tee time for the Old Course at St. Andrews, try the par-64 Winterfield Golf Course maintained by the city of Dunbar. Call Dunbar 63434 to get a tee time.

There is a bowling green on the right-hand side of the Station Road as you proceed toward town. We asked an old Scot, "How can such a green be so smooth and flat?" "It's easy," he explained, "you just plant the best of grass seed and then roll it for a few hundred years."

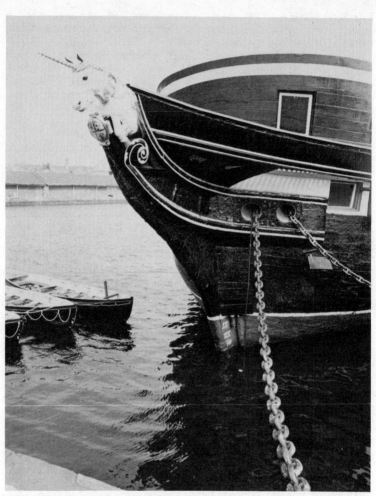

Unicorn figurehead of the frigate *Unicorn* glistens at the bow of Britain's oldest warship still afloat. Moored at the Victoria Dock in Dundee, the vessel is open to visitors from April to October and features an exhibition of Royal Navy development.

A DAY EXCURSION TO DUNDEE
DISTANCE BY TRAIN: 60 miles (96 km)
AVERAGE TRAIN TIME: 1 hour, 30 minutes

As your train approaches the city of Dundee, you will be able to witness a scene of railroading history—one of disaster and yet one of triumph. Following the station stop at Leuchars, where you detrain for St. Andrews, watch as the train passes through the local station of Wormit and on to the railway bridge crossing the Firth of Tay inbound to Dundee. The bridge, a double-track structure 11,653 feet long, was opened in 1887 and was considered at that time (as it is even now) to be a triumph of railroad engineering. Look alongside the present bridge and you will see a series of old bridge piers. These once supported a single-track bridge that was swept away during a violent storm in 1879, along with a train and seventy-five of its passengers.

Turn your gaze to the east during the crossing of the great Firth (estuary) where the Tay River empties into the North Sea and you will see a two-lane vehicular bridge 7,365 feet in length that was opened by Queen Elizabeth II in 1966. The River Tay and its rail and vehicular bridges are a vital part of Dundee's existence.

Dundee, the capital of Tayside and Scotland's third largest city, lies in a magnificent setting between the Sidlaw Hills and the banks of Britain's finest salmon river, the Tay.

Dundee was famous for generations as the city of "jute, jam, and journalism." Its prolific writers still abound, but jute is slowly sinking into the shadows of time as synthetic fibers take over in the cordage industry, and jam is made in England.

Dundee lies in the heart of Scotland, where the game of golf originated. The latest count reveals forty golf courses within one hour's drive of the city. Five actually lie within the city's district. In Dundee, the name of the game is golf, and its citizens have proven to the world that they can construct courses that can confound, confuse—but always entertain. In Dundee and throughout the area, you also will note that the hospitality in the nineteenth holes throughout the region is second to none.

By the way, if your original day-excursion plans were for St. Andrews but you failed to leave the train at Leuchars Station, you can still make it back to the golf capital by bus out of Dundee in less than one hour. You also can capitalize on your error, however, and enjoy Dundee.

Dundee's tourist information center is easy to find. Exiting from the rail station, turn left and then right along Whitehall Crescent until you come to

245

DUNDEE—*CITY OF DISCOVERY*

A Day Excursion from Edinburgh

DEPART FROM EDINBURGH WAVERLEY STATION	ARRIVE IN DUNDEE STATION	NOTES
0840	0956	(2)
0855	1020	(4)
1020	1137	(2)
1042	1156	(3)
1055	1231	(4)
1240	1356	(2)

DEPART FROM DUNDEE STATION	ARRIVE IN EDINBURGH WAVERLEY STATION	
1505	1620	(2)
1700	1815	(4)
1713	1828	(2)
1925	2045	(2)
2005	2120	(4)
2208	2323	(2)(4)

Distance: 60 miles/96 km
References: Thomas Cook Table 595

(1)	MON–FRI
(2)	MON–SAT
(3)	SAT
(4)	SUN

Train Information
0382–28046
InterCity Services: 071–278–2477

Dundee Tourist Information Centre
0382–27723

Crichton Street. Turn left up this street until you reach the top. Turn right again and you have reached the City Square. The tourist information center is at No. 4. You can phone the center from the railway station on 27723. The center is open Monday through Saturday, 0830–2000; Sunday, 1100–2000 during May, June, and September. It closes one hour later during July and August. From October through April, it is open Monday through Friday, 0900–1800 and Saturday, 1000–1600.

The cultural aspects of Dundee are enhanced by its McManus Galleries as well as the University Botanical Gardens. Camperdown Park and the Wildlife Centre are also stellar attractions for those who prefer outside activities. Among Dundee's many other attractions, one that we feel will prove to be of interest to all is the frigate *Unicorn,* Britain's oldest warship still afloat. The *Unicorn* is one of the world's four remaining frigates, those fast, lightly armed sailing ships of yesteryear now replaced by the destroyer class of naval vessel. Launched in 1824, the *Unicorn* remained in naval service until 1968. Ask the information center for the *Unicorn* and *RRS Discovery* brochures and instructions to reach the pier in the city's Victoria Dock. Sharing Victoria Dock with the frigate *Unicorn* is Captain Scott's Royal Research Ship *Discovery*. Built in Dundee, Britain's first scientific research vessel set sail on her voyage to the Antarctic in 1901. *Discovery* will move in 1991 to become the focal point of the new waterfront development "Discovery Quay."

Dundee's other points of interest include its old steeple, its four castles—Dudhope, Mains, Claypotts, and Broughty—and the Mercat Cross, which is moved about as the population center changes. The old steeple, standing at a height of 156 feet above the ground, dates from the fourteenth century. The steeple has withstood many storms, both natural and manmade. It was the site of the siege of 1651, when the town was invaded by Cromwell's army. The old steeple and all of the castle sites can be reached by public transport buses from the city bus station close to the British Rail terminal.

The Mercat Cross, a replica of the old structure that was demolished in 1877, is currently located at the end of High Street. The original cross was erected in the Seagate area. About the beginning of the fifteenth century, however, the city's population began to increase, and the town began to spread westward. The Seagate was abandoned as the principal center of the city in favor of a more open space to the west, which is now High Street.

Dundee has a passion for plaques and has erected a number of them on buildings having historical associations. At latest count, twelve such monuments are located throughout the city. Of particular interest to visitors is the plaque marking the Greyfriars monastery, which was granted to the city as a burial site by Mary Queen of Scots in 1564.

Humble weaver's cottage in Dunfermline (above), birthplace of steel millionaire Andrew Carnegie, is open to the public. Carnegie's benevolence brought amenities such as a concert hall, library, and sports center to the city. Old Pug Engine No. 11 (below) stands in Pittencrieff Park close by the Carnegie memorial statue.

A DAY EXCURSION TO DUNFERMLINE
DISTANCE BY TRAIN: 17 miles (27 km)
AVERAGE TRAIN TIME: 32 minutes

Dunfermline was once the capital of Scotland and holds an important position in Scottish history. The majestic spires of the Dunfermline Abbey dominate the town's skyline. Within the abbey are the graves of seven Scottish kings, including the tomb of Robert the Bruce. The abbey was founded by Scotland's King David in the twelfth century as a Benedictine monastery. In the course of time, through royal gifts and other extensive endowments, it became one of the most magnificent establishments in Scotland. In its time, the monastery has played host to a wide range of people, from Edward I of England to Oliver Cromwell.

A second attraction to Dunfermline is Pittencrieff Park, a lovely area with its flower gardens, music pavilion, aviary, and museum. It was given to the town by Andrew Carnegie, the Scottish-American philanthopist who was born in a humble weaver's cottage in Dunfermline in 1835. His birthplace is open to the public, and it attracts thousands of visitors every year. A statue of the steel millionaire stands in the center of Pittencrieff. It was erected by the citizens of Dunfermline in grateful appreciation of his many gifts to his native city.

Arriving in Dunfermline by train, you can go to the center of the city either by bus or by taxi. The walk is not too distant to the abbey and the other attractions in town. It is a bit longer, however, than the stationmaster's advice, "Not more than a four-minute walk from here." Allow fifteen minutes to cover the ground between the train station and the tourist information center on Chalmers Street. The abbey, Pittencrieff, and Carnegie's birthplace lie between these two points. Taxis queue at the front of the station. About £2.00 will see you to the city center. The bus stop is close to the station at an underpass on the left. The fifteen-pence fare will take you anywhere you may want to go within the city.

The tourist information center is on Chalmers Street at the entrance of the Glen Bridge car park. Its location again points out that Britain is still automobile oriented insofar as touring is concerned. Perhaps more information centers will change their locale to train stations, however, as automobile fuel costs and availability continue to worsen. The Dunfermline center operates daily, 1000–1800, through the summer season, including Sunday and holidays. It is closed during the winter. The printed information available at the center features the abbey and Carnegie's cottage. The staff is very helpful in suggesting other things to do.

DUNFERMLINE—*ANDREW CARNEGIE BIRTHPLACE*

A Day Excursion from Edinburgh

DEPART FROM EDINBURGH WAVERLEY STATION	ARRIVE IN DUNFERMLINE STATION	NOTES
0815	0842	(2)
0915	0942	(2)
0942	1019	(4)
1015	1042	(2)
1115	1142	(2)
1120	1202	(4)

DEPART FROM DUNFERMLINE STATION	ARRIVE IN EDINBURGH STATION	
1501	1535	(2)
1601	1635	(2)
1611	1644	(4)
1701	1735	(2)
1808	1844	(2)
1811	1842	(4)
1901	1932	(2)
2011	2042	(4)
2101	2132	(2)
2201	2232	(2)

Distance: 17 miles/27 km
References: British Rail Table 242

(1)   MON–FRI
(2)   MON–SAT
(3)   SAT
(4)   SUN

Train Information
031–556–2451
InterCity Services: 01–278–2477

Dunfermline Tourist Information Centre
0383–720999

To reach the tourist information center from the middle of town, orient yourself on Bridge Street in front of the Dunfermline City Chambers. Walk down Bridge Street toward the entrance to Pittencrieff Park to where you can turn right onto Chalmers Street. Follow Chalmers Street, staying on its right-hand side. The car park entrance is a short distance up Chalmers Street.

The triangle of interest is the Dunfermline Abbey, Pittencrieff Park, and the Andrew Carnegie birthplace. We suggest visiting the park first, due to its close proximity to the information center. Stop at the abbey, next, then the Carnegie cottage as you proceed back to the rail station.

The site of the Dunfermline Abbey has had continual Christian worship for about 1,500 years. In the fifth or sixth century, the first building on the site was the Culdee Church. Later, it was rebuilt on a larger scale by Malcolm III, father of King David I, and was dedicated in 1072. Traces of both buildings are visible beneath gratings in the floor of the abbey's Old Nave.

April through September, the abbey church is open 0930–1700 daily and 1400–1700 on Sunday. Between October and March, the closing hour is 1600. The abbey shop is open during the same hours as the church between April and September. At other times, sale goods are available from the church officer.

It was Andrew Carnegie who generously gave funds to Dunfermline for the upkeep of Pittencrieff Park. It has become a popular place for visitors to pause and reflect on his donations of a library, public baths, and a theater in addition to the park. During your stroll through the park, swing aboard Old Pug and marvel at the advances that have been made in railroading since its engine's fires were banked for the last time.

Andrew Carnegie's birthplace is open to the public daily from 1100 to 1700 (Wednesday closing is 2000; Sunday opening, 1400). From his humble beginnings, Andrew Carnegie found his fortunes in the new world. Nevertheless, with his philanthropist attitude, he never forgot his home town of Dunfermline. At age thirty-three, with an annual income of $50,000, Carnegie said, "Beyond this never earn, make no effort to increase fortune, but spend the surplus each year for benevolent purposes." This, he certainly did. His generosity in Dunfermline is administered today by a trust fund.

When you visit Dunfermline, you will be following in the footsteps of British royalty. Both Queen Victoria and Queen Mary visited there, and in 1972, Queen Elizabeth and Prince Philip were present to dedicate a Royal Pew in celebration of the abbey's 900th anniversary. You'll find, however, that Dunfermline extends a royal welcome to all of its visitors.

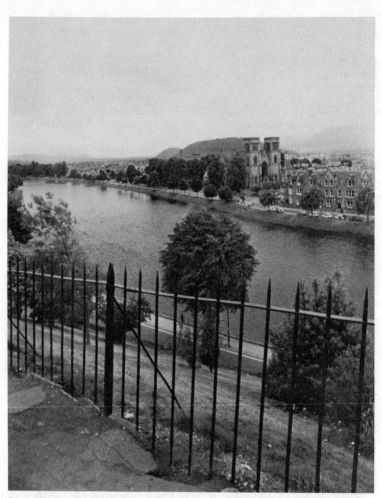

River Ness, as viewed from Inverness Castle, leads southwest to Loch Ness, mythical lair of "Nessie," the Loch Ness monster. Known as the "capital of the Highlands," Inverness, because of its increasing popularity, has expanded its hotels and recreational facilities to meet its visitors' needs.

From Edinburgh . . .

AN "OUT-AND-BACK" EXCURSION TO INVERNESS
DISTANCE BY TRAIN: 176 miles (283 km)
AVERAGE TRAIN TIME: 4 hours, 20 minutes

The position of Inverness at the eastern head of Loch Ness, Scotland's famous inland sea, earns the city its title, "Capital of the Highlands." From Inverness, you can get to more places in the Highlands than you can from any other location in Scotland. For this reason, we have termed the excursion to Inverness an "out-and-back" excursion, for you may want to use Inverness as your "base city" for exploring the Highlands.

If you plan to do a considerable amount of traveling throughout the Highlands, you may want to consider purchasing the Scottish Highlands and Islands Travelpass. You will find an expanded explanation of this unique travel bargain beginning on page 285 of this edition.

Should your schedule for visiting Inverness be limited, you may want to utilize the excellent British Rail sleeper services. For example, you could board a sleeper one night in Edinburgh and awaken the following morning in Inverness. You could spend an entire day sightseeing, followed by boarding another sleeper back to Edinburgh or Glasgow.

It is an ambitious program, but going in and out of Inverness by sleeper could permit you to board the 1010 train from there to the Kyle of Lochalsh (see page 257), where you arrive at 1252, then ferry to the Isle of Skye, soak in the sights, and leave Lochalsh on the 1640 to be back in Inverness by 1919 with several hours to spare before boarding the sleeper again.

But why hurry? The scenery is superb and the climate is invigorating. Take our advice and plan to spend at least several days in hospitable Inverness, exploring the Highlands at a leisurely pace.

The tourist information center in Inverness is at 23 Church Street, close to its junction with High Street. The shortest route to the information center lies down Union Street, which runs perpendicular to the front of the Inverness train station. Union Street ends one block further on at Church Street, where a left turn will bring you to the information center after a few more steps. There is a problem, however—Union Street is lined with shops loaded with Highland lore, and as a matter of fact, so is Church Street.

The tourist information center is open Monday through Saturday, 0900–2030; and Sunday, 0900–1800. During the off-season, we suggest that you call the center at (0463) 234353 for information.

There is so much to do in and around the "Capital of the Highlands" that not even a series of action-packed days could absorb all the possible activities.

INVERNESS—*HIGHLAND GATEWAY*

An "Out-and-Back" Excursion from Edinburgh

DEPART FROM EDINBURGH WAVERLEY STATION	ARRIVE IN INVERNESS STATION	NOTES
0925	1305	(2)(4)
1010	1402	(2)
1210	1546	(2)
1440	1820	(2)
1520	1920	(2)
1637	2000	(1)
1659	2030	(3)
1809	2140	(4)
1910	2254	(2)

DEPART FROM INVERNESS STATION	ARRIVE IN EDINBURGH WAVERLEY STATION	
0640	1009	(2)
0750	1114	(2)
1010	1416	(2)
1015	1350	(4)
1438	1821	(2)
1750	2128	(4)
1835	2209	(2)
2000	2338	(1)

Distance: 176 miles/283 km
References: Thomas Cook Table 600
(1)   MON–FRI
(2)   MON–SAT
(3)   SAT
(4)   SUN

NOTE: London-Inverness sleeper service: Depart London Euston Station 2110 weekdays; 2100 Sundays. Arrive Inverness 0730 + 1. Returning, depart Inverness 2115 (at 1940 on Saturdays); arrive London 0750 + 1 (at 0919 + 1 on Sundays).

Train Information	*Inverness Tourist Information Centre*
0463–238924	0463–234353
InterCity Services: 071–278–2477	

Here are but a few of the sightseeing possibilities in and around Inverness. Visit the castle grounds and walk along the garden paths at the River Ness. Cruise on Loch Ness, as far away as Urquhart Castle if you like, where most of the sightings of the Loch Ness "monster" (or "beastie," as the locals call it) have occurred. Journey on the renowned railway line between Inverness and Kyle of Lochalsh along eighty-two miles of railroad right of way that involved beauty, romance, history, and endurance in its building. Forge northward to Thurso, Scotland's most northerly town, on a dramatic rail route holding 162 miles of Scotland's better scenery captive for your viewing. If you prefer the solitude that surf breaking on a shore can bring, take a train east to Nairn, fifteen miles from Inverness. Or train south a mere thirty-five miles to Scotland's St. Moritz—where the ski boom has transformed the town of Aviemore into a continental sports village.

Eons ago, Loch Ness was carved out along a geological fault between two land masses in northern Scotland. The earth's forces formed a long narrow lake of approximately twenty-four miles with depths of up to 750 feet, possibly 1,000 feet in some parts. To go to Inverness and not have a look at Loch Ness would be like eating one potato chip and throwing the rest of the bag away. We urge you to dip into the mystery, the history, and the beauty of Loch Ness.

Loch Ness is reportedly the home of "Nessie," the Loch Ness monster, which has often been described as one of the world's greatest mysteries. The first recorded sighting of Nessie was made by an unimpeachable witness (Saint Columba, no less) in A.D. 565. According to the report, the monster attacked one of the members of his group. Since then, there have been too many visual and photographic sightings of the monster for it to be easily explained.

Fact or fiction, there is a continuing similarity in the descriptions of Nessie given by most of those who claim to have seen the monster over the years. Photographs also support a common description, that of a small head at the end of a long thin neck with an overall body length between twenty to thirty feet. Underwater evidence gathered by every means from space-age technology to yellow submarines suggests that it may have four flippers. Zoologists recognize this description as a plesiosaur, a type of marine dinosaur that existed more than seventy million years ago and should have become extinct.

Scientific data notwithstanding, the fact that malt whiskeys have been produced in large volumes throughout the area since the beginning of recorded time may account for many or all of the sightings!

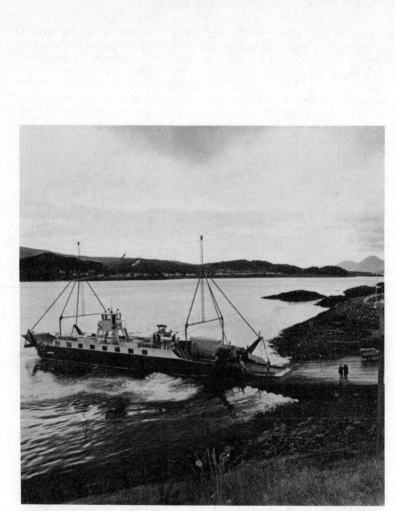

Kyle of Lochalsh, a narrow channel (Kyle) connecting Loch (Lake) Alsh with the open sea through the Sound of Raasay, offers superb views to its visitors. The Lochalsh Hotel is located conveniently beside the ferry dock for transport to the Isle of Skye, seen in the background.

From Edinburgh . . .

A DAY EXCURSION TO KYLE OF LOCHALSH
DISTANCE BY TRAIN: 258 miles (415 km)
AVERAGE TRAIN TIME: 7 hours, 35 minutes

The railway between Inverness and Kyle of Lochalsh has been accorded the distinction of being the premier scenic rail line in Britain. It offers a lovely journey through the Highland towns of Dingwall, Garve, Achnasheen, and Stromeferry before terminating on the western shores of Scotland overlooking the Isle of Skye. The rail line passes through a region of superlative natural beauty loaded with Scottish folklore. This eighty-two-mile journey, which appears rather uninspiring in the cold prosaic type of the timetable, is in reality a rare mixture of beauty, romance, history, and endurance.

When the railroad opened in 1870, the western terminal was the town of Stromeferry on the saltwater Loch Carron. Although the original intention was to build right through to Kyle of Lochalsh, construction money ran out and Stromeferry remained the terminus for twenty-seven years. Completing the remaining twenty-six miles of right of way proved to be a formidable task of engineering. Most miles were forged through solid rock, requiring cuts up to eighty-eight feet deep. Even the area of the train terminal at Kyle required blasting and removing rock. When you reach Kyle of Lochalsh, pause to appreciate the backbreaking toil that created the train station and the right of way leading to it.

A ferry plies between Kyle of Lochalsh and Kyleakin on the Isle of Skye. The ruins of Castle Moil stand on a promontory close to the Kyleakin ferry dock. During the time of the Vikings, the castle was the home of a Norwegian princess. History relates that the princess made quite a bundle during her stay in the castle by exacting a toll from ships passing through the narrow straits. To insure prompt payment, she had a heavy chain attached between the castle and the Kyle of Lochalsh, which was drawn taut when a ship approached. The chain was probably depreciated and charged off as a business expense, for there's no evidence of its existence today.

During the summer, the 1010 train from Inverness includes a special observation car, for which a supplement is payable. The special car returns to Inverness in the late afternoon, departing from Kyle of Lochalsh at 1700. A guide aboard the observation car offers interesting commentary en route. If you're unable to obtain a seat in that car, ask at the railway-station magazine stand for the British Rail illustrated booklet *Inverness to Kyle of Lochalsh*. It describes much of the scenery en route, along with a sprinkling of Scottish folk tales.

In Kyle of Lochalsh, you'll find the tourist information center conve-

257

KYLE OF LOCHALSH AND THE ISLE OF SKYE

A Day Excursion from Edinburgh Through Inverness

DEPART FROM INVERNESS STATION	ARRIVE IN KYLE OF LOCHALSH STATION	NOTES
0655	0927	(2)
1015*	1304	(2)(4)
1225*	1450	(2)
1755	2028	(2)(4)

DEPART FROM KYLE OF LOCHALSH STATION	ARRIVE IN INVERNESS STATION	
0700	0930	(2)
1030	1303	(4)
1135	1403	(2)
1530	1749	(2)
1700*	1945	(2)(4)

Distance: 82 miles/132 km
References: Thomas Cook Table 597
* Conveys observation car

(1)   MON–FRI
(2)   MON–SAT
(3)   SAT
(4)   SUN

Train Information
0463–238924
InterCity Services: 071–278–2477

Kyle of Lochalsh Tourist Information Centre
0599–4276

niently located midway between the train station and the ferry dock. It is open Monday through Saturday, 0930–2100, and Sunday, 1430–1730. To reach it, use the stairs to the overpass and then walk downhill.

Don't pass up the opportunity of visiting the Isle of Skye. You'll be treated to one of the finest land-and-seascapes in the world during the seven-minute crossing. The ferry departs every fifteen minutes during peak season, but check its return schedule to Kyle of Lochalsh to assure that you are not left on the Isle when your train departs the Kyle. Holders of the special Scottish Highlands and Islands Travelpass (page 285) may start their exploration of Skye from this point. For a quick review of the village of Kyleakin and its points of interest, check the tourist-information three-sided sign just outside the Castle Moil Restaurant, a short distance from the ferry dock.

It is a relatively short walk from Kyleakin to Castle Moil. For other diversions, check on both sides of the strait at the ferry dock for special excursion craft that explore the area by sea. There are daily boat cruises departing from the Kyleakin pier every two hours. Special cruises to the white coral beaches of Sandaig, where seals can often be seen basking and cavorting, run every Sunday.

Scottish legends leap out at you as the train plies between Inverness and Kyle. The castle at Dingwall was said to have been ruled by Finlaec, the father of MacBeth. In a graveyard opposite the castle ruins, the ghost of a young girl wanders nightly in search of her faithless lover. Approaching Garve, you'll pass Loch Garve, where even in the dead of winter there is a small part that never freezes—attributed to the water-horse monsters who carry off local girls. The inn at Garve purveys Athole Brose, a libation of whiskey, oats, and honey, several drafts of which could produce a whole herd of water horses.

The right of way passes areas that stir the imagination. Departing Achnasheen en route to Stromeferry, passengers may get a fleeting glance at the Torridon range of mountains—the oldest mountains on earth. They are so old that geologists have been unable to find any trace of fossils, indicating the mountains were formed long before life of any description began. The range, consisting of peaks such as Liathach (3,456 feet), Beinn Eighe (3,300 feet), and Beinn Alligin (3,021 feet), has sparkling quartzite peaks, often mistaken for snow.

In the seventeenth century, Brahan Seer, the Highland's prophet extraordinaire, said, ''The day will come when every stream will have its bridge, balls of fire will pass rapidly up and down the Strath of Peffery and carriages without horses will cross the country from sea to sea.'' And so it came to pass when, on 10 August 1870, the railroad steam engines began operating from sea to sea.

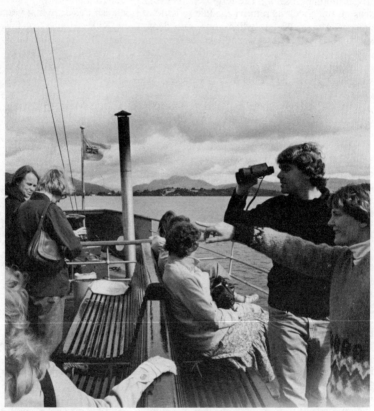

Superb view of the scenery surrounding one of Scotland's most famous bodies of water, Loch Lomond, is enjoyed by passengers aboard the steamer *Countess Fiona*. The vessel steams daily from its pier in Balloch from mid-April through September.

From Edinburgh . . .

A DAY EXCURSION TO LOCH LOMOND
DISTANCE BY TRAIN: 69 miles (111 km)
AVERAGE TRAIN TIME: 1 hour, 30 minutes

The enchantment of Loch Lomond is one of Scotland's most prized assets. The largest body of freshwater in Great Britain, Loch Lomond abounds with magnificent scenery along its shoreline, and in our opinion, it is best viewed from the decks of the steamer *Countess Fiona*.

Loch Lomond is twenty-three miles in length, five miles wide at its broad southern end, and enhanced by a scattering of small islands silhouetted against a background of dark blue water and rugged mountains. As the loch gradually narrows to the north, until only a few hundred feet of water separate the shores, Loch Lomond begins to look every bit like a Norwegian fjord.

Loch Lomond enjoys a worldwide reputation as one of the most beautiful places in Scotland. Loch Lomond's "bonnie banks" have been praised in song for more than two hundred years. Oddly enough, the ballad was written by a supporter of Bonnie Prince Charlie, a Jacobite monk, in a prison cell of the Carlisle Castle. America's senior citizens began dancing to the syncopated version of the tune when the Benny Goodman orchestra played in the "Swing Era" of the mid 1930s, and there's not a tenor, baritone, or bass singer alive today who hasn't extolled in voice the virtues of the "Bonnie Banks, Bonnie Braes and the steep, steep sides of Ben Lomond."

Loch Lomond is a cross section of Scotland and, as such, bears much evidence of man's history down through the ages. There is evidence of some of the earliest settlements in Scotland still visible on its shore and islands. Many of its islands are associated with the first Christian missionaries. Along its shores, armies have marched and drovers have herded their cattle from the grazing lands of the highlands, and it was on the "bonnie banks" where the kingdoms of the area came together to make the nation of Scotland.

History even records in the thirteenth century that the Vikings raided and plundered the loch area—which is somewhat astonishing when you consider that Loch Lomond is landlocked. Establishing a beachhead on the saltwater Loch Long at Arrochar to the west, the Vikings dragged their boats across two miles of land separating Loch Long from Tarbet on Loch Lomond. Tarbet is a port of call on the cruise of the *Countess Fiona*. It shouldn't be too difficult to envision a dragon-headed boat lying at anchor as you round the headland to Tarbet. Anyone with an imagination is welcome to try it.

Your BritRail Pass is valid for train service to Balloch, but you must

LOCH LOMOND—*BY YON BONNIE BANKS*

A Day's Cruise on Scotland's Famous Lake, Loch Lomond

DEPART FROM EDINBURGH WAVERLEY STATION	ARRIVE IN GLASGOW QUEEN STREET STATION
0700	0750
0730	0820
1130	1220

DEPART FROM GLASGOW QUEEN STREET STATION	ARRIVE AT BALLOCH CENTRAL STATION
0811	0858
0841	0927
1241	1327

NOTICE

At press time, the sailings on Loch Lomond for the 1991 season had not been announced. Readers are advised to telephone the Balloch Tourist Information Centre, Old Station, Balloch Road (0389) 53533 for current information concerning schedules and rates.

DEPART FROM BALLOCH CENTRAL STATION	ARRIVE IN GLASGOW QUEEN STREET STATION
1438	1523
1708	1753
1908	1953

DEPART FROM GLASGOW QUEEN STREET STATION	ARRIVE IN EDINBURGH WAVERLEY STATION
1530	1618
1800	1848
2000	2048

NOTE: Rail schedules shown apply Monday–Saturday only. Sunday rail services operate from Glasgow Central Station. Consult local schedules. Proceed on foot (allow fifteen-twenty minutes) between Balloch Central Station and Balloch Pier.

Steamer cruises operate on Loch Lomond from April through September. Check train information/tourist information office for complete details. Purchase cruise tickets aboard. References: Thomas Cook Table 590 and British Rail Tables 226, 228.

purchase separate tickets for the cruise on the *Countess Fiona*. We recommend the cruise to Inversnaid at the head of the loch and the return to Balloch Pier. For this, you should purchase a "day return" ticket—the American equivalent of a round-trip. Payment is made at the ticket office aboard the vessel. Since the Loch Lomond cruise is a popular attraction, particularly in high season during July and August, it is best to call ahead to assure space availability. A recorded message containing that information—together with any possible schedule changes—may be dialed on 041–248–2699 twenty-four hours a day. For any other information, contact the cruise operator's office during regular business hours by dialing 041–226–4271. By the way, the company that operates the cruise is the Alloa Brewery in Glasgow. You might just want to "ring them up" on another subject—a tour of their facilities.

The day-return ticket between Balloch and Inversnaid costs £8.50 throughout the sailing season. During low season between April and June and again in September, senior citizens can take advantage of half-price fares; children under sixteen are also half-price, and for children under five years of age, twenty-five pence will see them aboard any voyage. A family ticket—two adults and two children on the full round-trip between Balloch and Inversnaid—can be purchased for only £21.50. There is a variety of fares available between the ports of call on Loch Lomond, as well as "walkers' tickets," where one disembarks at one port then embarks at another. Too numerous to mention here, we suggest that, if you are interested, you should call 041–226–4271 for details or check with the city tourist information office in either Edinburgh or Glasgow.

During the high season (July and August), there is an afternoon-cruise schedule. The *Countess Fiona* departs the Balloch Pier at 1410 and returns at 1830 in the evening. To connect with the cruise, the latest you can leave Edinburgh for Glasgow is 1130. From Glasgow, you take the 1241 train to Balloch from the Queen Street Station, arriving in Balloch at 1327. The connecting train back to Glasgow departs at 1908 from Balloch, arriving at 1953; transferring to the Edinburgh shuttle at 2000, you'll be back in Edinburgh's Waverley Station at 2048.

The two daily cruises on Loch Lomond by the *Countess Fiona* during July and August (high season) make it possible for you to disembark at any one of its en route stops, explore the area, and return to Balloch on the later afternoon cruise. Getting off at Rowardennan, for example, you could scale the 3,192-foot summit of Ben Lomond. It's a five-hour round trip, but the view from this vantage point is spectacular.

In addition to the cruise aboard the *Countess Fiona*, there is a wide variety of other attractions available around Loch Lomond as well as some excellent restaurants to round out your day excursion.

263

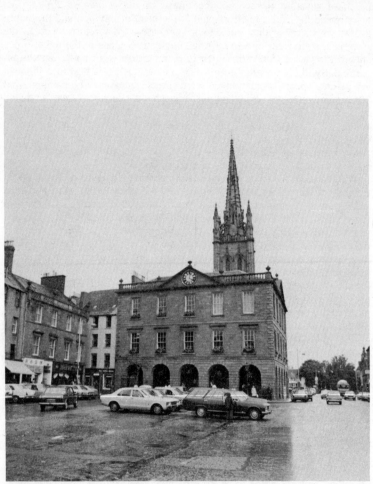

Eighteenth-century Town Hall dominates the broad main street of Montrose, a city that has served as a fashionable Scottish spa for almost three centuries. Montrose profited from trade with the Low Countries, consequently bringing Flemish-style architecture into its own decor.

A DAY EXCURSION TO MONTROSE
DISTANCE BY TRAIN: 90 miles (145 km)
AVERAGE TRAIN TIME: 2 hours, 10 minutes

Travelers who have visited many villages, towns, and cities throughout Continental Europe and the British Isles can "read" the history of a place in its architecture and street names. Montrose is an outstanding example of this point.

Even at first glance, Montrose does not look like a typical Scottish town. Its broad main street, High Street, has many elegant houses with the gabled ends on the street side. There was a time in the city's history when only Edinburgh surpassed it in prosperity and elegance. The Town House of Montrose—Americans would more properly term it the city hall—is fronted by a broad piazza. From its facade, Montrose looks more like a page out of a Flemish picture book rather than a Scottish one. Its great houses are surrounded by garden walls—not ordinary ones, but remarkably high garden walls. There are oddly named streets, such as "America" and "California"—another hint that the history of Montrose is different in many ways.

When Glasgow was still a village, Montrose was one of Scotland's principal ports. For centuries, the merchants of Montrose traded with the Low Countries. It was only natural that they would bring back to Montrose some of the things they admired on the Continent: for example, houses with gabled ends to the street side as they are constructed in Holland. The wide streets? From the promenades of Europe, no doubt. And what about the street names? Almost within living memory, ships sailed from Montrose to America carrying emigrants and returned ladened with lumber.

For many years, Montrose was Scotland's primary port for tobacco with its fleet sailing regularly to and from Virginia. Today, North Sea oil is virtually pumping life back into the city's harbor, where, until the recent past, an air of sleepiness prevailed as the trade with America began to subside. The first part of the civic motto of Montrose—*Mare ditat* (the sea enriches)—is again coming true.

Baffled by the high garden walls? History relates that more than 300 years ago, the streets of Montrose ran red with blood when a band of Highlanders raided the town. Its inhabitants were defenseless as they slept without the protection of a city wall and with only low garden walls about their residences. The carnage was swift and horrible. Within months, the majority of the walls within the town were built up to their present height to prevent attacks from intruders.

MONTROSE—*SEASIDE RESORT*

A Day Excursion from Edinburgh

DEPART FROM EDINBURGH WAVERLEY STATION	ARRIVE IN MONTROSE STATION	NOTES
0640	0826	(2)
0840	1031	(2)
0855	1050	(4)
1020	1209	(2)

DEPART FROM MONTROSE STATION	ARRIVE IN EDINBURGH WAVERLEY STATION	
1627	1815	(4)
1637	1828	(2)
1854	2045	(2)
1932	2120	(4)
2132	2323	(2)(4)

Distance: 90 miles/145 km
References: Thomas Cook Table 595

(1)   MON–FRI
(2)   MON–SAT
(3)   SAT
(4)   SUN

Train Information
0224–594222
InterCity Services: 071–278–2477

Montrose Tourist Information Centre
0674–72000

When you arrive in Montrose from Edinburgh, take a moment at the train station to direct your gaze to the west, away from the town. You will see a tidal basin where thousands of wild fowl forage for food, including the pink-footed Arctic goose during the winter. Seasonally, there is a great gathering of swans in the basin dotting the water with their white tufts of plumage like so many bread crumbs scattered on a watery lawn.

From the station, turn right on Western Road until it reaches Hume Street, where a quick left followed by a right turn one block away onto High Streets puts you in view of the town hall and its grand piazza. Stay on the right-hand side of High Street and walk a short distance south. Just before reaching the town's public library, you will come to the tourist information center at 212 High Street.

The office has a wealth of information available regarding both Montrose and the area surrounding it. A Heritage Trail leaflet provides information on walks through Montrose. It is available at the information office for a nominal fee. The information office also has a street map for sale that lists many points of interest.

Montrose is one of Scotland's leading seaside resorts, and it can become crowded during the peak summer season. Four miles of magnificent sandy beaches attract many an inlander to seek the sea. Beaches have a way of indicating their latitudes, however, just as places reflect their history in their names and facades. Beaches in Britain, for example, attract huge crowds in summertime, but note the distribution of the people on the beach. With exception of a hardy few, the majority of holiday makers are on the sands and not in the water.

The city's large indoor swimming pool and two eighteen-hole golf courses, plus numerous other sports facilities, make up for the other-than-tepid temperature of the North Sea waters off Montrose. The seaside also offers something rather unusual—something you'd never find at Atlantic City. On the beaches beside Elephant Rock, you can search for semiprecious stone such as agates, amethysts, cornelian, and onyx.

Cultural life is not lacking in Montrose. The name of William Lamb immediately relates to the world of art in fine sculptures and etchings. This well-known artist maintains a studio at 24 Market Street. On Panmure Place, the Montrose Museum houses an excellent collection of art relating to the natural and maritime history of the area.

If you've been waiting for us to drop the other shoe, the second part of the Montrose civic motto is *rosa decorat* (the rose adorns). If you walk in the Mid Links Park on a summer day, the air is scented with the perfume of roses. Although the city's name has nothing to do with roses—it was originally called "Monros" (the mossy promontory)—there are few towns in Scotland where roses grow more abundantly.

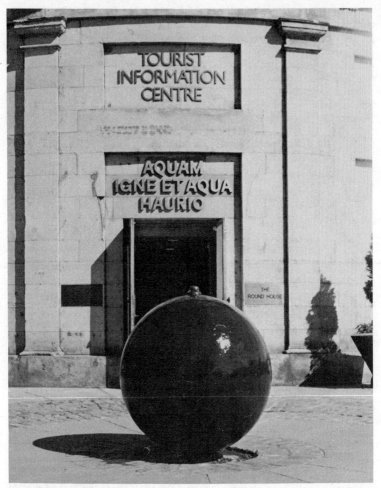

The Round House of Perth, the city's water pumping station since 1832, was restored in 1974. The Latin motto over the main door, *Aquam Igne et Aqua Haurio* (I draw water by fire and water), is attributed to its designer, Dr. Adam Anderson. The Tourist Information Centre has moved to High Street, the city's pedestrianized area. The unique Round House of Perth still warrants a visit to explore its vaults and machinery.

A DAY EXCURSION TO PERTH
DISTANCE BY TRAIN: 58 miles (93 km)
AVERAGE TRAIN TIME: 1 hour, 30 minutes

"Behold a river more mighty than the Tiber!" History relates that these words were uttered by a Roman commander as, approaching what is now the city of Perth, he caught his first glimpse of the river Tay. Beginning as a mountain stream at Ben Laoigh, the Tay trickles down the hillsides, gaining tributaries as it flows on its 120-mile journey to the sea. Perth stands astride the Tay, her history inexorably linked with the "river more mighty than the Tiber."

Two vehicular bridges, plus a rail bridge (all with pedestrian footpaths), cross the river Tay today, but "Old Man River" Tay kept the locals quite busy in earlier years, when floods swept away the first bridge in 1210 and its successor in 1621, leaving travelers no alternative but ferries for the 150 years to follow.

Perth is often referred to as "the gateway to the Highlands," but this is far from being its only attraction. Its prominent position in the history of Scotland has left a legacy of distinctive buildings in an area that is compact enough so that they can easily be examined on foot. Perth's architecture mixes the modern with the ancient. City fathers are justly proud of Perth's sports centers with an ice rink, swimming pools, tennis courts, and indoor bowling stadium.

Tay Street fronts the river on the city side. Without straying too far from the river, it is possible to enjoy the riverside and visit places of interest such as St. John's Kirk, the Perth Art Gallery and Museum, and the Fair Maid's House, as described in Sir Walter Scott's novel *The Fair Maid of Perth*. Turn left off Tay Street at Queen's Bridge and proceed two blocks to sight St. John's to your right. One of Perth's most famous landmarks, St. John's Kirk is where the Protestant reformer John Knox, following his return from exile in Geneva, preached his famous sermon against idolatry in 1559. The congregation was so taken with his sermon that as a result, they wrecked the church and then went on to create similar outrages on the monastic houses of the friars. Originally founded in 1126, St. John's is a fine example of Gothic-style architecture from the mid-sixteenth century.

Returning to Tay Street, continue to walk to the Perth Bridge, where you will find the art gallery and museum on George Street close to the bridge approach. In quest of the Fair Maid's House, ask directions when leaving the museum. It is at North Port, a short distance away, but there are several ways to reach it.

PERTH—*FIRST CAPITAL OF SCOTLAND*

A Day Excursion from Edinburgh

DEPART FROM EDINBURGH WAVERLEY STATION	ARRIVE IN PERTH STATION	NOTES
0740	0854	(2)
0925	1049	(2)(4)
0940	1053	(2)
1010	1143	(2)(4)

DEPART FROM PERTH STATION	ARRIVE IN EDINBURGH WAVERLEY STATION	
1659	1821	(2)
2015	2128	(4)
2055	2209	(2)

Distance:	58 miles/93 km
References:	Thomas Cook Table 599
(1)	MON–FRI
(2)	MON–SAT
(3)	SAT
(4)	SUN

Train Information: 0738–37117
InterCity Services: 071–278–2477

Perth Tourist Information Centre
0738–38353

Close by the Fair Maid's House is the North Inch, a beautifully situated park bordered by Georgian terraces and the River Tay and overlooked by Balhousie Castle, the historic home of the Black Watch Regimental Museum. Across the river lies the colorful Branklyn Garden, owned by the National Trust for Scotland and said to be "the finest two acres of private garden in the country." It sits on the wooded slopes of Kinnoull Hill and offers an excellent view over the town.

For centuries, Perth has been a prosperous market town, serving a rich agricultural hinterland and profiting from its geographical position in the heart of Scotland. The town's livestock markets flourish, with the famous Perth Bull Sales in February and October attracting buyers from all over the world. Perth's reputation as a trading center, however, rests principally with its excellent shops. Much of Perth's center is traffic-free and makes for excellent shopping.

In the pedestrianized High Street, call at the modern Perth Tourist Information Centre, located at the interesection of Kirkgate and Skinnergate. Operated by the Perthshire Tourist Board, the center is open from Easter to 30 June and 1 September to 31 October from 0900 to 1800 on weekdays and 1200–1800 Sundays. From 1 July to 31 August, the hours are daily 0900–2000. From November to Easter, the office is open only from Monday through Saturday 0900–1700.

Scone Palace, a mile north of Perth, stands close to the historic spot where Scottish kings were crowned through 1651. The Moot Hill, which stands in front of the palace, is an artificial mound that was constructed in the Dark Ages. Traditionally, Scottish chiefs and lairds came to Scone to pledge their allegiance to the king. This they did, filling their boots before they left home with the earth of their own districts. Thus, with the earth still in their boots, they were standing on their own land when they swore allegiance to their king. Afterwards they ceremoniously emptied their boots on the Moot Hill (or Boot Hill, as it is more appropriately known today).

The palace is open to the public, and there is an admission charge. You can reach it by bus No. 58 from the Leonard Street bus station. Check with the information center for details if you plan to go. By the way, don't plan to heist the stone of Scone—it's safely back in Westminster Abbey.

Home of golf, St. Andrews *lives* golf. The clubhouse of the Old Course (above) lies almost within the city itself. Founded in 1160 and consecrated in 1318, St. Andrews Cathedral (below) was destroyed by fire in 1380, then rebuilt, only to be destroyed again during the Reformation.

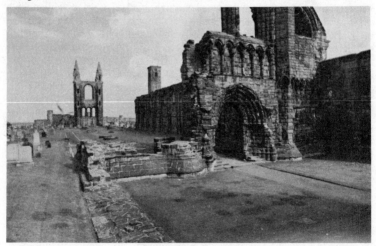

A DAY EXCURSION TO ST. ANDREWS
DISTANCE BY TRAIN: 57 miles (92 km)
AVERAGE TRAIN TIME: 1 hour

No town in the world is so completely identified with one game as St. Andrews is with golf. No matter where in the world they have played the game, there is nothing as exhilarating to devoted golfers as a round on the Old Course at St. Andrews. Anyone may play the Old Course, provided they can produce a current, official handicap certificate or a letter of introduction from a bona fide golf club, together with proof of identity. This rule applies only to play on the Old Course. Play on the other four courses at St. Andrews is not affected. The links belong to the townspeople and, as such, are open to all.

In summer and autumn, most available tee times on the Old Course are reserved—in many instances, a year in advance. To be certain of obtaining a starting time for the Old Course, it is essential to make application well in advance of the date of play. Latecomers still have a chance because some starting times are retained each day for issue by a random ballot procedure. To enter your ballot, it is necessary to apply to the starter by 1400 on the previous day. (The Old Course is closed on Sunday.)

To obtain full details and reservations for golf in St. Andrews, we suggest you telephone the St. Andrews links secretary at (0334) 75757 at least one day in advance of your intended visit. In total, St. Andrews and its surrounding area list sixteen courses from which to choose.

How old is the game of golf? Apparently, no one knows. Seemingly it originated on the stretches of grassland along Scotland's east coast next to the sandy beaches—the ground known in Scotland for centuries as "links." The sand dunes interspersed throughout the grasslands became the original traps or bunkers. A round of golf consisted of whatever number of holes were possible in the terrain of a particular link. For more on the history of golf, ask the tourist information center about the new British Golf Museum.

At first, the pastime of golf was indulged in predominantly by the Scottish aristocracy. With the advent of the inexpensive golf ball, however, golfing in Scotland soon became a mass sport. Aristocracy again moved to the fore by establishing clubhouses for the leisured gentlemen, where they could attend dinners to observe the end of matches between players.

Such was the case at St. Andrews in 1754 when twenty-two "noblemen and gentlemen being admirers of the ancient and healthful exercise of the golf," founded the Society of St. Andrews Golfers, which is now known throughout the world as the Royal and Ancient Golf Club.

ST. ANDREWS—*WORLD'S GOLF CAPITAL*

A Day Excursion from Edinburgh

DEPART FROM EDINBURGH WAVERLEY STATION	ARRIVE IN LEUCHARS STATION	NOTES
0640	0738	(2)
0840	0937	(2)
0855	0950	(4)
1020	1119	(2)

DEPART FROM LEUCHARS STATION	ARRIVE IN EDINBURGH WAVERLEY STATION	
1713	1815	(4)
1726	1824	(2)
1939	1045	(2)
2018	2120	(4)
2221	2323	(2)(4)

Distance: Train, 51 miles/82 km; bus, 6 miles/10 km
References: Thomas Cook Table 595

(1)   MON–FRI
(2)   MON–SAT
(3)   SAT
(4)   SUN

Train Information
0382–28046
InterCity Services: 071–278–2477

St. Andrews Tourist Information Centre
0334–72021

St. Andrews and history go together hand in hand. Such stellar sights as the St. Andrews Castle, with its bottle dungeon and secret passage, vie for your attention along with the ruins of St. Andrews Cathedral, once the largest in Scotland. Mary Queen of Scots had a house in St. Andrews that you can still see. The town is the home of Scotland's oldest university (1412). Long before Columbus discovered America or Cooke discovered Australia, students were attending classes at St. Andrews University. Another attraction is St. Mary's College and its unique quadrangle. Founded in 1537, St. Mary's is a part of the university complex. To visit St. Andrews and to roam its streets and scenes is to establish a tangible link with the past.

Leuchars is the rail station serving St. Andrews. This becomes rather obvious when you arrive, for there are signs at both ends of the station announcing "Leuchars Alight for St. Andrews." Buses meet all the express trains arriving from Edinburgh and Glasgow. The bus fare to St. Andrews is inexpensive, and taxis are readily available for about £5–£6.

From the bus station in St. Andrews, walk to your right on City Road, which changes its name to Alfred Place, before reaching South Street. Turn left on South Street and walk on the right side to Queens Gardens and the tourist information center, located directly across South Street from the Holy Trinity Church and the *Citizen* newspaper office. The center is open 0930–1700 Monday through Friday and 1400–1700 Saturday from October through April. May through September, it's also open on Sunday.

St. Andrews Castle may be reached by proceeding again along South Street (with no name changes, by the way) until reaching Castle Street, where you turn left and then proceed two blocks to the castle. Continuing one block farther on South Street will put you in front of the cathedral ruins.

Golfer or not, you must see the Royal and Ancient Clubhouse of St. Andrews during your stay. Though founded in 1754, the present clubhouse was built in 1854. The Royal and Ancient Golf Club is now the ruling authority of the game, and its clubhouse is recognized as the world headquarters for the game of golf. From the castle ruins, walk along The Scores until you come to Gillespie Terrace. From this point, the clubhouse and the eighteenth hole of the Old Course come into view.

Of all the places and views in St. Andrews, we give our nod to St. Andrews Castle overlooking St. Andrews Bay. Initially constructed in 1200, the castle was destroyed and rebuilt during a war between Scotland and England, only to be demolished again during the Reformation. The savagery of those times may be noted on a stone outside the castle gate where George Wishart was burned at the stake. The castle has lain in ruins since the seventeenth century, when much of its stone was removed for repairing the harbor.

Stirling Castle, astride its great 250-foot rock promontory, has dominated much of Scotland's history. Showplace of Stirling City, the castle and its surrounding buildings house a variety of exhibitions, including the Regimental Museum of the Argyll & Sutherland Highlanders.

From Edinburgh . . .

A DAY EXCURSION TO STIRLING
DISTANCE BY TRAIN: 37 miles (59 km)
AVERAGE TRAIN TIME: 50 minutes

Stirling Castle cannot be ignored. Standing on a 250-foot rock overlooking the River Forth valley, it offers one of the finest panoramic views in Scotland. The area surrounding the crag on which the castle sits has given up relics of early man's presence from the Stone Age down through the Bronze Age. There is no evidence that the Romans occupied the area, but it seems implausible that they didn't "take the high ground."

Stirling Castle has witnessed endless struggles for power. Kings and Queens have been crowned in its halls and great battles fought on the plain below it. Originally named Striveling—which may be translated as "a place of strife"—Stirling has been the scene of strife within the Scottish nation since before the time of recorded history. The town of Stirling and its castle truly stand at the crossroads of Scotland. Its position overlooking the Forth Valley and the crossing of the River Forth at its tidal limits has contributed to its past and present importance.

The castle, as seen today, began to develop around 1370 with the accession of the Stewart kings. It served as a royal residence from then until Mary Queen of Scots' son, James VI of Scotland, departed for London in 1603 to become James I of England. Scotland's tragic queen spent the first five years of her life in and around Stirling Castle. The castle is perhaps the finest example of renaissance architecture in Scotland, most of its buildings dating to the fifteenth and sixteenth centuries. It having been the royal Stewart residence, Scotland's kings and queens held court there, and parliaments met on its premises.

Between the castle and the old town of Stirling stands a National Trust for Scotland Visitor Centre. The center combines a multiscreen theater and exhibition with a bookstore and a crafts shop. According to its innovators, it is the first building in Europe to be designed specifically to bring alive the history of a town. Ten projectors and stereophonic sound create an audio-visual presentation not unlike Cinerama. The theme is Stirling Castle through seven centuries. All is bustle and noise as ships from France and Holland unload their cargoes and farmers drive their cattle to market. Stirling's market, now the city's Broad Street, is shown lined with shops selling everything from swords to spices. Meanwhile, back at the castle, a roistering banquet is being held in the great hall, packed with honored guests.

All of the information you might need for an enjoyable day excursion in

STIRLING—*AND STIRLING CASTLE*

A Day Excursion from Edinburgh

DEPART FROM EDINBURGH WAVERLEY STATION	ARRIVE IN STIRLING STATION	NOTES
0748	0833	(2)
0848	0933	(2)(4)
0948	1033	(2)
1148	1233	(2)

DEPART FROM STIRLING STATION	ARRIVE IN EDINBURGH WAVERLEY STATION	
1702	1755	(2)
1739	1833	(4)
1811	1857	(2)
1902	1955	(2)

Distance: 37 miles/59 km
References: Thomas Cook Table 599
(1)   MON–FRI
(2)   MON–SAT
(3)   SAT
(4)   SUN

Train Information
0786–64754
InterCity Services: 071–387–7070

Stirling Tourist Information Centre
0786–75019

278

Stirling is available in Stirling's tourist information center on Dumbarton Road. To get there from the train station, make a left turn onto Murray Place, a short distance in front of the station. Walk to the first traffic light and turn right onto Dumbarton Road, immediately opposite the city wall. The center's hours of operation during July and August are Monday through Saturday 0900–1930, and Sunday, 1000–1800. The center operates on more restricted hours during winter.

By purchasing Stirling's *Mini Guide* you will have a document that contains details of "Top of the Town," a thorough examination of the castle and the old town below it. The guide is packed with other interesting facts, including the development of Stirling's rich heritage from the Stone Age into the twentieth century. The guide is illustrated and will certainly be among those items you'll want to take home with you.

Other publications describing similar walks around Stirling are available in the center. One of particular interest is *Stirling Old Town Walk,* published by the Stirling District Council. It covers a course of one and a half miles and starts at a brass plaque set in the town wall opposite the information center.

Throughout Stirling during the summer months, the presence of flowers is always evident. You will notice this first in the railway station, and it continues all around town. Possibly Stirling developed its love for flowers from the King's Knot, an octagonal, stepped mound that was laid out as the royal gardens in 1627–28 beneath the walls of Stirling Castle by an Englishman, William Watts, who was brought from London to supervise the project. The raised central portion of the Knot is thought to have originated as a Bronze Age burial mound. It was probably used as an outdoor royal court for tournaments before being incorporated into the formal gardens by Mr. Watts.

There are many historic buildings in Stirling. Below the castle stands the imposing Church of the Holy Rude. It has seen great moments in history. Here, at its altar, the infant son of Mary Queen of Scots, James VI of Scotland and subsequently James I of England, was crowned at the tender age of eighteen months to succeed his exiled mother. The tower of the church still bears the marks of the 1745 rebellion, during which Bonnie Prince Charles's troops attempted to capture Stirling Castle. In the overture to the Reformation, the strident voice of John Knox boomed from the church pulpit.

Stirling is indeed a historic center that has played a vital role in the making of Scotland. It purveys an atmosphere that is hard to match in any other part of Scotland. Over the centuries of its involvement in historical events, it has preserved its heritage.

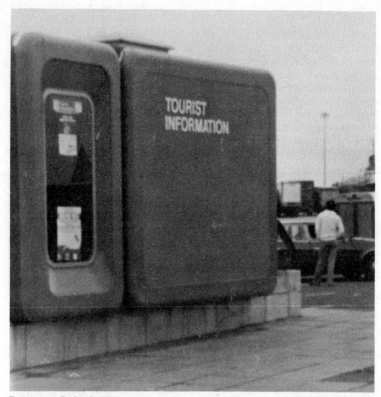

Gateway to Ireland, Stranraer's importance stems primarily from its being the terminal for ferry service to Larne in Northern Ireland. In keeping with this functional motif, the city tourist information office is located at the ferry-pier entrance to assist travelers arriving in, or departing from, Scotland.

A DAY EXCURSION TO STRANRAER
DISTANCE BY TRAIN: 147 miles (237 km)
AVERAGE TRAIN TIME: 4 hours, 45 minutes

Stranraer is primarily the terminal for passenger and car ferry service to Larne in Northern Ireland. Rail connections from Larne to Belfast take about forty-five minutes, so it's possible for rail travelers to go to Northern Ireland via this route. We emphasize, however, that BritRail Pass *is not accepted* for travel on trains operated by the Northern Ireland Railways. Travelers wanting to cross from Stranraer to Larne and then on to Belfast are advised to purchase regular rail tickets.

All arrangements for visiting Northern Ireland should be completed prior to departing on the journey rather than en route. One important requirement is a control ticket each passenger *must* have prior to boarding the Larne-Stranraer ferry. These tickets are issued free of charge.

The crossing between Stranraer and Larne usually takes two and a quarter hours, and trains are waiting at the terminals to take travelers to their final destinations. In both ports, the train terminal is directly alongside the ferry dock. Porter service is available.

Stranraer has direct, express-train connections to London, including overnight sleepers. Frequent train service connecting with the ferries to and from Larne is also available out of Glasgow. Edinburgh passengers should use the Edinburgh-Glasgow train service for the fastest connections to Stranraer. Holders of the Scottish Highlands and Islands Travelpass should note that the Travelpass cannot be used for travel from Edinburgh or Glasgow to Stranraer.

As we have indicated in the picture caption on page 280, the Stranraer tourist information center operates from a strategic position at the entrance to the ferry port. During June, July, and August, it is open daily, including Sunday, 1000–1800. Hours vary during the remainder of the year.

This office is equipped primarily to assist motorists using the ferry service. Rail passengers must walk back along the quay from the train terminal to the information center. The walk can be made in about five minutes, but we do not recommend making it if you plan to board the ferry. Ferry vessels have been known to depart as much as fifteen minutes ahead of schedule. Sealink's Stranraer ferry terminal is directly across the street from the information center. Ticketing and reservations are available in the ferry terminal, along with a comfortable passenger lounge with rest rooms and refreshments.

The old section of Stranraer clusters around its port area. There are

STRANRAER—*GATEWAY TO NORTHERN IRELAND*

A Day Excursion from Edinburgh or Glasgow

DEPART FROM EDINBURGH WAVERLEY STATION	ARRIVE IN GLASGOW QUEEN STREET STATION	NOTES
0700	0750	(2)(4)
1030	1120	(2)(4)

Transfer to Glasgow Central Station (See chapter 11)

DEPART FROM GLASGOW CENTRAL STATION	ARRIVE IN STRANRAER STATION†	
0813	1026*	(2)
0840	1054	(4)
1153	1406	(2)

DEPART FROM STRANRAER STATION	ARRIVE IN GLASGOW CENTRAL STATION	
1430	1645	(2)(4)
1830	2047	(4)
1845**	2102	(2)

Transfer to Glasgow Queen Street Station (See chapter 11)

DEPART FROM GLASGOW QUEEN STREET STATION	ARRIVE IN EDINBURGH WAVERLEY STATION	
1730	1820	(2)
2130	2220	(2)

Distance: 147 miles/237 km
References: Thomas Cook Tables 590, 591

*   Connects with steamer service to Belfast, via Larne
**   Connects with steamer service from Belfast, via Larne. Consult train information offices for train/steamer schedules for Sundays and holidays.
†   Food service is available at entrance to Stranraer Pier, across the street from the city tourist information office.

(1)	MON–FRI	(3)	SAT	(5) Daily
(2)	MON–SAT	(4)	SUN	

Train Information: 041–204–2844
InterCity Services: 071–387–7070

Stranraer Tourist Information Centre: 0776–2595

282

interesting streets and small alleyways with a variety of sights. The Stranraer Castle, a relic of the sixteenth century, adds a certain attraction to the area. The information center can provide you with a map of Stranraer and suggest various sights to see on a walking tour. The area is renowned for its golf, fishing, and swimming activities and becomes heavily populated with vacationers during the summer.

The Stranraer Castle, with the formal title of Castle of St. John, is known locally as the "Old Castle." Built in what is now the heart of Stranraer around 1510, it was erected on a site that gave the settlement its original name, Chapel. The name was later changed to Chapel of Stranrawer and finally shortened to Stranraer. *Stranrawer* was believed to have referred to a row of original houses on the strand, or beach, now buried beneath the town's streets.

There is an interesting hotel in Stranraer, one which you might mistake as the town's castle when you first see it. Its name is the North West Castle Hotel, and it's complete with a castle tower that cleverly conceals two well-stocked bars. Again, if you are anticipating a long train trip, you may want to bolster your spirits here in the quaint tower. In the lower bar, there are some fossiliferous wooden beams (no, they are not former patrons), while topside in the Explorers Lounge you are treated to a fine view of the harbor.

The hotel was originally the home of Sir John Ross, the famous Arctic explorer. He gave it the name North West Castle as a reminder of his journeys to the northern and western reaches of the Arctic. Although the "castle" has been transformed into the largest hotel in southwest Scotland, its origins with Sir John have been carefully preserved. Here you will find an indoor ice rink to cater to curling fans, and the hotel proprietor has also added a swimming pool, sauna baths, and several restaurants. A brochure at the hotel desk gives the full history of this most interesting hostelry.

Stranraer lies at the southern end of Loch Ryan, known since Roman times as a safe harbor. At the point where Loch Ryan meets the Irish Sea, the granite bulk of Ailsa Craig stands as a sentinel guarding the enclosed waters of the loch from the ravages of the storms that sweep into the area from the Atlantic across Ireland.

At one time Stranraer was a small fishing community, but it was propelled into its present status during World War II when the Allies constructed a huge port as an alternate to the Scottish port of Gourock on the Clyde River. Involved in the shipment of ammunition from the United States at the end of the conflict, the shipping firm of Townsend-Thoresen turned the port into a ferry terminal for what is now the shortest sea route to Ireland.

Isle of Skye, one of Scotland's major attractions, stands starkly against the skyline as visitors approach aboard the ferry from Kyle of Lochalsh to Kyleakin. From Kyleakin, bus service via Broadford and Sligachan serves Portree, the island capital.

13 SCOTTISH HIGHLANDS AND ISLANDS TRAVELPASS

For those with a roving spirit, the Scottish Highlands and Islands Travelpass provides a wonderful way of seeing the far north and west of Scotland. Only one ticket, the Travelpass gives you access to a holiday of unlimited travel over virtually the whole of the Highlands and islands of Scotland by train, bus, and ferry. Rail routes take you through some of the most beautiful scenery in the Highlands—areas often inaccessible by car. Buses take you to remote villages, and ferries take you to all the major islands clustered along the northern and western coastline of Scotland, some of which are a real sea journey away.

The Travelpass is for the serious visitor and is a true bargain in that it allows considerable savings over normal fares. It provides a convenient and low-cost way of seeing some of Scotland's most beautiful countryside, such as Kintyre, the Isle of Mull, the Outer Hebrides, Northwest Sutherland, Orkney, and the Spey Valley. With your pass, you'll receive a booklet with maps and timetables.

There are two types of travelpasses, based on season. There is a Travelpass valid for unlimited travel from June through September, which is issued for a period of seven days or fourteen days. (The Scottish Highlands and Islands Travelpass prices are listed on page 287.) The other type of Travelpass is valid for travel during March through May or during the month of October. This pass also is issued for a seven- or fourteen-day period.

During the validity period of your pass, you may travel over any route marked in your public-transport map, provided to you free when your Travelpass is validated. You may follow *Britain By BritRail*'s "base city-day excursion" satellite system of establishing yourself in a favorite city, town, or village and using it as a base from which to venture on a different excursion each day. Or you can plan an extensive tour, moving to a new place either daily or as the mood moves you. For hotel accommodations, take advantage of the "Book-a-Bed-Ahead" program. Any of the Scottish tourist information centers will make guaranteed hotel reservations for a small charge.

There is no limitation as to the number of times you can travel over a particular route. For example, you could travel daily from Inverness to Kyle of Lochalsh during the period your pass is valid. The Travelpass is also good for through-services between the areas it covers and Glasgow or Edinburgh.

Put a Travelpass in your pocket and you can explore by train, bus, and ferry deep into the Highlands and the islands in the north and west of Scotland. In addition, the Travelpass provides for one-time round-trip transportation between Glasgow or Edinburgh and the Highlands and islands area.

The Scottish Highlands and Islands Travelpass may be used as follows:

By Train (Economy Class)

On all regular services provided by British Rail in the Scottish Highlands north and west of Crianlarich, north of Dalwhinnie, and west of Nairn, and on through-services between the area and Glasgow or Edinburgh.

By Bus

On all regular services provided within the area by Highland Omnibuses Ltd., W. Alexander & Sons (Northern) Ltd., W. Alexander & Sons (Midland) Ltd., Scottish Omnibuses, Ltd. (Eastern Scottish), Western SMT Co. Ltd., Sutherland Transport & Trading Co. Ltd., Westerbus, Morar Motors Ltd., A. MacDonald of Acharacle, D. MacLennan of Shieldaig, Arran Coaches, West Coast Motor Service Co., John Mitchell (Stornoway) Ltd., and Scottish Postbus Service. Also includes a one-time round trip on British Rail through-services between the Highlands and islands area and Glasgow or Edinburgh.

By Ship

1. On all regular services of Caledonia MacBrayne Ltd. on the west coast of Scotland.
2. On the following Caledonia MacBrayne Ltd. services on the Firth of Clyde: Gourock-Dunoon; Wemyss Bay-Rothesay; Colintraive-Rhubodach; Ardrossan-Brodick; Claoniag-Lochranza; and cruises between Gourock, Dunoon, Rothesay, Brodick, and Tighnabruaich.
3. On the Scrabster-Stromness service of the P&O Ferries and the Orkney and Shetland Services.

Conditions of Use. Travelpasses may not be used as a partial payment for first- class rail travel, nor can they be used on tours and excursions that are not part of the operator's normally scheduled services. Travelpasses do not include refreshments or sleeping-berth charges on trains and ships. The passes are valid for a trip commencing before midnight on the last day of validity. There is no price reduction for children.

The Travelpass, which must be produced for validation at one of the following offices, is nontransferable and must be signed and shown upon request:

British Rail Waverley Station, Edinburgh
British Rail Central Station, Glasgow

British Rail Queen Street Station, Glasgow
British Rail (Inquiry Office), Inverness

Here are but a few of the great adventure trips that the Scottish Highlands and Islands Travelpass make possible:

• Travel north from Inverness to Thurso, the most northerly of Scotland's towns, then through the Port of Scrabster to the village of Stromness on the Orkney Islands. Vary your return route by busing through Tongue to Lairg to rejoin the rail route to Inverness.

• Lairg serves as a departure point to the coastal villages of Durness, Kinlochbervie, and Scourie by bus; alternately, Lochinver and Elphin to the west or Bonar Bridge and Dornoch east of Lairg.

• Journey by rail from Inverness to Garve, then by bus to Ullapool, where the ferry departs for Lewis Islands in the Outer Hebrides. Then bus to a trio of remote towns, Ness, Barvas, and Callanish, from the ferry port of Stornoway.

• From the Kyle of Lochalsh, the Isle of Skye bus-transportation network moves you about the island to Portree, Kilmaluag, Uig, and Dunvegan or to Armadale, where ferry service is available to the Inner Hebrides Islands of Canna, Eigg, Muck, and Rhum. Ferry runs from Armadale to Mallaig for rail service to Fort William.

• The rail head of Oban provides access to ferry boats to mountainous Colonsay or the northwest passage to the southern islands of the Outer Hebrides. From Oban, buses run through the long arm of Kintyre Peninsula to such ancient sites as Campbeltown, Machrihanish, and Southend.

HIGHLANDS AND ISLANDS TRAVELPASS

June through September: 7 days, $95; 14 days, $125

March through May; October: 7 days, $60; 14 days, $83

Prices effective January 1, 1990 and subject to change without notice.

To order, specify travel period and number of days, name, and complete mailing address.

Send cashier's check or money order to:

SCOTS–AMERICAN TRAVEL ADVISORS
26 Rugen Drive
Harrington Park, NJ 07640
(800) 247–7268

Please allow 2 weeks for delivery.

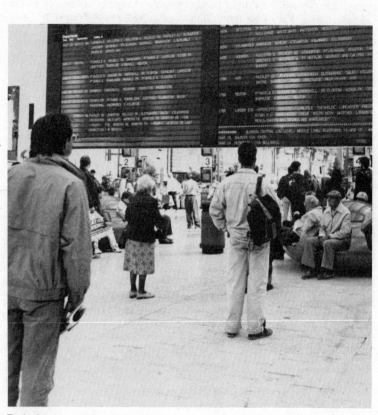

Train departure and arrival notices are posted throughout Glasgow's Central Station on digital boards. Always check at the station for departure time, destination, and loading platform prior to boarding your train.

RECOMMENDED READING LIST

The Best Bed and Breakfast in the World, England, Scotland & Wales. Guide to more than 900 lodging choices in England, Scotland, and Wales. 368 pages. $13.95.

The Best Pubs of Great Britain. Compiled by the Campaign for Real Ale, a guide to pubs in England, Scotland, Wales, and Ireland. 320 pages. $11.95.

Europe by Eurail, How to Tour Europe by Train. Guide for planning a Eurail trip, with up-to-date facts and tips. 640 pages. $12.95.

Guide to Recommended Castle and Palace Hotels of Europe. Good reading, plus a guide to 120 personally visited castle and palace hotels. 300 pages. $12.95.

Cadogan Guides *Ireland.* Explore the lush, magical Emerald Isle with this comprehensive guide. 320 pages. $13.95.

Cadogan Guides *Scotland.* What to see and do in this land of bagpipes, haggis, and the Loch Ness monster. 350 pages. $13.95.

Blue Guides. Comprehensive cultural guides published in Great Britain. Loaded with art, architecture, history, and suggested walks:

England	$19.95
London	17.95
Oxford & Cambridge	14.95
Scotland	19.95
Wales	16.95

The above-listed publications may be obtained in major bookstores or by writing to:

The Globe Corner Bookstore
3 School Street
Boston, Massachusetts 02108
To order by telephone (toll-free): (800) 358–6013

RECOMMENDED INFORMATION SOURCES

The Globe Corner Bookstore
3 School Street
Boston, Massachusetts 02108
(800) 358–6013

British Tourist Authority Offices in North America

New York: 40 West 57th Street, Suite 320, New York, NY 10019. Telephone: (212) 581-4700. FAX: (212) 265–0649

Chicago: 625 North Michigan Avenue, Suite 1510, Chicago, IL 60611–1977. Telephone: (312) 787–0490. FAX: (312) 787–7746

Los Angeles: World Trade Center, 350 South Figueroa Street, Suite 450, Los Angeles, CA 90071. Telephone: (213) 628–3525. FAX: (213) 687–6621

Toronto: 94 Cumberland Street, Suite 600, Toronto, Ontario M5R 3N3 Canada. Telephone: (416) 925–6326

BritRail Travel International Offices in North America

New York: 1500 Broadway, New York, NY 10036–4015. Telephone: (212) 382–3737

Los Angeles: 800 South Hope Street, Suite 603, Los Angeles, CA 90017. Telephone: (213) 624–8787

Toronto: 94 Cumberland Street, Toronto, Ontario M5R 1A3 Canada. Telephone: (416) 929–3333

Vancouver: 409 Granville Street, Vancouver, British Columbia V6C 1T2 Canada. Telephone: (604) 683–6896

George Ferguson & Company,
Eurail/BritRail Specialists
7215 Sawmill Road
Suite 50
Dublin, Ohio 43017–5001.
Telephone: (800) 722–7151.
FAX: (614) 764–0711

BRITISH TOURIST INFORMATION CENTERS

Below is a listing of British tourist information centers applicable to cities appearing in this edition of *Britain By BritRail*.

Key to Listing:
* Provides summer service only
† Accommodation services available to personal callers (for same or next night)
(B) "Book-a-Bed-Ahead" accommmodations service for personal callers (for same or next night) in any town with a Tourist Information Centre also offering this service

ENGLAND/WALES

Bath †(B)
8 Abbey Churchyard
General: (0225) 462831

Birmingham †(B)
2 City Arcade
(021) 643–2514

Brighton †(B)
Marlborough House,
54 Old Steine
(0273) 23755
Accommodations:
(0273) 27560

Bury St. Edmunds †(B)
6 Angel Hill
(0284) 764667
Accommodations:
57082

Cambridge †(B)
Wheeler Street
(0223) 322640

Canterbury †(B)
34 St. Margaret's Street
(0227) 766567
Accommodations:
455567

Cardiff †(B)
8–14 Bridge Street, South
(0222) 227281

Chester †(B)
Vicars Lane
(0244) 351609

Coventry †
Central Library,
Smithford Way
(0203) 82311/12

Dover †(B)
Townwall Street
(0304) 205108

Folkestone †(B)
Harbour Street
(0303) 58594

Gloucester †(B)
St. Michael's Tower,
The Cross
(0452) 421188
Accommodations:
504273

Greenwich †(B)
46 Greenwich Church
Street
(081) 858 6376

Hastings †(B)
4 Robertson Terrace
(0424) 18888

Ipswich †(B)
Town Hall,
Princes Street
(0473) 258070

Isle of Wight, Shanklin †
67 High Street
(0983) 862942

King's Lynn †
The Old Goal House
Saturday Market Place
(0553) 763044

Lincoln †(B)
9 Castle Hill
(0522) 529828
and 21 The Cornhill
(0522) 512971

**London British
Travel Centre**
12 Regent Street, Picca-
dilly Circus
(071) 730 3400

London Tourist Board
†(B)
(071) 730 3488
26 Grosvenor Gardens
Accommodations:
(071) 824–8844

Also at Harrods (Basement Banking Hall);
Tower of London*;
Selfridges (Basement Services);
and at Victoria Railway Station.

(071) 250 1039
Clerkenwell Heritage Centre

Margate †
Marine Terrace
Thanet (0843) 220241/2

Nottingham †(B)
14–16 Wheeler Gate
(0602) 470661

Oxford †(B)
St. Aldate's Chambers,
St. Aldate's
(0865) 726871

Penzance †(B)
Station Road
(0736) 62207

Plymouth
Civic Center
(0752) 264849/51

Portsmouth †(B)
The Hard
(0705) 826722

Ramsgate †
Argyle Centre,
Queen Street
(0843) 591086

St. Albans †(B)
Town Hall,
The Market Place
(0727) 64511

Salisbury †(B)
Fish Row
(0722) 334956

Sheffield †(B)
Town Hall Extension,
Union Street
(0742) 734671/2

Southampton †(B)
Above Bar Precinct
(0703) 221106

Stratford-upon-Avon†(B)
Judith Shakespeare's
House
1 High Street
(0789) 293127

Windsor *†(B)
Central Station
(0753) 852010

York †(B)
De Grey Rooms,
Exhibition Square
(0904) 621756

SCOTLAND

Aberdeen †(B)
St. Nicholas House,
Broad Street
(0224) 632727 or
Railway Station

Ayr †(B)
39 Sandgate
(0292) 284196

Dunbar †(B)
Town House,
High Street
(0386) 63353

Dundee†(B)
4 City Square
(0382) 27723

Dunfermline *†(B)
Glen Bridge Car Park
(0383) 720999

Edinburgh †(B)
Waverly Market, Princes
Street
(031) 557–1700

Glasgow †(B)
35 St. Vincent Place
(041) 204 4400

Inverness †(B)
23 Church Street
(0463) 234353

Kyle of Lochalsh *†(B)
(0599) 4276

Loch Lomond *†(B)
Balloch
(0389) 53533

Montrose *†(B)
212 High Street
(0674) 72000

Perth †(B)
45 High Street
(0738) 38353

St. Andrews †(B)
South Street
(0334) 72021

Stirling †(B)
Dumbarton Road
(0786) 75019

Stranraer *†(B)
Port Rodie
(0776) 2595

USEFUL PHONE NUMBERS—LONDON

Area Code (071)

Tourist Information	**Telephone No.**
London Tourist Board: Head office and bookshop at 26 Grosvenor Gardens SW1W ODU	730–3488
British Tourist Authority: British Travel Centre, 12 Regent Street, Piccadilly Circus SW1	730–3400
Accommodation Booking Service (credit cards only) Riverboat Information	730–4812

Rail Information

InterCity Services to:	
South and southeast England, East Anglia	928–5100
Southwest and western England, and south Wales	262–6767
Midlands, northwest England, north Wales, and west Scotland	387–7070
Eastern England and Scotland, except East Anglia	278–2477
Continental Europe, general inquiries	834–2345
Continental Europe, to make credit card bookings	828–0892
Recorded Timetable Announcements for Services to:	
Amsterdam	828–4264
Basel	828–7315
Brussels/Köln	828–0167
Paris	828–8747
Special Rail Offers	828–6708
Sleeper Reservations:	
Euston Station	388–6061
Paddington Station	922–4372
London Regional Transport (bus/underground)	222–1234
Hoverspeed Reservations	(0304) 240241

Scheduled Airlines

Aer Lingus (Irish)	437–8000/734–1212
Air Canada	759–2636
British Airways	370–5411
Delta Air Lines	668–0935
Icelandair	499–9971
Pan American World Airways	734–7292
Trans World Airlines	636–4090

Victoria Student Travel Service

Need student I.D. Approx. 50p charge per accommodation booking	730–8111

American Express
   6 Haymarket, Piccadilly   930–4411

Twenty-four-Hour Post Office & Long Distance Telephones
   Trafalgar Square Post Office at
   St. Martin's Place   930–9580

Express Bus Information
   National Express   730–0202

Bike Rentals
   Rent-a-Bike, Kensington Student Centre,
      Kensington Church Street   937–6089
   Saviles, 97 Battersea Rise   228–4279

U.S. Embassy, Grosvenor Square   499–9000

Canadian Embassy, Canada House,
   Trafalgar Square   629–9492

Emergency Police or Ambulance   999

Medical Help
   Middlesex Hospital, Mortimer Street   636–8333
   Westminster Hospital, Horseferry Road   828–9811
   Royal Dental Hospital, 32 Leicester Square   930–8831

USEFUL PHONE NUMBERS — EDINBURGH
Area Code (031)

Tourist Information

City of Edinburgh Tourist Information and Accommodations, Waverley
   Market, Princes Street. Tel: 557–1700

Scottish Tourist Centre, 14 South St. Andrew Street

Teletourist Service: recorded information on Edinburgh events and attractions.
   Tel: 246–8041

British Rail	
Waverley Station	556–2451
Sleeper reservations	556–5633
Scheduled Airlines	
Aer Lingus (Irish)	225–7392
British Airways	225–2525
British Caledonian Airways	225–5162
City Transport Information	556–5656
Student Travel Centre	668–2221
American Express	
139 Princes Street	225–7881
Emergency	
Fire, Police, Ambulance	999

USEFUL PHONE NUMBERS — GLASGOW
Area Code (041)

Tourist Information	
Tourist Information, 35 St. Vincent Place	204–4400
British Rail	
Passengers inquiries	204–2844
Sleeper reservations	221–2305
Scheduled Airlines	
Aer Lingus (Irish)	248–4121
Air Canada	332–9141
British Airways	332–9666
British Caledonian Airways	332–1681
Northwest Orient Airlines	226–4175
American Express	
115 Hope Street	221–4366
Emergency	
Fire, Police, Ambulance	999

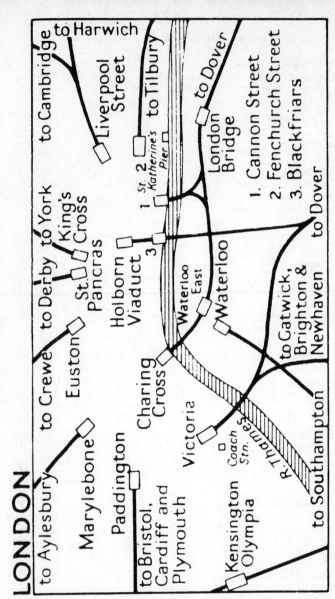

LONDON

to Aylesbury

Marylebone

Paddington

to Bristol,
Cardiff and
Plymouth

Kensington
Olympia

to Crewe

Euston

Charing
Cross

Victoria

Coach Stn.

to Derby

St. Pancras

Holborn Viaduct

to York

King's Cross

3

Waterloo East

Waterloo

R. Thames

to Cambridge

to Harwich

Liverpool Street

to Tilbury

1 St. 2
Katherine's Pier

to Dover

London Bridge

1. Cannon Street
2. Fenchurch Street
3. Blackfriars

to Dover

to Gatwick,
Brighton &
Newhaven

to Southampton

Courtesy Thomas Cook Timetable

Inter-terminal links
by London Underground

Courtesy London Transport

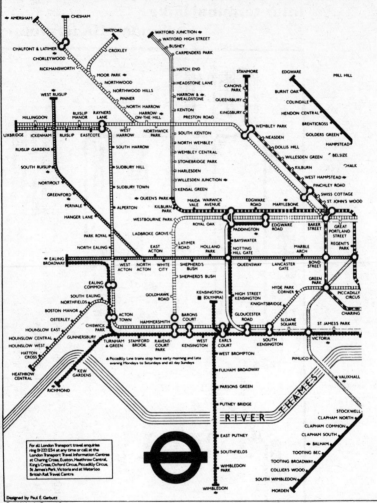

For all London Transport travel enquiries
ring 01-222 1234 at any time or call at the
London Transport Travel Information Centres
at Charing Cross, Euston, Heathrow Central,
King's Cross, Oxford Circus, Piccadilly Circus,
St James's Park, Victoria and at Waterloo
British Rail Travel Centre.

△ Piccadilly Line trains stop here early morning and late
evening Mondays to Saturdays and all day Sundays

RIVER THAMES

Designed by Paul E. Garbutt
Copyright London Transport Executive

THE LONDON UNDERGROUND

Courtesy Thomas Cook Timetable

Figures indicate table numbers

Les numéros renvoient aux tableaux

DOVER

to Chatham
to Ramsgate
Eastern Docks — Car Ferry
Market Square
Priory
Camden Crescent
to Ashford and London
Hoverport
Train Ferry
Western Docks
Marine Stn.
.... Bus service

The plans shown here are provided for orientation of readers
for those day excursions to points on the English Channel
with cross-channel port facilities. (Ref: Dover p-119;
Folkestone p-123; Ramsgate p-175)

FOLKESTONE

to Dover
to Ashford and London
West
Central
Bus Stn
Car Ferry
Harbour
.... Bus service

RAMSGATE

....Bus
to Margate and London
Dumpton Park
to Canterbury and London
Ramsgate Station
Harbour
Hoverport
Pegwell Bay

Courtesy Thomas Cook Timetable

BEST WESTERN HOTELS

For instant, computerized hotel reservations for Britain, from the United States and Canada, call (toll-free) (800) 528–1234 or write to Best Western Worldwide Hotels, P.O. Box 10203, Dept. 7036, Phoenix, AZ. A partial listing of Best Western Hotels throughout Britain, both in base cities and others mentioned in this edition of *Britain By BritRail*, follows:

ENGLAND

Bath: Bath Hotel***, Widcombe Basin (0225) 338855
  Lansdown Grove Hotel***, Lansdown Road (0225) 315891
Birmingham: The Copthorne Birmingham***, Paradise Circus (021) 2002727
Bury St. Edmunds: The Priory Hotel, Tollgate (0284) 66181
Chester: Mollington Banastre Hotel***, Parkgate Road (0244) 851471
Coventry: Hylands Hotel***, Warwick Road (0203) 501600
Gloucester: Hatherley Manor Hotel***, Down Hatherley Lane (0452) 730217
Hastings: The Beauport Park Hotel***, Battle Road (0424) 51222
King's Lynn: Knights Hill Hotel, Knights Hill Village (0553) 675566
London/Bayswater: Coburg Hotel, 129 Bayswater Road, Hyde Park (071) 2293654
  Mornington Hotel, 12 Lancaster Gate (071) 2627361
London/Kensington: The Gore Hotel, 189 Queen's Gate (071) 5846601
  John Howard Hotel, 4 Queen's Gate (071) 5813011
  London Tara Hotel****, Scarsdale Place (071) 9377211
London/Marble Arch: Bryanston Court**, 56 Great Cumberland Place (071) 2623141
London/Marylebone: Harewood Hotel, Harewood Row (071) 2622707
Plymouth: Duke of Cornwall Hotel***, Millbay Road (0752) 266256
St. Albans: Sopwell House***, Cottonmill Lane (0727) 64479
Salisbury: Red Lion Hotel***, Milford Street (0722) 23334
Stratford: Grosvenor House Hotel***, 12–14 Warwick Road (0789) 69213
  Windmill Park Hotel***, Warwick Road (0789) 731173
York: Dean Court Hotel***, Duncombe Place (0904) 625082
  York Pavilion Hotel***, Main Street, Fulford (0904) 622099

SCOTLAND

Edinburgh: Bruntsfield Hotel***, 69–74 Bruntsfield Place (031) 2291393
    Roxburghe Hotel***, Charlotte Square (031) 2253921
Glasgow: Buchanan Hotel***, Buchanan Street (041) 3327284
Inverness: Craigmonie Hotel***, 9 Annfield Road (0463) 231649
St. Andrews: The Scores Hotel*** (0334) 72451

WALES

Cardiff: Cardiff International Hotel, James Street (0222) 464141
Holyhead: The Beach Hotel***, Lon St. Ffraid (0407) 860332
Swansea: Langland Court Hotel**, Langland Court Road (0792) 361545

Thomas Cook
European Timetable

Each issue of the Timetable generally contains:

- **800+ tables of rail timings** in the 24-hour clock over every British and European main line railway.
- **Detailed, individual tables** for Europe's most important trains, including the high-speed EuroCity network, TGV services and the through routes from Britain to the Continent.
- **Quick-reference index maps** of the routes covered, with their respective table numbers.
- **Shipping services linking Britain**, Ireland, Continental Europe and Scandinavia, and throughout the Mediterranean.
- **Steamer services on the Rhine**, the Danube, the Gota Canal and the Swiss and Italian lakes.
- **Expanded coverage of Hungary**, now a Eurail pass country.
- **Plans of railway termini** for London, Paris, Rome and 33 other European cities.
- **Rail links between European cities** and their international airports.
- **Cross Channel** hovercraft, services with connections to and from London and Paris.
- **Monthly temperature figures** and annual rainfall for many cities and resorts.
- **List of principal resorts** not served by rail, with nearest railhead and means of access.
- **Foreign geographical names** with corresponding English forms.
- **Passport and visa regulations** for all countries in Europe.
- **Comparative international times** in Europe, with dates of daylight saving time where adopted.
- **Plans of the London Underground** and Paris Metro.

- Tables of European currencies with notes and coin values.
- Advance details of Continental Summer services in each monthly issue from February to May.
- Editorial page with last-minute alterations and additions and a summary of recent changes.

The *Thomas Cook European Timetable* is published in England on the first of each month. The Timetable is available in the U.S. and Canada through FORSYTH TRAVEL LIBRARY, distributor for the Timetable in North America.

Prices:
Current Edition *Thomas Cook European Timetable*
  $19.95 + $4.00 Priority Mail Postage

Rail Map of Europe by Thomas Cook
  Only $9.95 + $2.00 Postage

Special: The Current *Thomas Cook European Timetable* &
The Rail Map of Europe - Only $28.95 + $4.00 Priority Mail Postage

----

ORDER FORM

Forsyth Travel Library, Inc.
9154 W. 57th Street • P.O. Box 2975, Dept. ER
Shawnee Mission, KS 66201

My payment is enclosed for the following order:

❑ $23.95 Current Timetable, including postage

❑ $11.95 Rail Map, including postage

❑ $32.95 Special - Timetable and Rail Map, including postage

❑ $ 1.49 Timetable protective plastic cover

Departure date: _____

Name: _____

Address: _____

_____ Zip Code: _____

Please enclose check or money order payable to:

Forsyth Travel Library, Inc.
In a hurry? Order Toll-Free: 1-800-FORSYTH

EURAILPASS*

Eurailpass is a convenient card that entitles you to *unlimited 1st class rail travel* throughout 17 countries of Europe. Eurailpass gives you unlimited mileage to travel the length and breadth of Europe, to explore one, two or more countries, to stop and go where you want, when you want.

15 days ..............................U.S. $390	2 months ....................U.S. $840
21 days ..............................U.S. $498	3 months .................U.S. $1,042
1 month ..............................U.S. $616	

EURAIL SAVERPASS*

For three or more people traveling together. Valid for 15 days of unlimited 1st class rail travel. Same privileges as regular 15-day Eurailpass, but requires that the group travel together. (Saverpass for two people traveling together is valid between October 1 and March 31 only.)

15-Day Eurail Saverpass ....U.S. $298

EURAIL FLEXIPASS*

Unlimited 1st class rail travel for any 5 days within a 15-day period, or 9 days within a 21-day period, or 14 days within a 1 month period with the same privileges as the regular Eurailpass.

Any 5 days within 15 days Flexipass ....U.S. $230
Any 9 days within 21 days Flexipass ....U.S. $398
Any 14 days within 1 month Flexipass ....U.S. $498

EURAIL YOUTHPASS

Eurail Youthpass is a convenient card especially designed for people under 26 years of age. It entitles you to 1 or 2 full months of unlimited 2nd class rail travel throughout 17 countries of Europe.

Eurail ....U.S. 1 mo. $425
Youthpass ....U.S. 2 mo. $560

EURAIL YOUTH FLEXIPASS

Designed for people under 26 years of age, entitles you to unlimited 2nd class rail travel for:

Any 15 days within 3 months ....U. S. $340
Any 30 days within 3 months ....U.S. $540

Passes not refundable in case of loss, theft or once validated. In any other case, passes must be submitted to the issuing office within one year of issue date. Any refund is subject to a 15% cancellation charge. Please read the "Conditions of Use" on your pass. Prices applicable as of January 1, 1991.
✳*Children under 12 pay half price; under 4 travel free.*

ORDER BLANK

Please rush a: (check one)

1st Class EURAILPASS valid:

❑ 15 Days   ❑ 21 Days   ❑ 1 Month   ❑ 2 Months   ❑ 3 Months

2nd Class EURAIL YOUTHPASS valid:
❑ 1 Month   ❑ 2 Months

1st Class EURAIL SAVERPASS valid:

❑ 15 Days for 3 or more persons traveling together.

❑ 15 Days for 2 persons traveling together between October 1 & March 31 only.

1st Class	2nd Class
EURAIL FLEXIPASS	**EURAIL YOUTH FLEXIPASS**
❑ Any 5 Days Within 15-Day Period	❑ Any 15 Days Within 3 months
❑ Any 9 Days Within 21-Day Period	❑ Any 30 days within 3 months
❑ Any 14 Days Within 21-Day Period	

Please add $5.00 to total order for Certified Postage/handling, or $7.00 for 2-business days delivery.

Full Name _____

Full Name _____

Full Name _____

Street _____

City _____

State _____ Zip _____

Daytime Phone (   ) _____

Departure Date _____ Date of Birth _____

(for Eurail Youthpass & children under 12)

Enclose certified check or money order (including Postage/Handling) payable to:

GEORGE FERGUSON & CO.

7215 Sawmill Road, Suite 50 • Dublin, Ohio 43017-5001 or . . .

Charge: (check one)   ❑ Visa ❑ MasterCard ❑ American Express

Card No.: _____

Cardholder Name: _____

Expiration Date: _____

Signature (Required) _____

TELEPHONE ORDERS - TOLL-FREE
Payment only by Visa, MasterCard or American Express

1-800-722-7151
FAX ORDERS: 1-614-764-0711

With your order, you receive a FREE Eurail Timetable a FREE "Eurail Traveler's Guide" booklet with rail map, and FREE 24-hour assistance to replace lost/stolen Eurail pass.

BritRail Pass
ORDER FORM
Prices Effective January 1, 1991

BRITRAIL PASS gives you unlimited rail travel in England, Scotland, and Wales for periods ranging from 8 days to one month.

	First Class		Economy	
	Adult	**Senior** (60 & over)	**Adult**	**Senior** (60 & over)
8 days	❏ $319	❏ $289	❏ $209	❏ $189
15 days	❏ $479	❏ $429	❏ $319	❏ $289
22 days	❏ $599	❏ $539	❏ $399	❏ $359
1 month	❏ $689	❏ $619	❏ $465	❏ $419

YOUTH PASS (ages 16-25 inclusive)

8 Days Economy	❏ $169	22 Days Economy	❏ $319
15 Days Economy	❏ $255	1 Month Economy	❏ $375

LONDON VISITOR TRAVEL CARD

Buy yourself the freedom of the subway and red doubledecker buses in Central London. Hop on and off at will during the validity of the "VISITOR TRAVELCARD." Save valuable time, no waiting in line to purchase separate tickets, just show your pass and travel as often as you please in Central London.

	Adult	**Child** (5-15 years)
3 Days	❏ $18	❏ $ 8.00
4 Days	❏ $23	❏ $10.00
7 Days	❏ $40	❏ $16.00
LONDON DAY TOUR	❏ $65	❏ $49.00

FLEXIPASS

Flexibility for rail travelers. Choose to travel by rail for **any** 4 days within an 8-day period, or **any** 8 days within a 15-day period, or **any** 15 days within one month (within two months for Youth). (Days of travel need not be consecutive.)

		Adult	**Senior Citizen**	**Youth**
4 days	First Class	❏ $269	❏ $239	-
out of 8	Economy	❏ $179	❏ $159	❏ $145
8 days	First Class	❏ $379	❏ $233	-
out of 15	Economy	❏ $255	❏ $229	❏ $199
15 days	First Class	❏ $549	❏ $495	-
out of 1 month	Economy	❏ $369	❏ $329	-
15 days out of 2 months	Economy	-	-	❏ $295

NOTE: Children under 5 travel free; Children 5 thru 15 years pay 1/2 Adult fare for BritRail Pass and Flexipass; Youth = 16 thru 25 years; and Senior Citizen = 60 years & over.

ORDER FORM

Full Name _____

Street Address _____

City _____

State _____ Zip _____

Daytime Phone (____) _____

Expected Departure Date _____

Date of Birth _____

(senior citizen & child)

Please mail my BritRail Pass to: (If other than above.)

_____

_____

Any refund subject to 15 percent cancellation fee.
Please add $2.00 for Postage/Handling.
Enclose certified check or money order payable to:

GEORGE FERGUSON & CO.
7215 Sawmill Road • Suite 50
Dublin, Ohio 43017-5001
or

Charge: (check one) ❏ Visa ❏ MasterCard

Card No.: _____

Cardholder Name: _____

Card Expiration Date: _____

Signature (Required): _____

TELEPHONE ORDERS - TOLL FREE
Payment only by Visa or MasterCard
1-800-722-7151
FAX ORDERS: 1-614-764-0711
With your order, you receive a FREE BritRail Timetable
and a FREE British Rail Passenger Network Map.

A SELECTION OF BRITISH RAIL ONE-WAY FARES

Deciding whether or not you should purchase a BritRail Pass becomes a matter of simple arithmetic. Plan your trip to Great Britain, decide what places you want to visit, and use the fares listed below to determine if the cost of the individual rail segments has exceeded the cost of a BritRail Pass. Round-trip fares are slightly less than double the one-way charge. Children five to fifteen years of age, inclusive, pay half fare. All fares are applicable as of press time and subject to change without prior notice. Fares are given in pounds sterling. To convert to U.S. dollar equivalents, apply current rates of exchange. For example, at press time, the rate was approximately £1.00 = $2.01.

	One-Way Fares			One-Way Fares	
	First Class (£)	Economy Class (£)		First Class (£)	Economy Class (£)
From London to:			**From London to:**		
Aberdeen	95.00	64.00	Nottingham	34.00	22.50
Aviemore	94.00	63.00	Oxford	14.80	9.90
Ayr	71.00	51.00	Penzance	64.50	46.50
Bath Spa	30.00	19.50	Perth	81.00	56.00
Birmingham	31.00	20.50	Plymouth	51.00	37.00
Brighton	13.40	8.90	Portsmouth	18.30	12.20
Cambridge	14.00	9.30	Salisbury	20.90	13.90
Canterbury	14.50	9.70	Sheffield	43.00	28.00
Cardiff	39.00	26.00	Southampton	19.70	13.10
Chester	47.50	32.00	Stratford-upon-Avon	26.50	17.00
Coventry	27.00	17.00	Windermere	61.00	42.50
Dover	18.60	12.40	Windsor	5.50	3.80
Dundee	83.00	57.00	York	53.00	35.00
Edinburgh	76.00	54.00			
Folkestone	17.10	11.40	**From Glasgow to:**		
Glasgow	71.00	51.00	Aberdeen	34.00	22.50
Gloucester	26.50	18.50	Birmingham	62.00	41.00
Inverness	96.00	64.00	Dundee (Tay Bridge)	17.50	11.50
Hastings	16.30	10.90	Inverness	41.00	29.50
King's Lynn	22.40	14.90	Manchester	47.50	21.50
Leamington Spa	26.50	17.00	Oxford	74.50	48.50
Lincoln	35.00	23.00	Perth	10.40	6.80
Manchester	51.00	34.50	Sheffield	54.00	36.00
			Stirling	3.60	2.40
			York	46.00	30.50

MAPS OF GREAT BRITAIN

A good map can add greatly to your pretrip planning and your total trip enjoyment. Know where you are going and how to get there. We are happy to offer a fine selection of of British Maps specially imported for use by travelers.

CITY MAPS
- All are fully indexed indexed complete, current and comprehensive. Showing streets, railroads, stations, attractions, lakes, parks, etc. Folded with protective cover.

____ Aberdeen	$3.95	____ Glasgow	$6.95
____ Bath	3.95	____ Leeds	5.95
____ Belfast	6.95	____ Leicester	5.95
____ Birmingham	5.95	____ Liverpool	4.95
____ Bournemouth	4.95	____ London	6.95
____ Brighton	5.95	____ Manchester	6.95
____ Bristol	4.95	____ Newcastle-upon-Tyne	4.95
____ Bromley	3.95	____ Nottingham	4.95
____ Cambridge	4.95	____ Oxford	5.95
____ Canterbury	3.95	____ Plymouth	4.95
____ Coventry	4.95	____ Portsmouth	4.95
____ Croydon	3.95	____ Southampton	4.95
____ Dublin	7.95	____ Stratford-upon-Avon	4.95
____ Ealing	3.95	____ Weymouth	4.95
____ Edinburgh	6.95	____ Wimbledon	4.95
____ Exeter	3.95	____ Windsor/Slough	4.95

GREAT BRITAIN ROAD MAPS
- By Geographers A-Z Maps/U.K. Detailed road maps showing all major highways, roads, bridges, railways, cities, towns, canals, etc. In full color, with booklet index and mileage charts. Folded with protective cover.

____ South East & Central England (Scale: 1" = 5 miles) $6.95

____ South West England & South Wales (Scale: 1" = 5 miles) $6.95

____ Wales & Central England (Scale: 1" = 5 miles) $6.95

____ Northern England (Scale: 1" = 5 miles) $6.95

____ Scotland North & South (Scale: 1" = 5 miles) $6.95

____ Great Britain Road Map (Scale: 1" = 11 1/2 miles) $6.95

____ SPECIAL: All 6 maps .... Only $39.95

TO ORDER:
1. Indicate quantity desired in front of each title.
2. Calculate postage charge: 75¢ per map - minimum $1.55/maximum $3.75
3. Enclose check or money order payable to — FORSYTH TRAVEL LIBRARY
4. Send complete page with payment to:

FORSYTH TRAVEL LIBRARY, INC.
P.O. Box 2975, Dept. ER, Shawnee Mission, Kansas 66201-1375

24-HOUR TIME CONVERTER

NOON · MIDNIGHT

AN EASY GRAPHIC MEANS OF CONVERTING STANDARD 12-HOUR TIME TO 24-HOUR TIME AND VICE VERSA

Courtesy of Thomas Cook Ltd.
Thomas Cook International Timetable
Peterborough, England

U.S. PASSPORT OFFICES

Certain post offices are designated to accept passport applications. Inquire at your local post office in advance to determine whether they accept passport applications.

Applications also are accepted by mail or in person at the following passport agencies:

Boston: Thomas P. O'Neil Federal Building, 10 Causeway Street, Room 247, Boston, MA 02222. Tel: (617) 565–6998/90

Chicago: Kluczynski Federal Office Building, 230 So. Dearborn Street, Suite 380, Chicago, IL 60604. Tel: (312) 353–5426 or 353–7155

Honolulu: New Federal Building, 300 Ala Moana Blvd., Room C-106, Honolulu, HI 96850. Tel: (808) 541–1918/19/20

Houston: Concord Tower, 1919 Smith Street, Suite 1100, Houston, TX 77002. Tel: (713) 653–3153 or 229–3159/60

Los Angeles: Federal Building, 11000 Wilshire Blvd., Room 13100, West Los Angeles CA 90261. Tel: (213) 209–7070 or 209–7075

Miami: Federal Office Building, 51 SW First Avenue, 16th Floor, Miami, FL 33130. Tel: (305) 536–4681/82/83

New Orleans: Postal Services Building, 701 Loyola Avenue, Room T-12005, New Orleans, LA 70113. Tel: (504) 589–6728/29 or 589–6161/62/63

New York: Rockefeller Center, 630 Fifth Avenue, Room 270, New York, NY 10111. Tel: (212) 541–7700 or 541–7710/19

Philadelphia: Federal Office Building, 600 Arch Street, Room 4426, Philadelphia, PA 19106. Tel: (215) 597–7482

San Francisco: 525 Market Street, Suite 200, San Francisco, CA 94105. Tel: (415) 974–7972 or 974–9941/8

Seattle: Federal Office Building, 915 Second Avenue, Room 992, Seattle, WA 98174. Tel: (206) 442–7941 or 442–7945/6/7

Stamford: One Landmark Square, Broad & Atlantic streets, Stamford, CT 06901. Tel: (203) 325–4401/2/3

TIPS AND TRIVIA

Do not be surprised to see a 15 percent value-added tax (VAT) added to your bill for items purchased or services rendered. The VAT appears on just about everything, excluding bus/rail transportation.

Tipping: for luggage, generally tip twenty pence per bag; taxis, 15 percent, with a twenty-pence minimum; for service staff in hotels, 10-12 percent if service charge not included in bill.

Imports: you can import into Britain 400 cigarettes, two liters of table wine along with either two liters of sparkling wine or one liter of liquor, two ounces of perfume and nine ounces of cologne, and photographic film for your own use.

CLIMATE

	Jan	Feb	Mar	Apr	May	June	July	Aug	Sept	Oct	Nov	Dec
Average Low (F)	35°	35°	37°	40°	45°	51°	55°	54°	51°	44°	39°	36°
Average High (F)	44°	45°	51°	56°	63°	69°	73°	72°	67°	58°	49°	45°
Average Rainfall (in inches)	2	2	1	2	2	2	2	2	2	2	3	2

GEOGRAPHIC INDEX

All places that have a main entry appear in bold-face type.

AUTHORS' NOTE

We take this opportunity to thank the British Tourist Authority, British Rail, and BritRail Travel International for their cooperation. Thanks also to our European correspondents and all tourist information office personnel; both groups have been invaluable sources of information and are instrumental in making our annual revisions.

Most of all, we thank you, our readers. We appreciate hearing from you, and we do answer our mail. So if you have any comments or suggestions, please write to us.

George & LaVerne Ferguson
P.O. Box 194
Dublin OH 43017